VACATION DECISION MAKING

To Simeon, Catherine and Holena, with love

Vacation Decision Making

Alain Decrop
University of Namur, Belgium

CABI Publishing

CABI Publishing is a division of CAB International

CABI Publishing
CAB International
Wallingford
Oxfordshire OX10 8DE
UK

CABI Publishing
875 Massachusetts Avenue
7th Floor
Cambridge, MA 02139
USA

Tel: +44 (0)1491 832111
Fax: +44 (0)1491 833508
E-mail: cabi@cabi.org
Website: www.cabi-publishing.org

Tel: +1 617 395 4056
Fax: +1 617 354 6875
E-mail: cabi-nao@cabi.org

A catalogue record for this book is available from the British Library, London, UK.

Library of congress Cataloging-in-Publication Data
Decrop, Alain,
   Vacation decision making/by Alain Decrop.
p.cm.
   Includes bibliographical references.
   ISBN-13: 978-1-84593-040-0 (alk. paper)
   ISBN-10: 1-84593-040-1 (alk. paper)
   1. Tourism--Decision making. 1. Title.

   G155.A1D397 2006
   910'.68'8--dc22

ISBN-10:   1-84593-040-1
ISBN-13: 978-1-84593-040-0

Typeset by SPI Publisher Services, Pondicherry, India.
Printed and bound in the UK by Cromwell, Trowbridge.

Contents

Preface

Decision making is a never-ceasing human activity. Major decisions such as education, occupation, religion or marriage are pledging our life. But decisions are not limited to big occasions. In our daily life, we are tireless decision makers. Almost every day, we decide about time and money use. We commit ourselves to meet some people, we decide to buy products, to watch television, to perform certain activities and to go to bed. Human decisions are omnipresent whatever the domain. Since decisions direct one's behaviour and future, investigating them is worthwhile. Decision making has raised a lot of attention in many disciplines including economics, sociology, political sciences, law, psychology and the management sciences. In 2002, Daniel Kahneman was granted the Nobel Prize in economics for his famous works on judgements and decisions under uncertainty (e.g. Kahneman and Tversky, 1979; Tversky and Kahneman, 1981). The topic of decision making is a cornerstone of marketing and consumer behaviour as well. Choosing and buying products involves a broad range of decisions and a variety of decision-making processes.

The focus of this book is on vacation planning and decision making, which is of paramount importance in travel behaviour and tourism marketing. Choosing and buying tourism products and services includes a lot of decisions and subdecisions, many of which involve complex processes. Both the generic decision whether to leave or not and more specific vacation decisions are considered in this book, from an individual and social point of view. The first three chapters include an overview of decision-making paradigms and variables (Chapter 1), a critical review of existing tourist behaviour models (Chapter 2) and a description of the methods that may be used for studying vacation decision making (Chapter 3). The chapters that follow relate the findings of an in-depth qualitative interpretive study. During a whole year, we have followed the vacation decision-making process of 25 Belgian households. These were interviewed in depth up to four times: three times before their summer vacation and once after it. Following grounded theory methodology, a number of interesting findings emerged from data collection and interpretation. In Chapter 4, we discuss the context in which vacation decisions are made. In the next two chapters, the focus is on the decision-making process in itself both at the generic and vacation levels (Chapter 5) and at the destination level (Chapter 6). Post-experience processes are investigated in Chapter 7, whereas group processes are the particular focus of Chapter 8. Chapter 9 represents the integrative and conclusive part of the book where a new typology of vacationers is proposed.

Foreword

Viewing tourism as a subfield of vacation behaviour is useful for both theory and practice. Many individuals consciously and unconsciously engage in vacation behaviour that includes (or does not include) discretionary travel behaviour. Huge worldwide shifts towards other vacation behaviours and away from discretionary travel occurred following the 9/11 tragedy. Substantial numbers of people sometimes start engaging in behaviours other than domestic or international travel with little understanding by researchers of the drivers of such changing behaviours. For many countries general trends in vacation travel are sometimes negative rather than positive over several years; such negative trends have substantial negative influences on airline, restaurant, hotel and vehicle rental revenues and employment, as well as the quality of life in many households.

Thus, the need is substantial for adopting the broadening vision of tourism theory and research that Alain Decrop presents in this book. Surprisingly, most leisure researchers, consumer researchers and travel and tourism researchers rarely work jointly; the three groups read different sets of research journals and attend different professional meetings. The book in your hands bridges the three fields both in reviewing and creating new theory and in explaining the three extant literature streams. Decrop's innovative and eclectic approach serves to both broaden and deepen discussion and understanding of human work, leisure and travel behaviour.

Individuals' lives include work, leisure and discretionary behaviours, which mostly reflect causal historical explanations rather than rational or bounded rational reasoning. Often with or without conscious thought we become workaholics, golfers, television watchers, hobbyists, religious fanatics, domestic and/or world travellers – or some combinations of these and other activities. Decrop develops vacation research paradigms moving towards understanding and explaining such lived experiences and life histories.

Ecological systems theory (e.g. Bronfenbrenner, 1986, 1992; Raymore, 2002) states that understanding an individual's environment is essential to understanding that individual's choices and behaviour. An ecological perspective of human development recognizes the importance of understanding the contexts in which individuals find themselves. This approach 'incorporates the interactions between the individual, other individuals and the social structures of society to explain human development' (Raymore, 2002, pp. 41–42). From an ecological perspective, individuals interact with the contexts in which they live. Therefore, a researcher must consider the contexts in which an individual lives in order to fully understand the individual's choices and behaviour.

Early choice theory centres on the idea that choices are deliberate, calculated and seldom unconscious. Rational choice theory states that people are inherently rational and will always look for the best course to the end that they seek. First, choosers identify the future consequences associated with an assortment of current choice alternatives. Then, they consider what their future preferences will be for the consequences associated with the choice alternatives.

Scholars identify fundamental flaws in this theory. The theory assumes that choosers estimate future consequences based on knowledge of all possible alternatives and are not influenced by the decision environment by which they are surrounded. Furthermore, observation of choice behaviour indicates that decisions are often much more spontaneous and less deliberate and extensive than rational choice theory proposes.

Constructive choice theory does not assume 'omniscient rationality' and instead focuses on the application of choice heuristics or information-processing shortcuts. These choice-making strategies can be complex or simple, involving the cognitive processing of a wide array of information, or involving little information and not much thought. Choosers seek to maximize the accuracy of the choice while minimizing cognitive effort spent while making a choice. In addition, choosers will also base their decision on how easy it will be to justify their choice to their peers. Choosers also take into account the desire to confront or avoid negative feelings created by choice alternatives possessing attributes that conflict on important values. Choices are created spontaneously as a result of subconscious heuristic processing, not as a result of the calculated pursuit of previously existing goals or preferences.

Practice theory forms the basis of the fits-like-a-glove (FLAG) model (see Allen, 2002). FLAG choice theory states that social and historical forces, or habitus, shape the human experience. FLAG choice emphasizes the role of the body in perception and comprehension that underlies the feelings, understandings and actions of the consumer. The FLAG model describes embodied sensing, where a person's body functions as an integrated unconscious and conscious sensing organ. A person's experience is a mixture of the meanings resulting from the combination of the person's touching with all things encountered in the world. For example, embodied experience is illustrated by a travelling violation in the game of basketball. A player's recognition of this violation often stems from an instantaneous sensing of the body, rather than an understanding of the rules of a travelling violation. Additionally, practical experience comprises all of the understandings, feelings and actions that are induced while a person is in motion and engaging in a specific context. For example, an athlete's performance is the result of the athlete's feel for the game that comprises both bodily and cognitive states in relation to context and environment, rather than the mind giving the body commands.

The social shaping of practice takes two forms. The first includes low-involvement socialization of the understandings, feelings and actions, which make up the habitus of members of a certain group. Because these members have been exposed to similar social conditions and relations, they share a similar habitus. Differences between street basketball and formalized basketball illustrate socialization effects. Because different social conditions cultivate these games, the style of play differs greatly even though the games appear to be essentially the same. The second form entails the way in which external factors shape practice. These external factors include family, peer groups, institutions and mass media. Low-involvement socialization and external factors combine to shape practice.

History also shapes history and habitus. People's feelings, understandings and actions are shaped by a particular historical period and evolve over periods of time. Some practices that are now unthinkable (i.e. medieval practice of public torture and execution of criminals) were once common. The historical shaping of habitus is linked to the past, but is always changing. The FLAG model (Allen, 2002) elaborates on practice theory and integrates elements of social context into a model of choice. People make decisions based on what feels right or seems natural given the conditions and circumstances surrounding them. Therefore, consumers make decisions in which the object of choice seems to be a predestined, perfect fit. FLAG choices are present in daily experience. Choices made for friends, occupation, particular styles of clothing and even travel can be explained by the FLAG framework.

How People Explain Behaviour

Displayed behaviour does not always coincide with the agent's explanation of that behaviour. Therefore, it is necessary to understand how people explain behaviour and make sense of the social world that surrounds them before behaviour itself can be explained. People are continuously adapting to this social world and reshaping it. Explanations of behaviour guide their perceptions, attitudes and actions towards each other. By describing and examining these explanations, we can gain a better understanding of choice behaviour. In the past, attribution theory has been used to describe people's explanations of behaviour.

Attribution theory focuses on the various causes that people assign to behaviour. Attribution theory assumes that people explain behaviour by identifying a cause that either lies in the agent (person cause) or in the environment (situation cause). Whether a person cites person or situation causes is a result of factors such as one's personal goals, the type of information available and one's beliefs and desires (Kelley, 1967).

However, criticism of attribution theory includes the proposal that the theory does not account for the difference between the way people explain intentional behaviour (reason explanations) and the way people explain unintentional behaviour (causal explanations) (see Malle, 1999). Malle develops a new theoretical framework for describing how people explain behaviour which accounts for this difference through a model that identifies cause and reason explanation as two modes of explanation with which people clarify different behaviours.

According to Malle (1999, p. 24), reason explanations are people's explanations of an intentional behaviour that 'cite the agent's reasons for acting that way' while causal explanations are people's explanations of an unintentional behaviour that 'cite the causes that brought about the behaviour'. Therefore, the main difference between causal explanations and reason explanations is that reason explanations cite reasons that lead to an intentional action through an intention itself. An agent forms an intention to act based on reasons, which are primarily beliefs and desires. These reasons explain the intention as well as the action that results from it. Conversely, causal explanations cite the causes that brought about unintentional behaviour without the mediating role of an intention (Malle, 1999). Malle's research concludes that different types of behaviour (intentional vs. unintentional) are explained by different modes of explanation. When people are asked to explain unintentional behaviour, they will offer causal explanations, but when they are asked to explain intentional behaviour, they will offer reason explanations. Reason explanations form the link between the agent's reasons and the intention to act. Reason explanations clarify what the point of the action was from the agents' perspective and refer primarily to the beliefs and desires the agent considered when deciding how to act. In addition to reason explanations, two other modes of explanation serve to clarify various aspects of intentional behaviour.

Because intentions are not always carried out due to unfavourable conditions, perceivers may require an explanation for how it was possible that the action was performed. These explanations are called enabling factor explanations, which refer to the agent's skill, efforts and opportunities or even removed obstacles (Malle, 1999). Therefore, enabling factors clarify how it was possible that the agent performed the action, not what motivated the action.

Causal history of reason explanations cite factors that preceded and brought about the reasons for an action. These reasons are offered primarily when the explainer does not know the agent's reasons or considers them obvious. Causal history factors do not deny that the reasons themselves motivated the action. Instead, they serve to further explain reasons by offering the context, background and origins of those reasons (Malle, 1999). Thus, causal history factors could be one's childhood, personality traits or particular life experiences, which shape one's wants and desires.

Using this folk theory of behaviour explanation provides the ability to delve beyond the linguistic explanations given by respondents to understand the assumptions and social context that underlie these explanations. Through a thorough analysis of explanations using this model, researchers can create meaning out of the behaviours and events that surround them. Additionally, researchers can gain an understanding of why respondents give such explanations, or the social aspect that explanations serve.

Facilitators and Constraints to Leisure: Building an Ecological Systems Theory

Constraints are factors that researchers assume and perceive or individuals report experiencing that guide the formation of leisure preferences and inhibit or prohibit participation and enjoyment in leisure (cf. Jackson, 1997, pp. 461). Prior research shows that leisure constraints help us understand the factors and influences that shape people's everyday leisure behaviour as well as to understand differences in leisure choices for different segments of the population (Samdahl and Jekubovich, 1997).

The classic model of leisure constraints identifies three primary sources for leisure barriers: structural, interpersonal and intrapersonal. Structural barriers are defined as factors that interfere between leisure preferences or choices and actual participation, e.g. financial resources, available time, health and climate. Interpersonal barriers are interaction and relationships between individuals such as family responsibilities and the absence or presence of leisure partners. Interpersonal barriers echo psychological states and individual attributes such as stress, self-esteem, depression and socialization into or away from specific activities (Samdahl and Jekubovich, 1997).

Samdahl and Jekubovich (1997) report that while structural constraints affect the type of leisure activity people do, they do not prevent people from engaging in leisure altogether. Additionally, social relationships substantially shape people's leisure. A lack of relationships prevents people from doing activities that they would enjoy, while certain relationships motivate others to engage in leisure activities in which they normally would not participate (Samdahl and Jekubovich, 1997).

Such findings lead Samdahl and Jekubovich to question the ability of leisure constraints as a mechanism for studying the factors that shape people's leisure choices and behaviour since constraints do not accurately capture all factors that influence people's leisure behaviours. Therefore, after analysing individuals using the classic model of leisure constraints, they used grounded analysis on the same data and four common themes resulted. In spite of time constraints, people are able to alter their routines or establish rules that reconcile the busyness of their lives with their desire for some private space. Thus, time for leisure activities is created and protected. Another theme is the strong influence of coordinating leisure time with others. Having free time is not enough; individuals want to spend their precious free time with friends and family. The significance of sharing and refusal of individuals to travel alone is the third major theme of Samdahl and Jekobovich's study. Because the coordination of leisure time is so important, individuals are often willing to compromise on an activity if it will result in time sharing with a valued friend or family member. Based on these four themes, it is evident that interpersonal relations underlie and pervade the meanings that people give to leisure in very general terms and are not simply just one of three types of leisure constraints (Samdahl and Jekubovich, 1997).

Raymore (2002) recognizes a problem with the constraints approach, namely that the absence of constraints does not necessarily lead to participation. Raymore stresses the need to ask individuals about the resources they have that help them access and experience leisure. Drawing upon Jackson's definition (1997) of constraints, Raymore defines facilitators to leisure as 'factors that are assumed by researchers and perceived or experienced by individuals to enable or promote the formation of leisure preferences and to encourage or enhance participation' (Raymore, 2002, pp. 39).

Raymore provides a model for facilitators, similar to the constraints model, which identifies intrapersonal, interpersonal and structural facilitators. Personality traits are virtually any personal attribute that influences the way an individual views the world form intrapersonal facilitators. Interpersonal facilitators include the participation and encouragement of friends and family. Structural facilitators include demographic characteristics such as race, social class, income and age as well as factors such as health and wellness (Raymore, 2002). Facilitators and constraints act together to produce participation or non-participation, and must both be considered when discussing participation or non-participation from an ecological perspective.

Microsystems and Macrosystems

In relation to ecological systems theory, Bronfenbrenner (1986) proposes that the microsystem and the macrosystem, two contexts, influence both behaviour and development. The microsystem includes activities and individuals a person has experienced as well as past and present roles of the individual. The macrosystem is the larger context in which the individual functions and includes belief systems such as societal conceptions of ethnicity, socio-economic status and gender as well as other structures of society and its institutions.

Within an individual's macrosystem, there also exist both facilitating and constraining factors to leisure behaviour. Macrosystem facilitating and constraining factors include social class, gender, culture, money and ethnicity (Floyd *et al.*, 1994). For example, variation in leisure patterns exists within racial groups. While middle-class blacks and whites have similar leisure preferences, poor or working-class blacks and whites have completely different leisure habits. Additionally, blacks exhibit higher involvement in sports and fitness activities than whites do (Floyd *et al.*, 1994).

Facilitating and constraining factors also exist within an individual's microsystem. Microsystem facilitating and constraining factors include the personal influences that affect an individual's decisions and choices. Activities that an individual has participated in before are part of an individual's microsystem because maintaining participation in this activity is relatively easy (Woodside *et al.*, 2004). For example, individuals who go to the gym every day are likely to continue this behaviour because the activity is part of their daily routine. Friends and family who encourage an individual's participation in an activity are also part of an individual's microsystem.

Defining and Measuring Work and Leisure

To study the travel and leisure behaviour of individuals, work and leisure must be defined in order to articulate the relationship between the two. Defining work and leisure and distinguishing between them is not easy because there are many activities that combine both work and leisure.

Past research defines leisure in three ways: the time-based approach, the activity-based approach and the intention-based approach. The time-based approach defines leisure as free time, or any time an individual is not working. Therefore, leisure is a quantity of time, and by definition, leisure and work are mutually exclusive (Cotte and Ratneshwar, 2001). While this approach appears to provide a simple, objective definition, it does not account for the fact that not all the time spent away from work is actually leisure time (Beatty and Torbert, 2003). For example, an individual may be home from work and spend his or her time doing the laundry or cleaning the house. While this individual is not officially at work, classifying this time as leisure time is unjustified.

The intention-based approach defines leisure activity generated by an inner attitude of voluntary engagement and inquiry. Beatty and Torbert's essay, 'The False Duality of Work and Leisure', states that the intention-based or attitude approach best distinguishes leisure from related concepts. They support this approach as primary and 'advocate a definition of leisure as the experiential quality of our time when we engage voluntarily and intentionally in awareness-expanding inquiry, which in turn generates ongoing, transforming development throughout adulthood' (Beatty and Torbert, 2003, pp. 243).

However, this study adopts the activity-based approach in accordance with Woodside *et al.* (2005) for defining and measuring work, leisure and other behaviours. The activity-based approach defines leisure as the activities that people do when they are not working. The activity-based approach allows for all individuals to take part in leisure, even those who are overworked and must 'create' time in order to participate in leisure. However, this theory leads to another important question: what defines an activity as leisurely? (Beatty and Torbert, 2003). This approach is useful because it allows for the analysis of microsystems and the fact that most thinking occurs unconsciously. Woodside *et al.* (2005) note that

> intention, volition, awareness-expanding inquiry, and 'ongoing, transforming development throughout adulthood' are not necessary or sufficient for leisure experiences; an individual may engage in a leisure activity with little prior thought, no planning, with no freedom, and without committing to an awareness-expanding inquiry.

In accordance with the activity-based approach, leisure refers to an activity context unrelated to a job, employment, trade, profession or to maintaining life. Therefore, work is an activity that does relate to a job, employment, trade or profession. This definition of work is similar to the one that Ransome (1996, p. 23) proposes which defines work as a 'purposeful expedient activity requiring mental and/or physical exertion, carried out in the public domain in exchange for wages'.

Many researchers advocate the time-based approach of defining leisure because of the difficulty in asking respondents to report only on leisure behaviour. As Cotte *et al.* (2004) report, respondents often veer off topic, and shift their thoughts from leisure activities to how they spend their time and the meaning that this time has to them. Therefore, their study lends itself to the time-based approach to examining leisure and time styles.

Time style is the customary manner in which one perceives and thinks about time and leisure decisions. In the essay, 'Timestyle and Leisure Decisions', Cotte and Ratneshwar suggest that individuals' time styles can be described through four key dimensions: social orientation, temporal, planning and polychromic orientation. They argue that a person's time style, or manner of time perception and time use, has a persistent influence on his or her choice of leisure activities (Cotte and Ratneshwar, 2001).

The social orientation dimension of time style refers to the priority that individuals value 'alone' time vs. 'time with/for others'. Time spent with others can be categorized as either voluntary (one chooses to spend time with friends) or obligatory (one feels that he or she should spend time with a sick relative). The temporal orientation dimension of time style is the relative emphasis that people place on the past, present or the future. Factors such as education, events experienced, social class, age and gender all appear to influence an individual's temporal orientation. The planning orientation dimension of time style describes the way in which people approach time management and planning. An individual can be characterized on a scale ranging from analytic to holistic, which refers to a person who extensively plans and accounts for every minute of the day vs. a spontaneous person who thinks of time in larger chunks. Lastly, the polychromic orientation dimension of time style refers to the extent to which individuals are multitaskers, or take on multiple tasks at the same time, in comparison to individuals who finish a single task completely before moving on to the next task (Feldman and Hornik, 1981; Cotte and Ratneshwar, 2001).

In advancing an ecological systems theory, it is necessary to identify activity contexts within the four dimensions of time style. It is also necessary to examine additional behaviours, such as the planning of future activities, or activities that an individual planned to do, but never participated in, in order to gain a full understanding of an individual's travel and leisure behaviour (Woodside *et al.*, 2005).

Components of Life Space

In Stanley Parker's Book, *Leisure and Work*, life space is the total blend of activities or ways of spending time that people have. It is impractical to allocate all the parts of life space to either work or leisure because there are activities that do not fit into either of these categories. The components of life space can be categorized into four main groups: work and work-related time, life maintenance time, resting and sleeping time, and leisure time (Parker, 1983; Woodside *et al.*, 2004). Life maintenance time includes activities that relate to the mechanics of living. Examples of such activities include eating, cleaning, running errands, doing the laundry, going to the doctor and sexual intercourse. While resting and sleeping time is a part of life maintenance, these activities form a separate component of life space because of the significant amount of time that it involves on a daily basis. To illustrate these components of life space, Woodside *et al.* (2005) create a model to visually represent these components. Figure 1 displays this model.

Several components of life space overlap in Fig. 1, which includes all two-way, three-way and four-way combinations of work, leisure, life maintenance and resting/sleeping. Some portions of life maintenance overlap with work, leisure and sleeping/resting activities. For example, while on vacation (leisure time), an individual still needs to perform life maintenance activities such as eating and sleeping. Therefore, area C of Fig. 1 maps these activities. Additionally, extra time spent on life maintenance activities may be better classified as leisure activities. For example, sexual activity beyond the call of purely physiological need or eating strictly for pleasure illustrates that it is not always easy to distinguish between existence needs and leisure activities (Parker, 1983).

Aside from the four stated components, three additional areas that relate to contexts in life are illustrated in this model. Life contexts that an individual does not engage in or activities in which an individual does not plan to engage in, but sometimes thinks about, or a special area of interest by a researcher brought up for discussion with the respondent are categorized as non-activity (shown in area E). When researching leisure behaviour, it is important to recognize activities

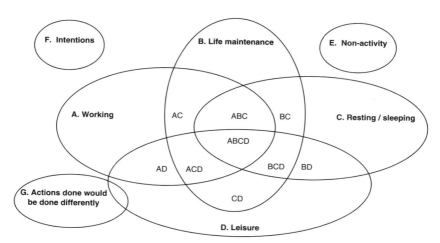

Note. A = working: performing activities related to job that usually provides household income.
B = life maintenance: personal hygiene activities; grocery shopping; home choirs; searching for work; other.
C = resting/sleeping: taking breaks from work; napping; sleeping at night.
D = leisure: hobby activities; leisure travel; visiting friends.
E = non-activity: actions not done (e.g. no overnight weekend travel away from home).
ABCD examples: time spent sleeping during honeymoon trip to France by an American couple with both the husband and wife attending work-related meetings during the visit in France.

Figure 1. Total Activities by Household Member.

that an individual has thought of participating in, yet has not taken any action to actually carry out (Woodside *et al.*, 2005).

Area F indicates intentions related to work, leisure, life maintenance or resting/sleeping. It is important for researchers on work and leisure to understand individuals' intentions and how dedicated they are to turning these intentions into reality. By understanding intentions, the researcher can gain a better understanding of how current life activities influence these intentions and the degree of dedication to carrying out the intentions. Woodside *et al.* (2005) state that 'area F recognizes the planning orientation dimension and asks what thinking processes and facilitators/constraints occur in informants' specific near and far term plans'.

In accordance with the temporal orientation dimension of time style, area G focuses on how past experiences affect the individual's interpretation of the present and plans for the future. Area G contains respondents' thoughts about what activities (regarding the areas of work, leisure, life maintenance, resting/sleeping or any combination of the four) they have done that they would like to have done differently or would do differently in the future. In this way, this area relies on the thinking process of the individual and how they feel about the decisions that they have made. These reflections about past decisions include whether or not activities were actually done, the recognition of alternative activities the respondent could have participated in, the overall evaluation of participation in the activity and whether or not the respondent would participate in that activity again (Woodside *et al.*, 2005).

Woodside *et al.* (2005) investigate the factors leading to participation or non-participation in travel behaviour among informants. Through long interviews, informants were asked to describe how specific travel behaviours came about. The focus of the interviews is to detail and explain behaviours informants exhibited: (i) today, yesterday evening; (ii) the past weekend; and (iii) last summer, this autumn and coming winter and spring.

While specific questions were posed, informants were given leeway to guide the direction of the interview. This interview method encourages informants to describe significant incidents in the context of their life history in relation to travel behaviour. The central focus, therefore, of these interviews is the perspective of the informant, not the expectations of the researcher (Stern *et al.*, 1998). At many points during the interview, informants were given the opportunity to clarify their explanations or add on to previous thoughts. These interviews include more than just informants' stated reasons for travel or non-travel behaviour; they include enabling factors and causal history of each respondent.

By describing choices using ecological systems theory and the FLAG model, we are able to better understand how and why these choices are made by gaining a holistic view of the entire life of informants and mapping out the paths that different respondents took to participate or not participate in travel behaviour. The research confirms Woodside *et al.*'s (2005) generalized model of the facilitating and constraining factors that are apparent in the case analysis. This model illustrates that ecological systems theory and the FLAG model are relevant and useful in explaining and describing the interactions of macro and micro facilitating and constraining factors affecting lifestyle, leisure and travel behaviour. An individual's choices may occur consciously or unconsciously, with or without rational thinking.

This new research paradigm indicates that the 'decision' to travel is often automatic and unconscious. The blending (i.e. interaction) of multiple factors, not one factor, causes an individual to travel. The result of an individual's lived experience leads to travel and alternative behaviours. The combination of an individual's lived experiences with their history, social environment and enabling factors make up a causal historical wave, which hits consumers when making a choice. Ecological systems theory and the FLAG model are much more accurate in explaining choice behaviour than rational choice theory or constructive choice theory.

The choice of a consumer to participate or not participate in travel activities is not usually one that is rational and planned. Consumers do not conduct a wide-ranging analysis of the consequences of travelling or not travelling and do not evaluate multiple alternatives. Instead, the decision to travel is one that is dictated by one's macrosystem and microsystem, and their causal history. Social, environmental and economic factors all play into consumers' decision to travel or not.

Additionally, some consumers will only travel if the behaviour fits directly into their lifestyle. It is not enough that a specified destination has a variety of activities, a reasonable price and an enticing ambiance. Instead, the location must have amenities that are specifically geared to the targeted consumer. For a family, this could mean that the location must be relatively easily accessible, good value and child-friendly. For a retired man interested in music, a special event such as an opera or special performance by a famous symphony orchestra might help to induce travel behaviour.

However, not all travel decisions are spontaneous and automatic. While the decision of whether or not to travel appears to be largely dictated by causal history, the decision of exactly where to travel and what activities to participate in are often much more rational and thought out. For example, the decision to go on a camping trip for a family of four who value time spent together and love the outdoors is one that fits directly into their lifestyle. However, which campsite the family decides to visit is often much more of a rational choice. In this situation, the family is likely to seek out alternatives, identify the consequences associated with the choice alternatives and make a decision based on choosing the alternative that maximizes value. In the camping example, this family may gather information on a few different campsites and choose the one that is the most cost-effective, close-by and has the best facilities.

The path that leads to participation or non-participation in travel behaviour illustrates the theory that facilitating and constraining factors combine to result in a given behaviour. These paths explain the travel behaviour of individuals and can be useful for building theories of travel and leisure behaviour. It would be inaccurate to evaluate the influence of a certain facilitating or constraining factor without taking into account its interaction with all of the other facilitating and constraining factors in an individual's lifestyle.

Decrop shifts thinking towards more generalized models of marketing strategy implications that are designed to stimulate domestic leisure travel developed. Marketing efforts are most effective when multiple strategies are implemented that enhance travel facilitators and reduce constraints. Thus, a blanket national advertising campaign will be less effective than a strategy that is more specific and targets different facilitating and constraining factors.

Creating mega or micro events that are specifically geared towards a certain hobby or activity may enhance facilitating factors. Additionally, advertising that reinforces an individual's need to attend a certain event would serve as facilitating factors to motivate travel to a specific location. Similarly, creating travel-friendly environments and events for young children would provide a couple with young children with viable travel options that would fit into their lifestyle. Similarly, travel products and advertisements, which emphasized strong relationships with friends and family, would appeal to the segment of the population that places a strong emphasis on their relationships.

In the same way, applying different marketing strategies may serve to reduce constraining factors. By offering travel options via credit cards and debt, people who do not immediately have the cash flow to travel will be able to do so. Marketeers can frame these trips as legitimate and worthwhile, which would justify the use of a credit card payment. Similarly, by creating themes that centre on life-changing epiphanies, marketeers can target the segment of the population that is consumed by work and may fail to notice the importance of the events which surround them. Such a strategy perspective suggests that traditional marketing efforts may be relatively ineffective in persuading individuals to participate in travel behaviour because of the automatic, subconscious nature of this choice. However, marketing efforts could be maximized by targeting consumers with causal histories that encourage travel and by utilizing the FLAG model to develop travel packages that are designed to fit into the lifestyle of a specific, targeted consumer.

Arch G. Woodside
Boston College
October 2005

Introducing Vacation Decision Making

1

1.0. Introduction

This chapter aims at introducing the three words of the title: vacation decision making (DM). First, the major paradigms that may be used to investigate DM will be presented; both general and consumer-specific theories will be discussed. Second, the major variables that may influence the vacationer's DM process (DMP) will be briefly described by outlining three categories: socio-psychological processes (perception and information processing, learning, attitude formation and change); personal variables (motivation and involvement, personality and self-concept, values and lifestyles, emotions); and environmental variables (socio-cultural, interpersonal and situational). Third, in order to make vacation and tourism unambiguous concepts, they will be introduced both in a socio-anthropological perspective (i.e. the phenomenon) and in economic terms (i.e. the product).

1.1. Major Paradigms in Decision-making Theory and Research

Since DM is so central to human activities, it is not surprising that a bulk of literature has focused on the topic. Economics, psychology and sociology are the most productive fields. In this section, we explore the major paradigms that have been used and are still in operation in order to theoretically conceptualize and empirically investigate DM. We discuss: (i) overall paradigms and examine (ii) more specific consumer DM paradigms.

1.1.1. Overall decision making

In the literature overview that follows, five moments[1] in DM theory and research are presented in a chronological order. The first starts with the classic books by von Neumann and Morgenstern (1944) on microeconomics and Edwards (1954) on psychology. DM is based on subjective expected utility (SEU), where utility refers to personal value rather than objective monetary value. This is a purely structural approach to DM (as contrasted with a process approach) that relates output choices to input variables. Decisions are modelled based on the mathematical principles of transitivity and consistency. Virtually nothing is said about the psychological processes leading to a decision. More broadly, SEU is related to the paradigm of *rationality*. The consumer is considered a rational decision maker or 'homo oeconomicus' who seeks to maximize his or her own utility or satisfaction under his or her budget constraint. In this framework, prediction is easy since the same actions are assumed to systematically lead to the same consequences.

The limitations of the SEU principle have been brought to light early enough (Papandreou, 1953; May, 1954; Coombs, 1958). Due to paradoxical situations, preference reversals, context or framing (task) effects, people's choices are often inconsistent with SEU's postulates and predictions. The shortcomings of SEU for a thorough explanation and a valid prediction of human DM have further been enhanced by more recent authors (Slovic *et al.*, 1977; Einhorn and Hogarth, 1981). A more probabilistic approach, the second moment, is proposed as an alternative to the deterministic approach of 'pure' rationality. The idea is to introduce *risk or uncertainty* about the consequences of an action; consequently, an alternative is no longer evaluated solely on the basis of its expected value but additionally on the basis of its level of risk. Prospect theory (Kahneman and Tversky, 1979) or regret theory (Bell, 1982; Loomes and Sugden, 1982) incorporates such probabilities. However, these theories still fail to describe the mediating processes that lead to a decision.

The work of Simon (1955) introduces a decisive step, which can be considered as the third moment in DM research. *Limited or 'bounded' rationality* (March and Simon, 1958; Cyert and March, 1963) is presented as a more realistic approach to DMPs. Although individuals are intrinsically rational, they are constrained by limited time and cognitive capabilities, and incomplete information. Consumers' attention, memory, comprehension and communication all have a selective effect on information. This results in actions that are not (always) completely rational. The goal is to choose an alternative that is 'good enough' rather than 'the best possible'. The *satisficing* principle replaces that of maximization (Simon, 1957). Experience and history influence the threshold of acceptability (or aspiration level). Since dynamic information search and processing lie at the core of these approaches, it has encouraged process-tracing studies of DM (see Svenson,

---

[1] This is partly based on Svenson (1996). She distinguishes four stages in the development of the psychological approach to DM research in the last 40 years. However, we prefer speaking of *moments* rather than *stages*.

1979 for a review). Through these studies, alternative rules to SEU (i.e. non-compensatory rules like elimination by aspect) and the principle of sequence (one rule is used after the other) were brought to light. Rule following (Anderson, 1983; March, 1994) parallels the rationality paradigms in that it also implies a logic of reason and order. However, in rule following, the reasoning process does not consist of evaluating alternatives in terms of expected consequences for preferences. Rather, it pertains to establishing identities and matching rules to recognized situations. There is a logic of appropriation instead of expectation. In that sense, rule following is more retrospective (one learns from the past to form useful identities), whereas rationality is clearly future-oriented (one anticipates the future to form useful preferences).

Besides satisficing, there is another major research tradition within bounded rationality, which is *incrementalism*. This tradition also assumes that the decision maker cannot have a comprehensive view of complex decision problems because of limited information and mental capabilities. However, incrementalism emphasizes a logic of amelioration: a decision is taken only if the new alternative is better than the status quo. Decision making implies a permanent incremental search that results in an endless series of ameliorations, which Lindblom calls 'seriality'. Incrementalism finds its best expression in the *muddling through* DM paradigm (Lindblom, 1959; Braybrooke and Lindblom, 1963). First developed in the political sciences, it assumes 'a myopic and fallible decision maker, who chooses by comparing the status quo to a few new options, and who tries in a groping manner to choose objectively better policies [or products] over poorer ones' (Bendor, 1995, p. 820). Lindblom (1959, p. 81) further describes the science of 'muddling through' as the method of successive limited comparisons (the 'branch' method) in contrast to the rational-comprehensive method (the 'root' method). The former continually builds out from the current situation, step-by-step and by small degrees, while the latter starts 'from fundamentals anew each time, building on the past only as experience is embodied in a theory, and always prepared to start completely from the ground up'. Bendor (1995) formalizes and extends the 'muddling through' paradigm to situations involving multiple decision makers, with either the same or conflicting objectives.

The inclusion of possible changes in the representation of decision alternatives is the new element in the fourth moment in DM theory and research. First, changes are necessary to solve decision conflicts since contradictory goals have to be negotiated and reconciled. This new assumption was introduced by Shepard (1964) and later refined by Kahneman and Tversky (1979) and Svenson (1979). Changes may also result from unexpected events. In that case, judgements will be based on norms or standards that are developed or retrieved through the events themselves (see Kahneman and Miller, 1986 for the norm theory). More generally, the adaptation of decision rules to the structure of a problem is qualified as *contingent* or *adaptive* DM (Payne, 1982; Payne *et al.*, 1993). This approach postulates that people use a variety of strategies to solve decision problems. The choice of a particular strategy depends upon personal characteristics (cognitive ability, prior knowledge), problem characteristics (task and context factors) and social context (accountability, group membership). Two major frameworks are used to explain contingent DM. On the one hand, the cost/benefit framework assumes that 'strategy selection is the result of a compromise between the desire to make a correct decision and the desire to minimize effort' (Beach and Mitchell, 1978, p. 64). On the other hand, the perceptual framework considers that DM is governed by basic principles of human perception such as the wording/framing of a decision problem (Tversky and Kahneman, 1981) or the perception of choices as offering gains or losses (Puto, 1987).

The *political model* of DM is a particular case of adaptive DM (Pettigrew, 1973; Pfeffer, 1981). It starts from the observation that most human decisions are not individual but rather involve groups. Theories of teams and games have first been proposed to explain group DM. However, these rely on the questionable assumptions that: (i) individuals have consistent preferences and/or identities so that no conflict can occur (theories of teams); and (ii) preferences and identities are inconsistent but partners strive to solve conflicts since they behave rationally (game theories). In contrast, the political DM paradigm assumes that multiple inconsistent actors are less inclined to emphasize eliminating conflict in preferences or identities (March, 1994). Struggle for power (through force or exchange) and coalition formation (through bargaining) are two usual expressions of a political DMP.

Postmodernism introduces the fifth moment in the study of DM. This renewed view on the social sciences paves the way for sharp critiques on the rationality and rule-following theories of human DM: 'the worlds that confront decision makers appear to be systematically less orderly, more ambiguous, and more symbolic than the worlds portrayed in most of the theories considered up to now' (March, 1994, p. 175). Reality is not unique, causality is often unclear and intentionality is a weak predictor of behaviour. New paradigms are developed in order to take this relativism into account. The *garbage can model* (Cohen *et al.*, 1972) incorporates the ambiguity and uncertainty that are observed in the world. It suggests that decisions are analogous to garbage cans into which problems, solutions, choice opportunities and decision makers are dumped and connected together by time proximity. As a consequence, almost any solution can be associated with any problem, provided they are evoked at the same time. The garbage can model is based on a temporal sorting perspective where 'any decision process involves a collection of individuals and groups who are simultaneously involved in other things' (March, 1994, p. 198). In that complex world, time is used as the simplest source of order.

1.1.2. Consumer decision making

Besides economics, psychology and sociology, DM has received a lot of attention in the management sciences, more specifically in organizational and consumer behaviour. Following this book's focus of interest, we will only look at consumer behaviour. Investigating purchase decisions (product, brand, store, mode of payment, etc.) is worthwhile as they allow businesses to sell their goods and services. Choice and use decisions are also of great importance, not only for the consumers themselves but also for marketeers and policymakers. In short, consumer decisions are omnipresent: 'there is no way that the consumer can escape making decisions' (Walters and Bergiel, 1989, p. 331). But here again, the final purchase is only the visible part of the iceberg, since that is the materialization of a whole DMP, thought to start with the recognition of a problem (need). Several theories were developed to explain consumer DM in line with the general paradigms discussed in Section 1.1.1. We make a distinction between classical theories and newer postmodern approaches.

Classical theories

Classical theories portray the consumer either as a risk reducer, a problem solver or an information processor. This is in line with moments one to three of Section 1.1.1. The view of the consumer as a *risk reducer* has first been proposed by Bauer (1960) and Taylor (1974). Risk may be defined as the personal anticipation that a particular action will result in a loss or the uncertainty about the consequence of a purchase. Risk can be psychological or physical; it may be connected with money, product performance or social acceptance. Risk-reduction theory assumes that consumers tend to reduce risk to an acceptable level in their market decisions. Information search is very limited, unless it helps to make safer choices. Risk reduction involves strategies like brand loyalty, repeat purchase and buying the most expensive or well-known brands.

Problem solving is the most popular approach to consumer DM. A substantial number of consumer behaviour models are based on that paradigm (Andreasen, 1965; Nicosia, 1966; Howard and Sheth, 1969; Engel *et al.*, 1973). Its basic assumption is that any consumer need or desire creates a problem within the individual. The consumer undertakes to solve that problem by deciding a course of action in order to satisfy this need or desire. Decision making entails these typical steps: need recognition, search for information (which is assumed to be very important), evaluation of alternatives (the consumer evaluates attributes and products), purchase, outcomes (post-purchase evaluation). Problem solving clearly refers to a thoughtful, reasoned action that postulates a rational decision maker (Fishbein and Ajzen, 1975). Buying decisions are located on a continuum between extended problem solving (EPS) and limited problem solving (LPS). The extensiveness of problem solving is positively influenced by the level of differentiation between alternatives, time availability and involvement (Engel *et al.*, 1990).

The *information-processing* approach assumes that consumers are continuously looking for and processing information in order to improve the quality of their choices (Bettman, 1979). In line with problem solving, it endorses bounded rationality, as it postulates that consumers have limited resources for processing information (i.e. limited working memory and computational capabilities). This goes parallel with the belief that 'preferences for options of any complexity or novelty are often constructed, not merely revealed, in making a decision'

(Bettman *et al.*, 1998, p. 188). Consumers do not have well-defined preferences but construct them on the spot when needed, such as when making a choice.

Postmodern theories

In the current market economy characterized by ever new technologies and competitive pressures, consumers are often confronted with a large number of alternatives (brands or substitutable goods), and are overwhelmed with information from many sources (e.g. family, friends, advertising, sales people). Uncertainty about product use and performance, as well as difficult trade-offs (such as price vs. quality), result in serious market dilemmas for consumers. 'This multifaceted nature of the consumer DM task has generated a number of important questions' (Bettman *et al.*, 1991, p. 50), and newer general explanations of consumer behaviour have emerged. Two major streams consider the consumer as hedonist or adaptive decision maker. The garbage can model is another recent paradigm that comes from organizational behaviour. These theories are in line with the last two moments of DM theory presented above.

In the *hedonic and experiential perspective* on consumer behaviour (Hirschman and Holbrook, 1982; Holbrook, 1984), the focus does not lie on the DMP as such but rather on the consumption experience of products. However, it has implications on DM and mental constructs. Hedonic consumption pertains to 'those facets of consumer behaviour that relate to the multisensory (i.e. tastes, sounds, scents, tactile impression and visual images), fantasy and emotive aspects of one's experience with products' (Hirschman and Holbrook, 1982, p. 92). Consumers seek to make the decisions that will maximize their pleasure and emotional arousal. Note that painful hedonic consumption is also possible, since 'consumers can utilize painful knowledge to expend emotions and construct fantasies that enable them to deal with unhappy realities better' (Hirschman and Holbrook, 1982, p. 96). Therefore, Holbrook (1984) suggests replacing the disenchanting classical CAB (cognition, affect, behaviour) sequence with a CEV (consciousness, emotion, value) model. This newer view of consumer behaviour focuses on product usage, consumption experience, and hedonic and symbolic dimensions of the product. Products are no longer considered as objective entities but rather as subjective symbols associated with emotional responses, sensory pleasures, daydreams or aesthetic perceptions. This hedonic and experiential perspective is particularly relevant for classes of products such as novels, cultural manifestations, sporting events or vacation.

Adaptive or *contingent* DM (Bettman *et al.*, 1991; Payne *et al.*, 1993) is based on the tenet that consumers are flexible in the way they respond to a variety of task conditions. First, DM is contingent in that decision strategies are adapted to the properties of the decision problem, such as the number of alternatives, time pressure (task variables) or the level of similarity and dominance of alternatives (context variables). Second, individual differences also affect how a person decides to solve a particular decision problem. Cognitive ability, prior (product) knowledge and expertise are major influences. Third, DM depends on many social factors. On the one hand, individual decisions can be influenced by the accountability to relevant others, such as friends or family members. On the other hand, many decisions involve multiple stakeholders. This leads to problems connected with group DM (communication, role-playing, conflicts, etc.). For example, Kirchler (1993) brings empirical evidence that marital purchase DM is a process of muddling through where spouses in disagreement use tactics to persuade or convince the other to yield. In short, 'problem, person, and social context factors provide an outline of the major aspects affecting contingent consumer decision making' (Bettman *et al.*, 1991, p. 63).

The *garbage can decision model* represents an even more radical break with classical theories. This paradigm has important implications for consumer DM (see Wilson and Wilson, 1988). First, problem definitions are variable: they change as far as new problems or people are attached to choice opportunities. Second, other tenets of classical consumer behaviour theory are disregarded: information is often collected but not used, preferences are unclear and may have little impact on choice. Third, evaluation criteria are not available beforehand but rather are discovered during and after the DMP. Fourth, a particular choice can be made even when no problem has been noticed or when the problem relates to other choice opportunities. In contrast, no choice is made when a number of problems are attached to the choice opportunity because it exceeds the energy of the decision maker.

1.2. Major Variables in the Decision-making Process

This section aims at explaining the concepts that are generally used to describe consumers' DMPs. The first subsection is about the socio-psychological processes involved in DM: how the tourist perceives information, processes it and makes decisions. Constructs like: (i) perception; (ii) learning; and (iii) attitude are defined and illustrated by appropriate examples. The second considers the personal variables that shape the DMP. This includes: (i) the tourist's motivation process; (ii) his or her personality and self-concept; (iii) lifestyles; and (iv) emotions. The third discusses environmental variables because they are necessary for a thorough understanding of the tourists' DMPs: (i) social and cultural influences, such as reference groups and social classes; (ii) interpersonal variables; and (iii) situational variables, such as time, money, health or marketing pressure, which may either inhibit or facilitate making a decision.

1.2.1. Socio-psychological processes

Perception
Perception helps us to know our environment through translating stimuli coming from the external, physical world to the internal, mental world that each of us experiences (Wilkie, 1990). Stimuli may originate from the marketeer (through the marketing-mix tools: product design, advertising message, etc.) or

from other sources (most of the time, previous experience and the social net-work). As external information becomes brain information, perception helps make sense of the world. Three basic cognitive operations make perception a very selective and interpretive process: sensation, attention and interpretation. Sensation or exposure refers to the interception of environmental stimuli by our sensory nerves. Attention pertains to the pattern recognition of the sensory input against the knowledge representation stored in our long-term memory. Interpretation or comprehension is concerned with sense making. Three key activities are involved in perceptual interpretation: organization (determining how bits of information belong together), categorization (identifying the stimulus to know what it is) and inference (thinking more about the stimulus, and developing beliefs about other stimuli).

For example, Belgium may be interpreted through a semantic network of mental connections with other concepts such as chocolate, beer or a flat land (organization); categorized as a small European country; and then perceived as beautiful in an inferential way (because 'small is beautiful'). Frances (1992) and Gordon (1989) provide more detailed discussions of perception. Perception is an absolute prerequisite for processing information that involves two additional steps after interpretation – acceptation and memorization. Acceptation involves the way incoming information is evaluated by the consumer. Memorization pertains to the transfer of the information from one of the senses to the short- and the long-term memory.

Learning

In cognitive psychology, learning is related to perception. Perceived information can be assimilated mentally or 'learned' by consumers in order to develop knowledge and skills that will allow them to give new responses to their environment. This process of knowledge acquisition involves storing information in the long-term memory in the form of associations. Those associations give birth to beliefs and feelings. For instance, a particular holiday destination may be connected with different attributes such as climate, culture or nature, as well as with how the tourist feels about it. Other theories of learning have been proposed in the literature: behavioural learning (through classical and instrumental conditioning) and vicarious learning (through social imitation).

Attitudes

Attitude is one of the most popular topics in the consumer behaviour literature so far. An attitude is classically defined as a 'learned predisposition to respond to an object or a class of objects in a consistently favorable or unfavorable way' (Allport, 1935). Classical theory (e.g. Rosenberg and Hovland, 1960; Fishbein, 1963; Fishbein and Ajzen, 1975; Ajzen and Fishbein, 1980) argues that attitudes include three components: cognitive (perception, belief); affective (evaluation, affect); and conative (action, intention). This CAB sequence implies cognitive consistency. It means that 'people are predisposed to organize their attitudes and beliefs into internally consistent structures' (Eiser, 1986, p. 14), and that attitudes in turn are consistent with behaviour. Following this multifaceted view, examples of a vacationer's attitudes towards destinations could be:

1. 'I think Greece has the most wonderful historical sites in the world' (belief).
2. 'I like Thailand very much' (affect).
3. 'I always choose Turkey for my vacation' (behavioural intention).

This view, however, is opposed by authors (e.g. Shaw and Wright, 1967; Zajonc, 1978; Peterson *et al.*, 1986; Holbrook and Batra, 1987) who narrow attitude down to its affective component and prefer to define it as 'feelings of liking or disliking' (Foxall and Goldsmith, 1994, p. 94).

Preference is a special case of the broader attitude construct. Preference is usually defined as the predisposition of choosing one product alternative over the other. It implies taking a position that is the result of a comparative process. Comparison may be explicit (ranking objects) or implicit (rating objects).

1.2.2. Personal variables

DM behaviour is much more than the result of socio-psychological processes. The tourist is a person who deserves to be considered as a human being with his or her own motives, personality, lifestyles and emotions. Of course, consumers may also be described in demographic terms (age, gender, marital status, education level and occupation, place of residence, etc.) and according to their resources (money, time and cognizance). However, these are more obvious characteristics that do not need further explanation here.

Motivation and involvement
In addition to *how*, the question of *why* consumers behave as they do is of paramount importance to understand DMPs. Motivation refers to the process by which an individual will be driven to act or behave in a certain way. It is characterized by a 'state of tension within the individual which arouses, directs and maintains behavior toward a goal' (Mullen and Johnson, 1990, p. 178). It is important to note that motivation is a generic term. More specific terms are often used when describing the motivation process. Four of them deserve a closer look: motives, needs, wants and benefits.

A motive is a lasting disposition, an internal drive or 'push factor' that 'causes the tourist to search for signs in objects, situations and events that contain the promise of reducing the prevalent drive' (Gnoth, 1997, pp. 290–291). Each motive has a different content in terms of goals of behaviour. Motives and personal characteristics determine a person's predisposition to act. A need is the materialization (on the consumer plane) of a motive (on the psychological plane). In the same way, the want (manifestation of the need) is the goal object and the benefit (whatever consumers derive from products), the result of behaviour (Foxall and Goldsmith, 1994). In addition to general theories of motivation by Freud, Murray and Maslow, a lot of motivation typologies were specifically developed for explaining tourist behaviour (e.g. Crompton, 1979; Fodness, 1994; Gnoth, 1997; see Ross, 1994 for a review).

Involvement is another concept connected with motivation. In contrast to basic motives and needs, which characterize the consumer alone, involvement is the result of a consumer–product interaction. There is a usual distinction between enduring and situational involvement. The former exists when a consumer shows interest in an object (product or activity) over a long period of time (Laurent and Kapferer, 1985), whereas the latter may be defined as 'the level of perceived personal importance and/or interest evoked by a stimulus within a specific situation' (Antil, 1984, p. 204). The level of involvement (low/high) is often used to categorize products or consumer problem-solving modes (see Section 1.1.2). It has major consequences on different aspects of the DMP, and more particularly, on the type and extent of information search.

Personality and self-concept

Personality may be defined as the reflection of a person's enduring and unique characteristics that urge him or her to respond in persistent ways to recurring environmental stimuli. Personality results from the person's history and goes far beyond socio-demographics. The individual's enduring characteristics are often called 'traits'. Following this approach, vacationers could be characterized as reflective, active, sociable, outgoing, inquisitive and confident. Air travellers could be described as very active, very confident and reflective while bus travellers are dependent, apprehensive, sensitive, hostile, belligerent and unrestrained (Mayo and Jarvis, 1981). Traits together form personality types. One popular type-casting approach makes a distinction between psychocentric persons, who are more concerned with themselves (introverted), anxious and inhibited, and allocentric persons, who tend to be more extroverted, self-confident and adventurous. This useful model was first adapted in tourism by Plog (1972): 'travelers who are more allocentric are thought to prefer exotic destinations, unstructured vacations rather than package tours, and more involvement with local cultures. Psychocentrics, on the other hand, are thought to prefer familiar destinations, packaged tours, and touristy areas' (Ross, 1994, pp. 33–34).

Self-concept is another way to explain how personality influences behaviour. The notion of self-concept, or self-image, derives from the Freudian psychoanalytic theory and pertains to the concepts that the consumer believes characterize him or her. Authors generally deal with two levels of self-concepts (e.g. Grubb and Stern, 1971):

1. The actual self-image refers to the individual's global perception of himself or herself (including his or her descriptions and evaluations of himself or herself).
2. The ideal self-image is the person's perception of what (including who) he or she would like to be. Note that vacationing and travelling are often mentioned as part of the ideal self.

Lifestyles

The term 'lifestyle' refers to unique patterns of thinking and behaving (like daily life routine, activities, interests, opinions, values, needs and perceptions) that characterize differences between consumers. Lifestyles (or 'psychographics') are reflections of the self-concept and offer insight into tourists' patterns of time, spending and feeling. In contrast with the purely descriptive demographic data, lifestyles give indications about how people really live. Plog (1994) identifies eight psychographic/personality dimensions of the tourist: venturesomeness, pleasure-seeking, impulsivity, self-confidence, planfulness, masculinity, intellectualism and people orientation. Another interesting typology comes from Mayo and Jarvis (1981). Based on a broad literature review, they describe five types of travellers: 'peace-and-quiet' traveller, overseas traveller, historian traveller, recreational vehicle traveller and 'travel now/pay later' traveller. Finally, the Austrian National Tourist Office condensed 16 styles from the *Eurostyles* typology into five socio-targets: prudent relaxation-seeker, young family, young hedonistic vacationer, demanding adventure-seeker and classic culture-seeker (Mazanec, 1994).

Emotions

Vacation decisions are much more than a question of cognitive information processing, lifestyle and motivation. Fantasies, feelings and fun, encompassed by the 'experiential view' of consumer behaviour, are a part of tourist experiences that has been omitted in many tourism textbooks and articles for a long time. Vacation is one of those phenomena that include 'various playful activities, sensory pleasures, daydreams, esthetic enjoyment, and emotional responses' (Holbrook and Hirschman, 1982, p. 132).

Emotion can be defined as 'a state of arousal involving conscious experience and visceral, or physiological, changes' (Mullen and Johnson, 1990, p. 75). In consumer behaviour, emotion is generally expressed in terms of feeling towards the product while, for Holbrook (1984), it encompasses a wider range of phenomena that entail four interacting components: physiological response, cognition, behavioural expression and feelings. Several typologies of emotions (see Holbrook, 1984) may be used accordingly in tourism marketing and advertising. A few studies have proven that advertising effectiveness depends upon the emotional content of messages. The use of repetition, classical conditioning, humour and fear appeals are particularly powerful in eliciting emotional responses towards products. Table 1.1 lists examples of Plutchik's eight primary emotions (1980) in the tourist experience.

1.2.3. Environmental variables

The previous paragraphs focused on socio-psychological processes and personal variables. To come to a complete understanding of tourist DMPs, the context must be taken into account as well. The context refers to the environmental

Table 1.1. Examples of Plutchik's eight primary emotions (1980) in the tourist experience.

Emotion	Example in tourism
Acceptance	Deep personal liking for one's favourite travel agent
Anger	Being stuck in a traffic jam to the airport as one is leaving for a holiday
Disgust	Discovering that one's hotel room is visited by cockroaches
Expectancy	Getting into the bus for the excursion to Egypt's pyramids
Fear	Being stung by a mosquito during a safari trip in Kenya when no malaria precaution has been taken
Joy	Listening to exotic music played by the locals
Sadness	Being 7 years old that summer and finding that there is no swimming pool in your hotel
Surprise	Finding a bottle of champagne in one's room even when one did not ask for it

variables affecting what and how the tourist thinks, feels, learns and behaves. We make a distinction between: (i) social and cultural influences; (ii) interpersonal variables; and (iii) situational influences on the DMP.

Social and cultural influences

All the facets of the individual consumer discussed earlier, as well as the psychological processes leading to choice, are influenced by the social and cultural structure in which the consumer is embedded. Often the consumer is unaware of these pervasive and intangible influences.

Culture refers to a 'set of values, ideas, artifacts, and other meaningful symbols that help individuals communicate, interpret, and evaluate as members of society' (Blackwell *et al.*, 2001, p. 314). According to McCracken (1988), culture serves both as a 'lens' through which all phenomena are seen and as a 'blueprint' of human activity, determining the coordinates of social action and productive activity. It includes beliefs, values, norms, signs, habits and non-normative behaviour. Thus, culture also influences the way the person behaves as a tourist. Sport is a good example to show how culture may influence travel behaviour. Sport has become such an important cultural value in the Western countries that it nowadays influences the content of the holiday experience. To many Europeans and Americans, golf, tennis, skiing or scuba-diving are, among other sports, no longer secondary activities but primary motives for leisure travel. There also exist 'subcultures' within the overall culture. These are groups based on region, race, language, religion, age, social class and other factors. The point is that members of a subculture typically conform to many of the norms of the dominant culture, but deviate from other norms that are not compatible with those of their subculture.

Social class is a special type of subculture. Social classes result from the division of society on the basis of status and prestige. Education and occupation are the basic factors that determine the belonging to one social class. Wealth and income are less decisive determinants. 'Each social class displays a distinctive lifestyle which is reflected in values, interpersonal attitudes, and self-perceptions that differ from those held by any other class' (Mayo and Jarvis, 1981, p. 236–237). Many tourist destinations like ski resorts have a definite social class orientation. For example, the Spanish Costa Blanca appeals to the lower middle class and the working class who are looking for sea, sun and fun to escape their daily life's stress and greyness. The Caribbean or the French Riviera are spots where higher social classes feel like fish in the sea. Other places, such as Florida, attract people from all social classes, but the different classes tend to segregate themselves once they arrive.

Interpersonal variables

Most vacation decisions are joint or syncretic in that they involve different members within a decision-making unit (DMU). Therefore, interpersonal or group influences may have a major impact on plans and choices. Following Shaw (1976, p. 11), a group involves members who share something in common: 'two or more persons who are interacting with one another in such a manner that each person influences or is influenced by each other person'. Groups may have a normative influence (the wording 'reference group' is often used), a value-expressive influence (the group strives to impose its norms, values or behaviour patterns), and/or a comparative/informative role in DM. Blackwell *et al.* (2001) suggest three group dichotomies: primary vs. secondary; formal vs. informal; and aspirational vs. dissociative. A primary group is regarded as 'a social aggregation that is sufficiently intimate to permit and facilitate unrestricted face-to-face interaction' (Blackwell *et al.*, 2001, p. 397) and characterized by a high level of cohesiveness. In contrast, a secondary group is more occasional; it also bears face-to-face interaction but 'it is more sporadic, less comprehensive, and less influential in shaping thought and behavior' (Blackwell *et al.*, 2001, p. 397; see also Ward and Reingen, 1990). Formal groups have a defined structure with established rules, a known list of members and requirements for membership, while informal groups have a looser structure and are more likely to be based on friendship or common interests. Both types develop norms, which can have a stringent effect on behaviour and DM, and involve membership, i.e. achieving a formal acceptance status in the group. Finally, aspirational groups refer to entities with which the individual aspires to associate by adopting its norms, values and behaviour; in contrast, dissociative groups are those with which individuals will try to avoid any association.

When considering the way DM takes place within a DMU, be it a couple, a family or a group of friends, major aspects need to be investigated such as the level of communication and group cohesiveness, the DM mode (consensus, bargaining, vote, dictatorship, etc.), and the result of confrontation (agreement vs. conflict). Role is another major variable that involves the following research questions:

1. How are roles (i.e. initiator, influencer, decider, purchaser and user) and tasks distributed within the DMU?
2. What is the relative influence of each member of the family (husband, wife or children; dominant vs. syncretic decisions)?
3. What is the specialization level (joint vs. autonomic decisions, depending on the level of communication)?

Situational influences

It is easy to argue that environmental variables such as time, money, health or marketing pressure can intervene as either inhibitors or facilitators on making a vacation decision. Belk (1975, p. 158) defines situations as 'all those factors particular to a time and place of observation, which do not follow from a knowledge of personal (intra-individual) and stimulus (object or choice alternative) attributes and which have a demonstrable and systematic effect on current behavior'. He distinguishes five types of situational variables, which are described and illustrated by appropriate tourism examples in Table 1.2.

1.3. Vacation as a Socio-economic Object

In this section, we want to make sure that tourism and vacation are properly understood throughout this book. These concepts will be discussed in a social (phenomenon) and economic (product) perspective, but first, the reasons why we prefer speaking of vacation instead of tourism are explained.

1.3.1. Why 'vacation' rather than 'tourism'?

When reading previous sections, maybe it has been noticed that tourism and vacation are used interchangeably. In the following chapters, we will prefer the words 'vacation' and 'vacationer' to 'tourism' and 'tourist', respectively. There are several reasons for this:

1. Tourism etymologically refers to touring, which is only one way to spend one's leisure days. In contrast, vacation is less restrictive, as there are more ways to spend one's vacation (e.g. touring, vacationing at the same spot or vacationing at home).
2. Only leisure tourism is considered here and not other forms of tourism, like business or religious tourism (see WTO, 1995). In this respect, 'vacation', which has a connotation of leisure time, is less ambiguous than 'tourism'.
3. Data from our study show that tourism has a negative connotation: informants do not like to be considered as tourists, which is related to crowd behaviour and lack of authenticity, but rather as vacationers.

Table 1.2. Situational variables in vacation decision making.

Type of variable	Definition	Tourism example
Physical surrounding	Includes the weather, geographical location, decor, sounds, lights, aromas, tangible signs and displays of merchandise and other materials	The weather in the home region, outdoor advertising and the decor of a travel agency's window may influence destination choice
Social surrounding	Includes the other persons, their characteristics, roles and interactions	People living in crowded cities tend to spend their holiday in open spaces where they can rest and be alone for a while
Temporal perspective	Includes the period (from time of the day to season of the year), time constraints, and elapsed or expected time	Many vacationers are limited by the period (depending on the school holiday) and by the available time (paid holiday)
Task definition	Stands for the orientation, intent, role or frame of a person, through which certain aspects of the environment may become relevant	The vacationer is not likely to use the same criteria in selecting a city trip for oneself and as a gift for one's parents
Antecedent states	Momentary moods or conditions, which 'colour' the perception, evaluation and acceptance of the present environment, that are stipulated to be immediately antecedent to the current situation	A couple who is very tired after a house move could choose a club vacation, even though they usually prefer a more culturally active holiday

A last question: why do we prefer the words 'vacation' to 'holiday' and 'vacationer' to 'holidaymaker'? The reason is etymological. The word 'vacation' was first used to designate the cessation of an activity (end of the 14th century). It comes from the Latin word *vacare*, which means being empty or doing nothing. Then, it received the sense of a suspension or a break from work, i.e. a period of rest. Since the mid-15th century, the term indicates the period of the year when judicial, school and university activities are suspended. Later, 'holiday', which etymologically means the holy day dedicated to a religious feast, was used as a synonym for rest and recreation (Rauch, 1993). 'Holiday' prevails in the UK, whereas 'vacation' is more popular in the USA.

1.3.2. A socio-anthropological perspective

A historical sketch

Vacation is a broad Western sociocultural phenomenon in modern history that does not hold for earlier periods and other societies. In the Middle Ages, travelling was automatically connected with trade or religion. Modern times gave rise to the concept of leisure tourism, together with the Renaissance and the refinement of society. However, non-trade travelling was still the privilege of the aristocracy and was related to well-defined goals, most often health and culture. After the French Revolution, blood privileges were replaced by wealth privileges. The gentry became the leisure class, when private income made idleness possible. At the beginning of the 19th century, travelling became a factor of social valourization and a cultural value. Veblen (1899), in his famous *Theory of the Leisure Class*, was the first to suggest that leisure reflects social class structure and the uneven distribution of work in society. He further presented the consumption of leisure as a symbol of social status. The first tourist-travellers had no other goal than spending their time for their own pleasure. These were the glory days of romanticism and sentimentalism: 'in their quest for unusual or historic sites, those tourists feed a meditation on time or existence' (Rauch, 1993, p. 9). The change of scenery was the requested feeling. This 'luxury' engendered the envy of lower social classes, who progressively claimed the right to leisure and vacation.

Since the mid-19th century, vacation became available to broader population strata. An imitation effect arose, as people longed for consumption patterns of higher social levels. The achievement of half-day and longer weekend breaks (since the second half of the 19th century in several European countries) paved the way for week-long holidays and paid vacation on a regular basis (1936 in Belgium). This lay at the origin of the development of mass tourism. Resting, relaxing and having fun in crowded places were the major vacation motives of these lower middle classes. Since the Second World War, the tourism industry has seen extraordinary growth. There are more factors that foster travel and tourism demand.

1. Discretionary time is continuously increasing. With the organization and standardization of work alongside the industrial revolution, working hours were gradually reduced. This reduction of labour time, which is still continuing today, contributes to an unceasing increase in available leisure time.

2. Discretionary income in the industrialized countries has been growing continuously for three decades. This has boosted the private consumption of goods and services, including tourism, and has opened the world of leisure to almost any social strata. Moreover, factors such as inflation and exchange rate favour the development of tourism demand in countries with stable currencies and expanding economies.

3. Technological evolution and new transportation systems (like charters for air travel) result, through economies of scale and energy, in cost reduction and a downward shift in retail prices. The ever-growing competition among destinations and tourism suppliers also explains this.

4. Political factors also come into play. With the passing decades, tourism became a powerful economical and social reality. States were induced to acknowledge its importance and have progressively used it to achieve sociocultural, educational and political objectives. Countries whose tourism receipts are (potentially) important take a particular care to maintain their image through political stability. As illustrated by the recent examples of the Iraq War, the civil war in Algeria or the bombing waves in Turkey and Indonesia, 'good reputation' is a key factor for success to hosting countries. Peace and security are necessary conditions for tourism demand.

In conclusion, throughout the 20th century the evolution towards a more open and integrated society has extended geographical and cultural borders. This, too, has fostered tourism demand. The narrowing gap between developed nations and social classes is influenced by factors such as communication and media development, and the evolution of mentalities.

A socio-anthropological interpretation

How to analyse this historical shift towards mass tourism? Urry (1990, p. 7) points out that 'there is relatively little substance to the sociology of tourism'. Nash (1996) comes to a similar statement with respect to the anthropology of tourism. The various socio-anthropological explanations of tourism may be subsumed under two general themes: one concerned with the problem of authenticity and alienation and the other related to the personal transition from everyday to vacation life. To a certain extent, this dichotomy parallels the distinction between push-and-pull factors[2]. The latter perspective is concerned with the interactions between hosts and guests, while the former focuses on the guests only.

After Veblen (1899), Boorstin (1964) offers one of the earliest formulations of tourism as a social phenomenon. He considers tourism as the prime example of 'pseudo-events' – mass tourists insulated in 'environmental bubbles' (i.e. guided groups isolated from the host environment and communities in the familiar American-style hotel) who find pleasure in inauthentic, contrived attractions. Boorstin observes that his contemporary Americans enjoy these 'pseudo-events' and disregard the real (strange) world outside. This idea of *alienation* and superficiality is further developed by Turner and Ash (1975). Tourists are

---

[2] The constructs of push-and-pull factors originate from migration theory and, in particular, from the question 'why do people move?' The 'push–pull hypothesis' is one of the first attempts to give a general explanation to such moves (Thomas, 1941). It suggests that migration is due to 'socio-economic imbalances between regions, certain factors "pushing" persons away from the area of origin, and others "pulling" them to the area of destination' (Jansen, 1969).

restricted by surrogate parents (travel agents, couriers, hotel managers) to strictly circumscribed and fumigated worlds where they are relieved of any responsibility and protected from harsh reality. Those parents make sure that tourists only go to and see 'approved' places and objects, in order to avoid too much contradiction with the home country. Characteristics of local cultures are oversimplified and mass-produced, resulting in 'tourist kitsch'. Cohen (1972, 1979, 1988) tempers this tradition by maintaining that there is no single tourist as such, but a variety of tourist types and modes of tourist experiences. 'Experiential', 'experimental' and 'existential' tourists do not rely on and, to varying degrees, even reject conventional organized tourist activity. Moreover, such environmental bubbles 'permit many people to visit places which otherwise they would not, and to have at least some contact with the "strange" places thereby encountered' (Urry, 1990, p. 8).

The major challenge to Boorstin's position comes from MacCannell (1976). He criticizes Boorstin (1964) and Lévi-Strauss (1955) because their accounts are exemplary of an upper-class view, where deriding tourists is 'intellectually chic': 'tourists dislike tourists', to quote MacCannell's own words (1976, p. 10). He further argues that the so-called 'pseudo-events' stem from the social relations resulting from tourism and not from an individualistic commitment to the lack of authenticity. For MacCannell, all tourists are looking for *authenticity*. This modern quest for authenticity is paralleled with the universal concern for the sacred. The tourist is a kind of modern pilgrim, seeking authenticity away from everyday life in other historical periods, other cultures as well as in purer, simpler lifestyles. Among these, tourists are particularly fascinated by the 'real lives', i.e. the daily work lives of others. Since direct observation of these real lives is difficult and ethically unacceptable, tourist attractions (or 'tourist spaces') are constructed backstage in a contrived and artificial manner. These constructions lie at the core of MacCannell's concept of 'staged authenticity'. Other authors (Pearce and Moscardo, 1986; Crick, 1988) have further elaborated on this concept. MacCannell also speaks of alienated leisure (since tourism involves a return to the workplace). He notes the extreme diversity of tourist centres of attraction and the regulation of these (tourist gazes cannot be left to chance: the gaze's object has to be there or to 'happen').

The second general socio-anthropological view focuses on tourists and their odysseys, or tourism as a *personal transition*. Based on the processual model in anthropology (i.e. all societies mark the passage of time through rituals and special events), vacation is seen as a kind of ritual of renewal in the annual cycle. Vacation marks a seasonal special and sacred break from the mundane and profane everyday work (Graburn, 1989). Further, particular tourist experiences such as honeymoon trips or retirement cruises are analogous to 'rites de passage' (van Gennep, 1909) or intermittent pilgrimages (Turner and Turner, 1978; Smith, 1992), which may be paralleled with the Muslim 'haj' to Mecca (Graburn and Moore, 1994). MacCannell (1976) proposes a number of stages involved in tourist rituals: naming the sight, framing and elevation, enshrinement, mechanical reproduction as new sights name themselves after the famous.

Turner (1973, 1974) makes a distinction between three ritual stages, which were adapted to tourism by other authors (Lett, 1983; Cohen, 1988; Shields, 1990):

1. Separation: the social and spatial separation from the conventional social ties and usual place of residence.
2. Liminality: the direct experience of the sacred (shrines) out of time, place and conventional social ties. This results in a kind of uplifting experience. This also gives room for 'liminoid situations' (Turner and Turner, 1978), where everyday obligations are suspended or even inverted, leading to permissive and playful behaviour and/or unconstrained social togetherness.
3. Reintegration: 'the individual is reintegrated in the previous social group, usually at a higher social status' (Urry, 1990, p. 10).

Tourism is portrayed as a quest for the inversion of everyday life: the upper middle-class tourist seeks to be a 'peasant for a day' while the lower middle-class tourist will seek to be a 'king or queen for a day'. Moreover, in their passages (since tourists are touring), tourists are moving from one experiential state to another, with greater or lesser consequences for themselves and their home societies (Nash, 1996).

Urry (1990) also neglects authenticity as the basis for the organization of tourism: tourists are not looking for authenticity but 'just' for an escape from everyday life. Another argument comes from Feifer (1985), who points out that some tourists ('post-tourists') almost delight in the inauthenticity of tourist experiences. They know that there is no authentic tourist experience, but merely a series of games that can be played. Based on Foucault's idea (1976) of the gaze, Urry proposes an alternative explanation of tourism. The tourist gaze arises from a movement (journey) of people to, and their stay in, various other destinations outside the normal places of residence and work. While tourist gazes may bear on a lot of different places and objects, they share common characteristics, such as:

1. Gazes are related to purposes that are not directly connected with paid work.
2. Tourist gazes have a mass character.
3. Features have to be out of the ordinary, in that they separate the tourist from everyday and routine experiences.
4. Tourist satisfaction stems from the anticipation of intense pleasures, especially through daydreaming and fantasy (Campbell, 1987). Such anticipation is constructed and sustained by advertising and the media, which generate sets of signs.
5. The gaze is constructed through signs and tourism involves the collection of such signs (Urry, 1995). Dann (1996) further elaborates on the language of tourism by underlining that tourism has a discourse of its own (revealed by the act of promotion and by the accounts of practitioners and customers).

In addition to the two major themes of authenticity and personal transition, other explanations of tourism have been proposed by anthropologists. First, tourism has been presented as a kind of *acculturation* or development.

Acculturation refers to 'the process wherein members of one culture react to another culture with which they are in contact' (Graburn and Moore, 1994, p. 237). This perspective emerges from the awareness that hosting societies are in the process of changing, often dramatically, as a result of contacts with the Western world. A few authors emphasize the asymmetry of hosts–guests interactions in tourism, as the more developed culture of the Western tourists dominates that of the lesser developed hosts (Nuñez, 1989). This view of tourism as imperialism (Crick, 1989; Nash, 1989) is criticized by Nash (1996).

Finally, tourism is considered a kind of *social superstructure*. In contrast with the acculturation paradigm, this perspective posits that the major forces that create tourism are to be found in the places where tourists are produced, i.e. in generating situations. The focus is on the guest, the demand side of tourism, and no longer on the host/destination supply side. Researchers have looked at the processes by which tourists are generated in their home societies. Why are there different rates or forms of tourism within and between societies? In order to answer this central question, Urry (1990) points at social class and Graburn (1983) at cross-cultural differences. In both cases, 'differences in mode of tourism are interpreted as being the result of basal sociocultural arrangements at home' (Nash, 1996, p. 90). Nash accommodates the different perspectives on the anthropological study of tourism in a bigger picture. His view involves a broadening of the acculturation paradigm according to which 'tourism may be seen to involve contact between agents of historically situated tourism generating and receiving situations with consequences for all parties involved in that contact' (Nash, 1996, p. 166).

1.3.3. An economic perspective

Vacation is a major human activity and social phenomenon, which involves large numbers of participants. In McIntosh *et al.* (1995, p. 10), four types of actors are distinguished: 'Tourism is the sum of the phenomena and relationships arising from the interaction of tourists, business suppliers, host governments, and host communities in the process of attracting and hosting these tourists and other visitors.' In this book, the focus is on tourists, and, more precisely, on vacationers as consumers of vacation products and services.

Tourism is a very particular product that, to a large extent, cannot be compared with any other consumer good or service. Speaking of *the* tourist product is even improper since tourism consists of a collection of items that can have physical and service features together with symbolic associations, all of which expect to fulfill the wants and needs of the consumer. This may include a place (the travel destination), a service (the tour operator's package including most of the time transportation and lodging) and sometimes even tangible items (like the travel bag). However, tourism is often categorized as a service since it entails the characteristics of a service such as described in Table 1.3 (Judd, 1964; Kotler, 2003).

Table 1.3. Tourism as a service.

Service characteristics	Tourism characteristics	Tourism consequences
Intangibility	Like any service, the tourist service cannot be tested or physically inspected before consumption	Increased perceived risk for the buyer
Heterogeneity	In contrast to tangible mass-produced goods like cars or refrigerators, it is very difficult to standardize tourist services	The tourist producer has no hold on destination characteristics like weather or local prices, and on the labour force that is providing tourism services
Perishability	The consumption of tourist and travel services is strongly time-bound; moreover, tourism demand is very seasonal, causing a discrepancy between a fluctuating demand and a stable supply	If not sold at the right moment, a plane seat or a cruise berth is lost forever
Inseparability	The tourist offer comprises a set of services and products, which cannot be sold or consumed separately	There is a need for inclusive packages: from the very moment the tourist has decided to go on holiday, he or she needs, among other things, transportation, lodging and meals
Ownership	In contrast to a consumer good, a tourist service cannot be owned, but is only temporarily accessed or used by the purchaser	The tourist owns the benefit of the service (flight, hotel or beach) and not the service itself; i.e. he or she has no enduring involvement in the product, but only in the benefit

At the aggregate level, tourism demand results from the 'activities of persons traveling to and staying in places outside their usual environment for not more than one consecutive year for leisure, business and other purposes' (WTO, 1995, p. 15). The Word Tourism Organization (WTO) further makes a distinction between overnight visitors (who are called tourists) and day visitors. Five types of travel motives are proposed: leisure, relaxation and vacation; visiting friends or relatives; business and occupational motives; medical care; religion and pilgrimages.

Tourism is not a product like others for several reasons. First, going on vacation involves a lot of decisions and sub-decisions, like where to go, what to do, how to go there and with whom. All those decisions entail a lot of perception and evaluation judgements, which are based on several different attributes. So, destination judgements may bear upon the climate, the landscape, cultural sights or the local people. A usual distinction (Lefkoff-Hagius and Mason, 1993) is made between: (i) characteristic or product-referent attributes (e.g. the mean temperature or spiciness of food at a tourist destination); (ii) beneficial or outcome-referent attributes (e.g. the friendliness of the local people or good taste of food); and (iii) image or user-referent attributes (e.g. vacationing in Monaco would give me a prestigious and rich image; going to Iraq would make an insensible adventurer of me).

Second, vacation decisions have a dynamic nature since plans evolve and travel decisions spread over time with absolute deadlines (i.e. the vacation periods). A few papers (Francken, 1978; van Raaij and Francken, 1984; Moutinho, 1987) show that vacation choices involve a long DMP, which takes place over many months. Moreover, the different vacation decision items have a different timing (Dellaert *et al.*, 1998).

Third, from the socio-economic point of view, vacation is very interesting since:

1. Tourism is an important human activity: many people spend a lot of time thinking, talking about, planning and experiencing their vacation.
2. Vacations represent joint economic decisions, i.e. they involve the whole household (Fodness, 1992).
3. Travel and vacation are a major recurrent entry in many household budgets. Ryan (1995, pp. 94–95) points out that 'for many families, it is often the largest single repeated expenditure that occurs at frequent intervals'.

For all these reasons, focusing on tourists' DMPs deserves a closer look. As shown in Chapter 2, it has already attracted a lot of interest in the recent tourism marketing research literature.

Models of Vacation Decision Making

2.0. Introduction

The vacationer's DMP has been investigated in a substantial number of papers and monographs in the last three decades. The majority of these are restricted in scope since they are limited to some specific aspects of vacation DM, such as motivation (Mansfeld, 1992; Fodness, 1994), information search (Fesenmaier and Vogt, 1992; Fodness and Murray, 1997; Mäser and Weiermair, 1998), or family DM (Jenkins, 1978; van Raaij, 1986; Nichols and Snepenger, 1988). However, a few general conceptualizations have been proposed. In this review, we make a distinction between: (i) microeconomic; (ii) cognitive; and (iii) interpretive models (a summarized description of all models is given in Appendix 1). Microeconomic models use traditional demand theory in order to explain tourism behaviour. A rational vacationer is depicted who tries to maximize the utility of his or her choices under the constraint of his or her budget.

Cognitive models do not pay attention to the price–demand relationship but to the mental processes that are involved in DM. We identify three types of cognitive models: input–output or 'consideration set' (CS), sequential and process. Most of these lean heavily on classical buyer behaviour theory and postulate a (bounded) rational and hierarchical tourist DM. In sequential models, the DMP is thought to take place in compulsory sequential steps, which are typically problem identification, information search, evaluation of alternatives, choice and post-choice processes. The second family of models can also be considered sequential, but the focus is on the evolution of product alternatives in CSs. That is why we categorize these approaches as 'consideration set (CS) models', even though this wording may sound a little strange. Finally, process models do not pay as much attention to the structural relationships between input and output as to the mental processes that underlie DM.

In contrast to both microeconomic and cognitive models, interpretive frameworks are not concerned with how vacationers *should*, but on *how* they *actually* make decisions. The personal, social and cultural context of DM is taken into account to present a more naturalistic view of the consumer. We will now discuss each type of model by first, presenting the different conceptualizations from extant literature, and second, by assessing strengths and shortcomings of those models, and enhancing the interest of revisiting tourist DM from a broader contextualized perspective.

2.1. Microeconomic Models

Microeconomic approaches to the study of vacation DM are based on the concept of the economic person, spending money to gain satisfaction, maximizing the utility or benefits of his or her choices under the constraint of his or her budget. Decisions are thought to be governed by price: the lower the price, the higher the volume of demand and vice versa. This normative approach aims to explain how the consumer should behave rather than how he or she really behaves. Decisions are individual, timeless and context-free ('other things being equal'). The questions of how and why the vacationer makes choices are dismissed.

Tourism demand analysis has benefited from considerable interest. Traditional demand theory is defined as 'the analysis of consumer choice under budget constraint and the consequent prediction of the change in a consumer's chosen collection of goods when prices change' (Lancaster, 1971, p. 2). In addition, any good (vacation alternative) is thought to possess objective characteristics or attributes that are used by consumers in their evaluations. Utility is ultimately derived from these attributes and maximizing utility requires choosing a bundle of goods that generates the optimum bundle of attributes. In tourism, Lancasterian demand models have been developed by authors such as Rugg (1973), Morley (1992) and Papatheodorou (2001).

Rugg

Rugg (1973) was the first to apply Lancaster's principles to tourism. He developed the following model in a system of N destinations:

Maximize $U = f(z_{tour})$
Subject to constraints:
$z_{tour} = G(d)$ (consumption technology),
$Y \geq p_{tour}d + p_{trans}m$ (budget),
$z, d, p_{tour}, p_{trans}, m\ c, t\ n \geq 0$ $Y, T \geq 0$

Where:

z_{tour} = the vector of characteristics of tourism (e.g. historical characteristics, scenic beauty);

G = the matrix of consumption technology coefficients;
d = the vector of the composite tourism product (i.e. the number of days spent in each destination);
p_{tour} = the vector of corresponding prices;
p_{trans} = the vector of transportation fares between all destination pairs;
m = the permutation column vector whose elements are either 1 or 0;
c = the permutation row whose elements are all 1;
t = the vector of transportation times between all destination pairs;
n = the permutation column vector whose elements are 1 or 0;
Y = the disposable income or the money budget allocated to tourism;
T = the discretionary time or the time budget allocated to tourism.

In his model, Rugg introduced three dimensions that were ignored by tourism demand economists at that time: time constraint, transportation costs (by modifying the budget constraint) and time costs (by modifying the time constraint). Rugg's model was empirically tested through a least-squared regression analysis.

Morley

Morley (1992) extended Rugg's work on tourism demand modelling. He suggested a decision process that incorporates: (i) the decision to travel or not; (ii) the allocation of time and budget; and (iii) the choice of the tour. All these elements are integrated in one utility function along with non-tourism goods or services. The major contribution of this model is the idea that changes in incomes and in the prices of non-tourism products may affect tourism behaviour. Moreover, in line with Lancaster and Rugg, Morley paid particular attention to tour characteristics, which are classified in three types:

1. Those common to all tours that are not dependent on the time spent on the tour (e.g. any overseas trip).
2. Those that are particular to a tour but that are not time-dependent (e.g. visiting friends in England).
3. Those that depend on the time spent on the tour (e.g. the activities that are carried out).

In Morley's words (1992, p. 259):

> [D]ifferent tours yield different utilities, because of attributes of the tours themselves and their contribution to the utility of the individual. For example, an individual may be looking for a holiday consisting mainly of lying in the sun on an exotically located beach. Tours will offer varying amounts of the important relevant factors: sunshine, attractive beaches, etc. The utility derived will depend on such factors.

Morley's discrete choice model (1994) has been empirically tested through experiments exploring the impact of three price variables on the choice of Sydney as a destination by tourists from Kuala Lumpur. Haider and Ewing

(1990) have used a similar experimental method to analyse the preferences of winter beach vacationers for various Caribbean destination attributes (i.e. characteristics of the accommodation, the distance to the tourist facilities and price).

Papatheodorou

Papatheodorou (2001) raises a few points against the application of traditional demand theory in tourism, as it ignores the particularities of the tourist product. First, he thinks that consumer heterogeneity is a stylized fact: '[T]he assumption of a representative tourist who visits simultaneously all the destinations under consideration is highly unrealistic' (2001, p. 165). Second, demand theory gives a static view and falls short on accounting for the evolutionary features of the tourism product (e.g. the emergence of new destinations and the decline of others). For Papatheodorou, one should distance oneself from the assumption of a homogeneous good: most of the time, tourist destinations cannot be compared directly because they are differentiated both horizontally (consumer preferences are asymmetric over the variety of destinations) and vertically (quality differs from one destination to the other). Third, the gradual emergence of large consolidated and coordinated business structures in tourism is in opposition with the assumption of classical demand theory – that producers are 'pathetic price takers' incapable of coordinating their strategies or manipulating tourist markets.

In order to face these caveats, Papatheodorou suggests applying the Lancasterian characteristics framework in line with Rugg (1973) and Morley (1992). However, he proposes a discrete choice model where the vacationer travels only to the resort or destination that is associated with the highest utility, thereby excluding multidestination tourism. Based on two dimensions (attractions and facilities), he makes a comparative exercise that focuses on the effects related to expenditure and time impediments, prices, consumer preferences, quality, information and advertising, agglomeration and, finally, the emergence of new destinations.

Seddighi and Theocharous

In another effort to explain tourism demand, Seddighi and Theocharous (2002) combined the Lancasterian approach and Koppelman's Consumer Transportation Model (1980). The latter differs from traditional economic demand models in that it incorporates psychological consumer-oriented variables such as perceptions, feelings and preferences. These act as mediators between the travel system characteristics and choice behaviour, and hence provide an improved understanding of tourism behaviour. Destination choice is seen as a multistep process depicted in Fig. 2.1.

First, tourists are identified by a series of socio-economic and demographic indicators. Each is faced with the generic decision to go on vacation or not. Second, the prospective vacationer has to choose between a domestic and a foreign holiday, which is mainly determined by his or her purchasing power. He or she then develops perceptions and feelings (attitudes) towards alternative (either

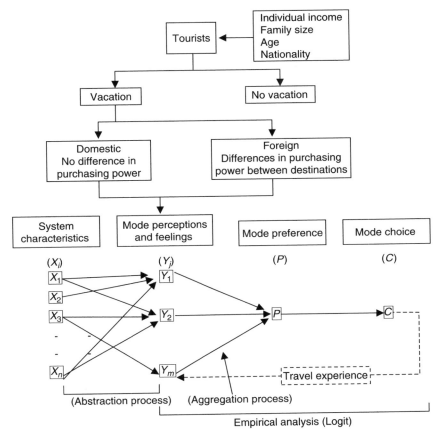

Fig. 2.1. Seddighi and Theocharous's model of tourist behaviour and destination choice.

domestic, foreign or a combination of both) destinations (Y_j) on the basis of their characteristics (X_i). These perceptions and feelings are assumed to serve as decision criteria through an abstraction process from the system characteristics. Third, perceptions and feelings are aggregated into a preference ordering of destination alternatives that is expected to lead to choice (this process is moderated by situational constraints such as holiday availability). Fourth, the tourist's travel experience acts as a feedback loop to modify the perceptions and feelings towards the visited destinations.

This conceptual model has been empirically tested through a field survey on a sample of 200 tourists in Cyprus. A multivariate Logit model was used to analyse the data. Conditional probabilities were computed as a measure of perceptions and feelings, given the characteristics of tourists and the tourism products. Thirteen characteristics were used as variables in the model: age, gender, marital status, income, education, previous experience, cost of living at the destination, price of the tourist package, facilities, cost of transportation, quality of promotion and advertising, quality of services and political instability. None of these variables proved to be significant at the 0.05 level when being tested one at a time. However, the overall fit of the model (all variables taken together) was considerably high ($pseudo$-R^2 = 0.679). Age and the quality of promotion proved to be the major factors for changing feelings and perceptions.

Criticism

Although they are useful for explaining and predicting tourist choices, microeconomic models show severe limitations. First, they do not address the substantive issues of information asymmetry and the possible inversions of the demand–price curve (i.e. snobbish effect). More importantly, the rationality paradigm raises serious questions for such an emotional and experiential product as tourism. Most characteristics of the tourist product do not match the economic tenets of tangible return on investment, spontaneous DM involving a small part of the consumer's assets, or material delivery of the product. For example, distance generally means economic disutility since it generates extra cost; in contrast, in tourism, distance is often associated with utility as extra miles mean more discovery and more exoticism. Moreover, microeconomic models do not incorporate a substantial number of variables (intrapersonal, interpersonal and contextual) that may be relevant in vacation DM. In the same way, they lack dynamism (decisions are assumed to be static and untemporal) and focus on the individual consumer although vacation decisions often evolve over time and are made in a group setting (e.g. family, party of friends). In summary, microeconomic models are useful to measure and predict, but not to understand, vacation DM in its full complexity.

2.2. Cognitive Models

The cognitive paradigm to consumer research and behaviour focuses on the socio-psychological variables and processes involved in DM. The consumer is no longer passive but becomes an actor of his or her choices: he or she thinks and develops rules and strategies in order to solve his or her problems, to satisfy his or her needs. Perception and information processing are the core processes for this. Svenson (1979) makes a distinction between structural and process approaches. Structural models are concerned with the relation between input, defined in terms of the information provided about each alternative, and output, represented by judgements of, or choice between, the alternatives. In contrast to this, process approaches pertain to how decisions are made in terms of the underlying cognitive processes. We will use this distinction here as well.

2.2.1. Structural models

A major stream of research about vacation DM focuses on the evolution of destinations (vacation plans) in CSs. This stream may be paralleled with the input–output principle that is typical of structural approaches. The CS (evoked set) comprises all the destinations the vacationer is contemplating for his or her current holiday. It is part of the perceived opportunity set (awareness set), which includes all the destinations known to the vacationer. As the latter is not omniscient, the awareness set is itself only a part of the total opportunity set, which entails all possible destination alternatives (Woodside and Sherrell, 1977; Goodall, 1991). Choice then consists of an evaluation and selection process where the different destinations in the CS are compared on an alternative or attribute basis.

Crompton and colleagues

Crompton (1977) presents a structural model of the tourist's destination choice process in two steps: first, there is the generic decision of whether or not to have a holiday, and, if the answer is yes, there is the second decision of where to go? He depicts destination choice as the result of the interaction of perceived constraints (e.g. time, money, skills) and destination images. Broadening Crompton's conceptualization, Um and Crompton (1990) developed a more complete framework based on the ideas of Howard and Sheth's DMP (1969), Fishbein and Ajzen's multi-attribute attitude model (1975), Belk's situational variables (1975) and Assael (1984). As illustrated in Fig. 2.2, the model is divided into three sets of variables:

1. External inputs, which represent influences from both social and marketing environments. Following Howard and Sheth (1969), these are classified into significative (destination attributes), symbolic (promotional messages) and social stimuli.
2. Internal inputs, which derive from the vacationer's socio-psychological characteristics (personal characteristics, motives, values and attitudes).
3. Cognitive constructs, which represent the 'integration of the internal and external inputs, into the awareness set of destinations and the evoked set of destinations' (Um and Crompton, 1990, p. 436). Two stages in travel destination choice are distinguished: (i) an evolution of an evoked set from the set of destinations the vacationer is aware of (awareness set); and (ii) selection of one destination from the evoked set. At both stages, attitude is the key construct in the destination choice process. Based on broader socio-psychological literature, three attitudinal dimensions are recognized: need satisfaction, social agreement and 'travelability'[1].

---

[1] 'Travelability' should be understood as the propensity to travel.

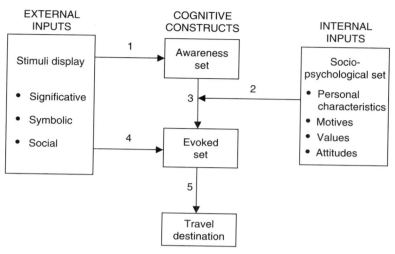

Fig. 2.2. Um and Crompton's model of the pleasure travel destination choice process.

There is thus a cognitive evolution, which Um and Crompton materialize in five sets of processes represented by arrows in Fig. 2.2:

1. Formation of beliefs about destination attributes (through passive information catching or incidental learning).
2. Initiation of destination choice process after the generic decision to go on holiday has been made (including consideration of situational constraints).
3. Evolution of an evoked set from the awareness set of destinations.
4. Formation of beliefs about evoked destination attributes (through active information search).
5. Selection of a specific travel destination from the evoked set.

The empirical testing of this model focuses on the differences between attitude scores (operationalized as the difference between perceived inhibitors and perceived facilitators, in order to take situational constraints into account) at the two stages of the model. Results suggest that 'attitude is a significant indicator for predicting whether or not a vacation place is selected as a final destination from the alternatives in the awareness set' (Um and Crompton, 1990, p. 445).

Woodside and Lysonski

Woodside and Lysonski's general model (1989) of traveller destination choice is probably the most popular conceptualization to date. To a large extent, this model is in line with Um and Crompton (1990), since it again heavily leans on Howard and Sheth's theory (1969) of buyer behaviour. Marketing variables (coming from the marketing mix's four *P*s) stand for the external inputs; traveller variables (i.e. previous experience, socio-demographics, lifestyles and value system) represent the internal inputs; and Woodside and Lysonski's evolution from destination awareness to choice can be compared with Um and Crompton's progression from awareness set to the final location choice. However, Woodside and Lysonski add more details since destination awareness is seen as the mental categorization process between CS (spontaneously evoked destinations), inept set (rejected destinations), inert set (destinations that are not actively considered) and unavailable but aware set. They also add important variables that were not identified in Um and Crompton's model, such as:

1. Affective associations: specific feelings related to a specific destination.
2. Traveller destination preferences: influenced by both destination categorizations and affective associations, and resulting in a ranking of destinations.
3. Intentions to visit: perceived likelihood of visiting a particular destination within a specific time period.

The arrows in Fig. 2.3 indicate how these variables connect with each other.

Destination awareness and, more particularly, the categorization process in four sets, is influenced by both marketing mix and the traveller's own variables (especially previous experience; see arrows 1 and 2). These increase the destination's likelihood of being included in the vacationer's CS. Affective associations are usually positive for a destination that is part of the evoked set ('Spain has breath-taking beaches and a wonderful nightlife') and negative for a destination that is in the inept set ('there is nothing to do in Austria'; arrow 4). Tourist preferences for particular destinations is a positive function of the rank order of those destinations in tourist CSs (arrow 5). Intention to visit a specific destination is influenced positively by the consumer's preference towards that destination (arrow 9). Based on bivariate tests, Woodside and Lysonski found empirical support for those hypotheses. Another interesting finding is that the average sizes of the CSs are rather small (three to five destinations on average; see also Woodside and Sherrell, 1977). Although the other relationships were not tested, the authors argued that:

1. Preferences are (at least partly) positively influenced by affective associations and are also affected by some of the traveller's variables.
2. Choice is predicted to be affected by the interaction of intention to visit and situational variables.

Criticism

Structural models are popular in vacation behaviour research because they describe the major cognitive, affective and behavioural variables involved in the DMP and suggest sequences to connect them. Moreover, they are limited to a few key variables, which makes them simple to understand and easy to use

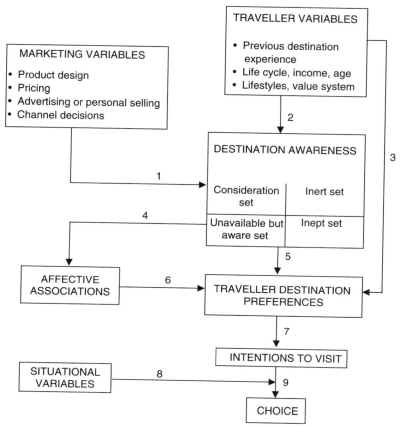

Fig. 2.3. Woodside and Lysonski's general model of traveller leisure destination awareness and choice.

for empirical studies (in the CS models described above, significant statistical relationships have been brought into light) and managerial decisions. However, structural models are reductive because they only deal with a small part of the variables and relationships that may be involved in DMPs. While useful for measurement and prediction, those models show severe limitations for a thorough understanding of tourist behaviour. They fail to explain the complexity of DM and its full range of variables. Ritchie (1994) has put a finger on this lack of a comprehensive framework describing the many components and processes of tourist DM. He further argues that inadequate attention is paid to the context of DM.

2.2.2. Process models

In CS models, the focus is on structural relationships between inputs (traveller and marketing variables) and outputs (preferences, intentions and choices). In the process approach to DM, the focus is not on decision itself but rather on psycho-behavioural variables that underlie DM and on *the way* consumers come to have cognitive and affective judgements, intentions and commitments prior to arriving at a final decision (Abelson and Levi, 1985). Most process models are sequential as they suggest an evolution of plans and decisions through different stages.

Early efforts

Wahab *et al.* (1976) have been the first to elaborate a sequential vacation DM model involving the following steps: initial stimulus, conceptual framework, fact gathering, definitions of assumptions, design of alternatives, forecast of consequences, cost–benefit of alternatives, decision and outcome. Moreover, the authors stress the uniqueness of the holiday-buying decision in that there is: (i) no tangible return on investment; (ii) considerable expenditure in relation to earned income; (iii) a purchase that is not spontaneous; and (iv) an expenditure level that necessitates saving and preplanning. However, their framework is very stereotypical (the authors believe that DM always goes through the same sequential process) and still imbued with economic principles.

Actually, Schmoll (1977) and Mathieson and Wall (1982) were the first to develop sequential vacation DM frameworks based on the grand models of consumer behaviour (those of Nicosia, 1966; Howard and Sheth, 1969). Motivation (travel desire) is responsible for triggering the whole DMP. The next 'classical' stages follow: information search, assessment of alternatives and decisions. For Schmoll (1977), this whole DMP is influenced by four sets of variables:

1. Travel stimuli (e.g. trade publications).
2. Personal and social determinants that contribute to shape motivations, desires or needs, and expectations.
3. External variables (e.g. confidence in the travel agent, destination image, previous experience, cost and time constraints).
4. Characteristics of service distribution.

For Mathieson and Wall (1982), travel desire is a function of the tourist's profile and his or her awareness of the destination resources and characteristics. It is followed by information collection, assessment of alternatives, actual decisions, travel experience and evaluation. A number of 'trip features' (including structural, personal and interpersonal aspects) influence these different aspects of DM (see Fig. 2.4).

Ten years later, Mansfeld (1992) came up with a more parsimonious version of Mathieson and Wall's conceptualization, with three major steps leading to choice: motivation (rather than desires), information search and the evaluation of alternatives. The role of motivation is enhanced as a large

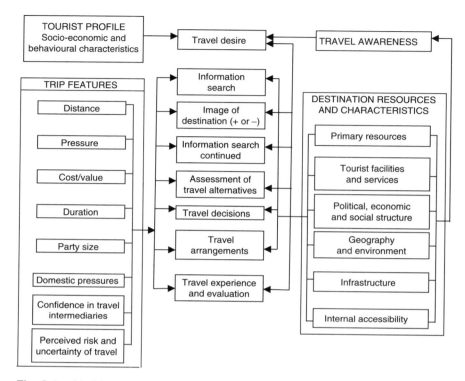

Fig. 2.4. Mathieson and Wall's tourist decision-making process.

number of complex motivators (both intrinsic and extrinsic) may influence travel behaviour. Moreover, Mansfeld introduces group constraints impinging on destination choice.

van Raaij and colleagues

van Raaij and Francken (1984) and van Raaij (1986) give an interesting description of 'the vacation sequence'. Based on Engel and Blackwell (1982), they distinguish five stages in tourist behaviour:

1. Generic decision (primarily depending on discretionary income and family life cycle).
2. Information acquisition (mainly a function of experience and educational level).
3. DMP (considered a joint family task).
4. Vacation activities (adventure, experience, conformity, education, health, social contacts and status).
5. Subsequent (dis)satisfaction (difference between expectations and actual 'performance'; the attribution of dissatisfaction determines complaint behaviour).

Other determinants of the DMP are 'advertising by travel agents, household communication and interaction style, level of education and experience with vacations, price sensitivity and sensitivity for other vacation attributes, loyalty to destinations, and types of vacations' (van Raaij, 1986, p. 4). van Raaij further underlines the importance of perceptions and preferences as a basis for understanding consumer research in tourism and recommends using behavioural constructs (e.g. DM behaviour, vacation activities and post-experience behaviour) to classify tourists. The focus of van Raaij's models is more on group DM (the interaction process) and on segmentation variables (e.g. lifestyle) than on psychological variables.

Moutinho

The most encompassing process model so far has been proposed by Moutinho (1982). In his '[i]nvestigation of vacation tourist behaviour in Portugal', the author makes a comprehensive overview of all major variables that intervene in the tourist DMP, and expands it to the proposition of a general flowchart model. He first develops an extremely complex framework (three full pages are needed to write it!) and then simplifies it into a more manageable, although still very detailed, vacation tourist behaviour model (Moutinho, 1987). As can be seen in Fig. 2.5, the model is divided into three parts based on the usual distinction between pre- and post-purchase stages in consumer decision processes (see Wilkie, 1990).

PRE-DECISION AND DECISION PROCESSES   This stage involves 'the flow of events, from the tourist stimuli to purchase decisions' (Moutinho, 1987, p. 39), and is made up of three fields: preference structure, decision and purchase. The preference structure for a particular destination is based on a set of factors, including internalized environmental influences (cultural norms and values, reference groups, social class) and individual determinants (personality, lifestyle, motives). Attitude and family also contribute to frame the preference structure. The intention to purchase depends on the tourist's degree of certainty towards the destination ('confidence generation') and on inhibitors, which can cause the tourist to respond differently from what his or her attitudes dictate. Finally, the psychological analysis of the preference structure is split into three subfields:

1. Stimulus filtration: filtering travel marketing stimuli enables the vacationer to organize information in a meaningful way. If some stimuli are ambiguous, he or she may feel the need to search for additional information.
2. Attention and learning: the process of comparison whereby inputs are confronted with the information stored in memory, shaping the individual's cognitive structure.
3. Choice criteria: the tourist product attributes that are important to the vacationer when evaluating the different alternatives that constitute his evoked set.

Logically enough, this preference structure then leads to decisions and purchase. A decision is defined as 'a psychological predisposition in terms of intention

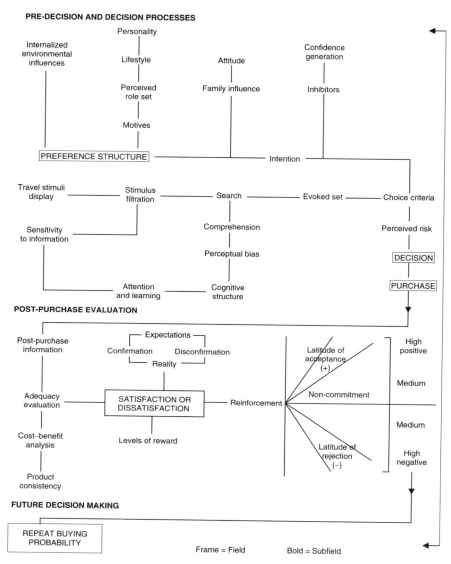

PRE-DECISION AND DECISION PROCESSES

Personality

Internalized environmental influences

Lifestyle   Attitude   Confidence generation

Perceived role set   Family influence   Inhibitors

Motives

PREFERENCE STRUCTURE ———————— Intention

Travel stimuli display ———— Stimulus filtration ———— Search ———— Evoked set ———— Choice criteria

Sensitivity to information   Comprehension   Perceived risk

Perceptual bias   DECISION

Attention and learning ———— Cognitive structure   PURCHASE

POST-PURCHASE EVALUATION

Post-purchase information

Expectations   High positive

Confirmation   Disconfirmation   Latitude of acceptance (+)

Reality   Medium

Adequacy evaluation   SATISFACTION OR DISSATISFACTION ———— Reinforcement   Non-commitment

Medium

Cost–benefit analysis   Levels of reward

Latitude of rejection (−)   High negative

Product consistency

FUTURE DECISION MAKING

REPEAT BUYING PROBABILITY   Frame = Field   Bold = Subfield

Fig. 2.5. Mountiho's vacation tourist behaviour model.

towards the buying act', whereas a purchase is 'the act of buying a vacation destination'. Moutinho points out that the total tourist product is often purchased in a sequence and not always as a tour package.

POST-PURCHASE EVALUATION   The tourist's purchase assessment process is fundamental since it adds to his or her store of experiences and provides feedback by adjusting his or her frame of reference for future purchase intentions. In the model, the post-purchase evaluation field is labelled 'satisfaction or dissatisfaction'. That dimension is considered in the light of the cognitive dissonance mechanism and results in three zones ('latitudes') of commitment to subsequent behaviour: positive (acceptance), negative (rejection) and neutral (non-commitment). Moutinho further introduces 'adequacy evaluation' as a subfield. This factor, resulting from a mental comparison process of costs and benefits, is related to 'the "ideal" point of each attribute of the tourist product as perceived by the tourist' (Moutinho, 1987, p. 42). This may be interpreted as a kind of quality/price ratio.

FUTURE DECISION MAKING   This last part of Moutinho's model can be seen as the practical interface with marketing decision planning. It concerns the study of the subsequent behaviour of the tourist by analysing repeat-buying probabilities of tourist products and services. Depending on return prospect, three cases are possible: straight rebuy, future rebuy and modified rebuy (change to new products or search for better quality). The fourth case, going to competition, results from either hesitation or refusal to buy the product again.

Goodall

Goodall (1988) makes a distinction between the holiday selection process and the choice of the resort. The holiday selection is described as 'systematic and sequential' and involves a bounded rational tourist, i.e. the tourist taking satisficing (rather than optimal) decisions 'within implicit and explicit constraints of an uncertain environment' (Goodall, 1988, p. 2). First, there is the generic decision to take a vacation, stemming from motivations. Then there is the evaluation of alternative vacations, which is made possible through the formation of mental images. Goodall introduces three different types of images: preferential (representing the ideal vacation); evaluative (expectation level against which actual vacation opportunities are compared); and naive or factual (pertaining to the perception of each vacation destination).

As to the resort choice (i.e. a package involving travel, accommodation and excursions), once the generic decision has been made, vacation requirements (subdecisions) must be specified and a search process initiated to find the vacation that best matches those requirements, within time and money limits. This search process may be more or less extensive depending on the vacationer type (e.g. impulse buyer vs. meticulous planner). The holidaymaker then evaluates the different alternatives following a satisficing rather than an optimizing rule, which leads to the final decision and purchase (booking his or her vacation).

Middleton and colleagues

Middleton's conceptualization (Middleton, 1994; Middleton and Clarke, 2001) is much more parsimonious and focuses on motivation as the driving force behind all decisions and as the origin of the dynamic process in the model. The model is split into four parts:

1. Stimulus input, consisting of the 'range of competitive products produced and marketed by the tourist industry' (Middleton and Clarke, 2001, p. 54).

2. Response outputs, pertaining to actual purchases that include product, brand, price, and outlet choices.

3. Communication channels, between input and output (divided into two parts: the formal commercial media and informal interpersonal communication), and between buyer characteristics and decision process where the central focus is on needs, wants and goals. These are influenced by three interacting elements: the vacationers' demographic, economic and social position, their psychographic characteristics and their attitudes. 'These three elements act sometimes as constraints upon purchase decisions and sometimes to provide or reinforce the motivation' (Middleton, 1994, p. 54).

4. Communication filters (learning, perception and experience), affecting the buying decision process in that only a small part of the information that is produced by the communication channels is received by the individual. Perception, itself influenced by attitudes, has a strong selective effect.

The last point in Middleton's conceptualization is the distinction between: (i) simple vacation purchases (car rental or motel accommodation), which are assimilated with convenience goods and routinized problem solving; and (ii) complex vacation purchases (a 2-week vacation abroad or a world cruise), which are considered shopping goods requiring extended problem solving. This distinction is used for building a spectrum of buyer behaviour characteristics.

Criticism

Process models are very traditional in that they have their roots in consumer DM models by Nicosia (1966), Howard and Sheth (1969), Fishbein (1970) and Engel *et al.* (1973). They have the merit of reviewing the major DM components and connecting them. However, process models propose only *one* hierarchical DMP, which rests on many stereotypical postulates and unproven hypotheses such as:

1. 'The *first* decision to be made is whether to go on a vacation trip or to stay at home' (van Raaij and Francken, 1984, p. 103).

2. 'A holiday is a *high*-risk purchase' (Goodall, 1988, p. 2).

3. 'Having gathered the travel information, the individual reaches a *stage* of feeling confident enough to establish several destination alternatives' (Mansfeld, 1992, p. 409).

Further, these models are arbitrary in the 'arrangement of the ubiquitous attitude-intention-behavior sequence' (Gilbert, 1991, pp. 93–94). Other taken-for-granted assumptions that tourism is a high involvement product or that information search is extensive may also be criticized. For example, the positioning of the generic decision to go or not to go on vacation as the first decision the vacationer makes before the other vacation subdecisions should be questioned. Does a last-minute decision to go on vacation mean that other aspects that are important for vacation have not been decided before? Finally, most process models lack empirical evidence. For example, Moutinho's model (1982) lacks simplicity and the formulation of precise research hypotheses.

2.3. Interpretive Frameworks

Both structural and process models lie in a cognitive positivistic approach to DM. Recently, this view has been challenged and new frameworks of DM and behaviour by tourists have been proposed. These lean on postmodern interpretive approaches. Based on the premise that DM is much more than a formalized multistage process, a naturalistic and experiential vision on tourist behaviour is enhanced. This results in alternative sets of propositions and frameworks of DM that include variables and hypotheses (such as low involvement or passive information search) that were not taken into account in the traditional models. The two major contributions of Woodside and MacDonald (1994) and Teare (1994) are discussed below.

Woodside and MacDonald

One of the first criticisms on structural and process models comes from Woodside and MacDonald (1994, p. 32): '[W]hile useful, such models fail to capture the rich interactions of decisions and behaviors of the travel party and the destination environment experienced by the travel party.' Woodside and MacDonald fill the gap to some extent by using qualitative data to validate a 'general systems framework' of how leisure visitors may make choices (Fig. 2.6).

What is new here is that they identify eight choice subsets, which may be activated by four principal 'start nodes' related to the information acquisition and processing sequence. In Fig. 2.6, double-sided arrows indicate that causality is not determined beforehand but depends on each individual tourist. This is in sharp contrast with the deterministic approach proposed in the previous models. The framework gives insight into how decisions, interactions between members of a travel party and activities or events occurring during pleasure trips relate to each other and lead to other activities or events. The model assumes that the activation of initial travel choices (due to 'triggering events') spreads over time to other travel choices. Based on the model, 25 research propositions are generated and discussed with 84 leisure travel parties visiting Canada's Prince Edward Island on the basis of a 22-page open-ended questionnaire in face-to-face interviews. Those propositions are listed in Table 2.1.

Hyde (1998) has extended three aspects of Woodside and MacDonald's framework as to the choice of vacation itinerary by independent travellers. First, he identifies a sequence in which travel subdecisions are made (i.e. subdestinations → travel route → attractions and activities). Second, he introduces a distinction between the processes that occur before a vacationer's arrival (i.e. information search and planning, leading to a 'researched before' set of subdestinations) and

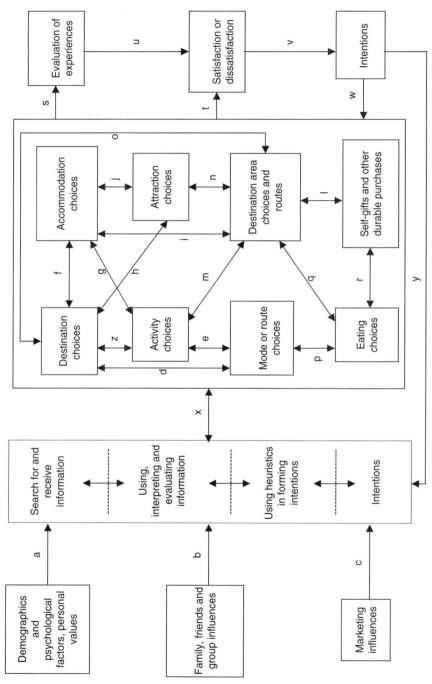

Fig. 2.6. Woodside and MacDonald's general systems framework of customer choice decisions of tourism service.

Table 2.1. Woodside and MacDonald's set of propositions (1994).

No.	Arrow	Proposition
1	a	Both leisure and business travel are influenced strongly by levels of income and education, and the value system of household members
2	b	Family, friends and group influences strongly affect the activation of choice sets and the selection of particular options in the choice sets
3	c	For some travellers, marketing influences in the form of: (i) travel agent recommendations; (ii) scheduled media advertising; (iii) direct mail, especially visitor information guides; and (iv) travel shows have substantial influences on activating traveller choice sets and the selection of specific options
4	w	Intentions towards returning to a previously visited destination affect traveller decision choices
5	x	Travellers' search for, and use of, information have dramatic impacts on their travel choices: destination visitors who are high-information users participate in more activities, spend more money per day in the destination area, have more positive evaluations about their experiences and have higher intentions compared to low-information users and non-users
6	d	Mode or route choices may cause destination choices, and vice versa
7, 8	e, p	For some important leisure traveller segments, mode or route choices often cause activity choices and eating choices, and vice versa
9–12	m, l, n, i	For some important leisure traveller segments, local area choices and travel routes in the destination area have bi-directional influences on activity choices, self-gifts and other durable purchases, attraction choices and accommodation choices
13–15	f, h, z	Substantial bi-directional influences occur between destination choices and accommodation choices, attraction choices and activity choices, respectively, for some important leisure traveller segments
16–18	j, n, i	For some important leisure traveller segments, accommodation choices, attraction choices and destination area choices substantially affect one another
19–21	l, q, r	For some important leisure traveller segments, self-gifts and other durable purchases, destination area choices and routes, and eating choices substantially affect one another
22	s	Leisure travellers evaluate the quality of many of their choice experiences
23	t	Choice experiences influence the leisure traveller's overall satisfaction or dissatisfaction with the total trip or visit experience
24, 25	v, u	Evaluations of the quality of experiences affect intentions through satisfaction or dissatisfaction

those that occur during the stay at the destination (i.e. again, an active search of information leading to the formation of a 'researched after' set, accompanied by the possibility of opportunistic considerations leading to final choices). Third, he makes more explicit which information sources are most influential before and during the vacation experience. He (1998, p. 185) concludes by highlighting three major characteristics of fully independent travel: (i) 'the traveler experiences an evolving itinerary rather than a fixed itinerary'; (ii) 'travelers are willing to take risks in their selection of vacation elements'; and (iii) 'the traveler possesses a desire to experience the unplanned'.

Teare

Another effort towards a more interpretive approach of tourist DMPs comes from Teare (1994). He conducted a case study of consumer DM in the UK hotel leisure market. After reviewing pre-purchase and purchase studies, he concluded that prior product experience and product involvement lie at the core of the DMP. This is especially in line with Reid and Crompton's taxonomy (1993) of leisure purchase decision paradigms that is based on the level of involvement. Starting from the belief that these two variables are interrelated, Teare summarizes their potential explanatory value in six research propositions (see Table 2.2). Four other propositions arise from the review of consumption and post-consumption studies. Prior experience is still an important factor: it influences the formation of expectations, assessment criteria and, finally, the tourist's personal rating system (which is derived from experience-based norms). These propositions were examined in a longitudinal study conducted over a 3-year period. Teare used Glaser and Strauss' grounded theory approach (1967) (Chapter 3, this volume) to analyse the data gathered on the basis of participant observations and personal interviews.

Criticism

The frameworks of Woodside and MacDonald (1994) and Teare (1994) propose a deeper and contextualized qualitative approach to vacation DM. This results in alternative sets of propositions and frameworks, which include variables and hypotheses (such as passive information search) that were not taken into account before. However, Woodside and MacDonald remain in the classical hypothetical deductive tradition. Their framework builds on intuition and on literature; propositions are generated and then examined empirically. We think one should go the other way round, using an inductive approach where propositions and theoretical frameworks emerge from the data and are not imposed beforehand (Chapter 3, this volume). This would result in a closer fit to reality and more room for discovery, alternative explanations and new theoretical leads. Open-mindedness should actually prevail: one does not start with preconceived ideas, one is not constrained by existing theoretical propositions or frameworks. Teare (1994) has already taken the first steps in that direction with a small ethnography of tourist DM in the UK hotel leisure-break market. However, his conceptualization sounds more like summary ethnography than an emerging grounded

Table 2.2. Teare's set of propositions (1994).

No.	Proposition
1	The propensity of consumers with extensive prior experience to engage in high-involvement DM is related to the perceived importance of the product
2	The propensity of consumers with extensive prior experience to engage in low-involvement DM is related to product familiarity and personal confidence in product class DM ability
3	The propensity of consumers with limited prior experience to engage in high-involvement DM is related to perceived risk, and limited personal confidence in product class DM ability
4	The propensity of consumers with limited prior experience to engage in low-involvement DM is related to pre-knowledge of product suitability and low perceptions of risk
5	The uses of pre-purchase decision rules, and their relative effectiveness during the assessment of choice criteria, are positively related to the consumer's prior product experience
6	Confidence in joint DM is positively related to product role specialization
7	The correlation between product expectations and experience is positively related to product familiarity
8	The degree of sophistication inherent in the operation of the consumer's personal rating system is positively related to the extent of prior product experience
9	Satisfaction during product consumption is a function of many differently weighted impressions and experiences, which are cumulative and which are continually being integrated into the consumer's personal rating system
10	Satisfaction during post-consumption evaluation represents the sum total of individual assessments made during consumption; this evaluation reinforces or modifies the consumer's preference structure and influences future DM

theory. Moreover, the theoretical propositions he generates pertain to the special case of hotel accommodation choice, and not to vacation DM in general.

2.4. Overall Assessment of Extant Models[2]

The integrated models described above all rest on the idea that the DMP is ordered and consists of discrete subprocesses following up on each other, sometimes with the possibility of feedback loops. Vacation planning takes up a large portion of this ordered process based on the assumption that tourists are problem solvers with bounded rationality, following a number of distinct cognitive

[2] This section has been adapted from Decrop and Snelders (2004, pp. 1010–1012).

information processes. This results from the fact that integrated models of vacation planning lean heavily on classical buyer behaviour theory (Nicosia, 1966; Howard and Sheth, 1969; Engel *et al.*, 1973), where decisions are thought to proceed in sequential and hierarchical steps. Those conceptualizations are useful for describing the major elements involved in the DMP and the way they are connected with each other. However, they also have a number of shortcomings.

Phillips *et al.* (1995, p. 280) point out that the traditional, sequential DM models are relatively irrelevant for describing choices 'for which consumers have little experience, or where the problem is less well-defined, or where emotional considerations play an important role'. There are many indications that vacation DM is not related so much to solving a problem as it is to creating enjoyable feelings (e.g. fantasizing while reading brochures), experiences (e.g. having fun with friends) and emotions (e.g. while gazing at the Pyramids). In line with this, Gilbert (1991, p. 98) argues that 'travel is a special form of consumption behavior involving an intangible, heterogeneous purchase of an experiential product'. A more experiential vision on tourist behaviour is thus needed, as a complement, to account for experiential aspects such as fun, feelings, fantasies (Holbrook and Hirschman, 1982; Pine and Gilmore, 1999), nostalgia and daydreaming (Phillips *et al.*, 1995), which can be very relevant in vacation choices. Holbrook and Hirschman identify leisure tourism as a product class where seeking emotional arousal is a major motivation, which is supported by Hyde (1998). Vacation planning is likely to be affected by those hedonic aspects as well.

The basic sequence of the integrative models is 'the ubiquitous attitude-intention-behavior sequence' (Gilbert, 1991, pp. 93–94). This assumed order of processes leads to statements like: '[H]aving gathered the travel information, the individual reaches a stage of feeling confident enough to establish several destination alternatives' (Mansfeld, 1992, p. 409). Other sequences are also proposed, such as 'the first decision to be made is whether to go on a vacation trip or to stay at home' (van Raaij and Francken, 1984, p. 103). In these examples, it is assumed that vacation planning is triggered off by a generic decision to go or not to go, and that attitude formation and evaluation of alternatives come about during vacation planning, after sufficient information has been collected. However, based on issues of individual differences, the contingency of DM and the adaptability of the consumer (Payne *et al.*, 1993), one should at least assume that there is not just one, but more possible types of vacation DMPs. For example, the growing phenomenon of last-minute booking means that the generic decision may come after decisions on the time period or the accompaniment. It also implies that choice sets remain unstable throughout the planning phase, and that vacationers may collect destination information on arrival.

Another point of concern is the individual focus of existing integrative models. Although there has been some research on family DM (Jenkins, 1978; van Raaij, 1986; Nichols and Snepenger, 1988), other groups, such as non-married couples and parties of friends, have not been investigated. Moreover, the influence of interpersonal relationships on the vacation planning process has been neglected. Ritchie (1994, p. 11) regrets that 'the great majority of tourism research continues to obtain data for the study of travel decisions by interviewing only one of the individuals involved in the choice process'. For these reasons, the social dimension of DM and the way it affects vacation planning deserve closer scrutiny.

Finally, most cognitive and interpretive models lack clear definitions of the vacation or tourist product, and of its components and attributes. Some models only deal with one particular aspect of vacation decisions, i.e. destinations (Crompton, 1977; Woodside and Lysonski, 1989), activities (Moscardo *et al.*, 1996) or accommodation (Teare, 1994). Other models implicitly take any vacation subdecision into account, but fail in detailing those subdecisions or do not explain how they relate to each other. This results in misconceptions and confusion. For example, Moutinho (1987) considers destination choice as a compulsory subdecision among other travel decisions. He places it in a group of other subdecisions (with travel mode, timing, budget, intermediaries), which come as a third step after tourism need has been aroused and gathered information has been deliberated on, and before travel preparation. He often takes vacation destination as one of the possible examples of tourist products. But sometimes he also explains it apart (e.g. when describing the evoked set theory and the tourist product utility concept). The only attempt to make a precise distinction between the different components of the vacation product, or the different vacation subdecisions, is by Woodside and MacDonald (1994). Eight choice sets are identified in their general framework of tourist choice decisions (see Fig. 2.6). The different facets of vacation decisions have further been explored by Jeng and Fesenmaier (1997) and Dellaert *et al.* (1998). Yet they do not give a precise description of what makes destination decisions special.

Given these problems with existing models, Ritchie (1994) concludes that there is a need for a comprehensive framework describing the many components and processes involved in tourist DM, and taking into account the context in which decisions are made. The models of Woodside and MacDonald (1994) and Teare (1994) can be seen as a response to this. Both propose a deeper qualitative approach to DM and behaviour by tourists. In this book, their efforts are extended to a larger study on the planning process for the summer vacation. Theoretical propositions will be generated from the data using the grounded theory methodology and confronted with the existing literature. The intended contribution is to arrive at a deeper and contextualized understanding of vacationers' DMPs, starting from a naturalistic interpretive perspective.

Methods to Investigate Vacation Decision Making　　3

3.0. Introduction

In this chapter, we present alternative ways for investigating tourist DM and behaviour. Research paradigms (e.g. positivism, interpretivism) are first discussed as a framework for the chapter. Next, theoretical and empirical methods that may be used to investigate consumer or tourist DM are presented. Three families are outlined: input–output techniques, process-tracing studies and naturalistic methods. The last section of the chapter is devoted to the presentation of the author's original research design used to investigate vacationers' DMP from a qualitative interpretive perspective.

3.1. Research Paradigms

3.1.1. Positivism vs. interpretivism

The opposition between positivism (and post-positivism) and interpretivism (and constructivism) is a usual dichotomy[1] when discussing general philosophies of science and research. Differences are ontological (what is the nature of reality?), epistemological (what is the status of knowledge?) and methodological (how to achieve this knowledge?). The major characteristics of positivism and interpretivism are summarized in Table 3.1.

---

[1] This is the simplest dichotomy. More detailed paradigmatic typologies have been proposed by Burrell and Morgan (1979) and by Guba and Lincoln (1994).

Table 3.1. Basic differences between positivism and interpretivism.

Assumptions	Positivism	Interpretivism
Nature of reality	Objective, tangible, single	Socially constructed, multiple
Goal of research	Explanation, strong prediction	Understanding, weak prediction
Focus of interest	What is general, average and representative	What is specific, unique and deviant
Knowledge generated	Laws: absolute (time, context, and value-free)	Meanings: relative (time, context, culture, value-bound)
Subject–researcher relationship	Rigid separation	Interactive, cooperative, participative
Desired information	How many people think and do a specific thing, or have a specific problem?	What do some people think and do, what kind of problems are they confronted with and how do they deal with it?
Research methodology	Hypothetical-deductive approach (experimental design)	Holistic-inductive approach (naturalistic inquiry)

Positivism postulates a 'real' and apprehensible reality, driven by immutable natural laws and mechanisms. Based on this, classical conceptions of DM postulate order and simplicity in the world. That order is based on three pillars: reality (there exists an objective world that can be grasped), causality (reality and history are structured by chains of causes and effects) and intentionality (any human behaviour is directed towards a goal and decisions are instruments of purpose and self). Considering tourist DM from the positivist perspective, the questions raised are of this kind: Which decisions do tourists make? In what sequence are they made? How do they relate to actual behaviour? How to predict them? Positivism relies on the traditional hypothetical-deductive approach as a research strategy. Hypotheses are first generated from experience, existing knowledge or intuition and then verified empirically. Experimental designs are developed where the conditions of the study can be controlled or manipulated, and in which a very limited set of outcome variables are measured.

The more recent interpretivist view on science departs dramatically from this approach. The focus is no longer on explanation in order to predict and control but on understanding and interpretation. As to DM, the relevant question is how people come to particular decisions and why. Interpretivism emphasizes relativism: reality is not objective, single and divisible but socially constructed, multiple, holistic and contextual (Ozanne and Hudson, 1989). This ontological premise implies the use of different methodologies. Interpretivism does not suggest a separation but rather an interactive and cooperative relationship between the investigator and the object of investigation. The focus is not on the quantity of information gathered but rather on its quality and richness. All aspects of observation are considered worthwhile: the interpretive inquirer watches, listens, feels, asks, records and examines. In-depth interview, participant observation and document analysis are favoured tools in this approach. Interpretivism is often assimilated with naturalistic inquiry as it strives to understand naturally occurring phenomena in their naturally occurring states (Lincoln and Guba, 1985). Naturalistic inquiry is a 'discovery-oriented approach that minimizes investigator manipulation of the study setting and places no prior constraints on what the outcomes of the research will be' (Patton, 1990, p. 41). In contrast with positivism, which is based on the hypothetical-deductive framework, interpretivism relies on a holistic-inductive approach. The research phenomenon is investigated as a whole and theoretical propositions are generated from the empirical field.

3.1.2. Quantitative vs. qualitative research

In contrast to positivism and interpretivism, the adjectives 'qualitative' and 'quantitative' originally pertain only to research methodologies. The former implies identifying distinctive observations, and the latter counting similar observations. Table 3.2 further details this distinction. Some qualitative techniques, like interviewing, are used both by positivist and interpretivist researchers. However, the latter will use verbal and visual data as such, whereas the former will strive to formalize any input data more stringently and to transform it into strings of numerical variables. In conclusion, the most relevant paradigmatical distinction is not qualitative vs. quantitative research but interpretivism vs. positivism. Nevertheless, interpretivism is often associated with a qualitative approach (and positivism with a quantitative approach) because interpretivist (positivist) problems can be better addressed by qualitative (quantitative) methods.

However, it should be kept in mind that the choice of a research method is not a question of paradigms but rather a function of the research problem. After having determined 'What do I want to investigate?', the researcher must choose the appropriate method. The decision depends not only on the nature of the topic to be addressed, but also on the investigator's personal interests and skills. The ideal situation is that of a researcher who is open to, and familiar with, both qualitative and quantitative methods. A non-passionate decision is possible that will only depend on the research question(s). But that situation is rare. Personal interest creates an allegiance to a particular paradigm and preference for a particular approach. There are still other factors determining the choice. Table 3.3 provides a checklist of some of the major questions that may influence the choice of an appropriate methodology. If positive or negative answers prevail, it is more likely that a qualitative or quantitative approach is the best way to investigate the research problem.

Table 3.2. Basic differences between qualitative and quantitative research.

	Qualitative	Quantitative
Problem Questioning Objective	Complex, diffuse, ambiguous Open-ended Identify and define categories that may evolve during the research process	Well-defined, unambiguous Closed Identify and define standard categories at the outset of the study
Sought models	Interconnections between a large number of categories: capturing complexity	Relations clearly specified between a limited set of categories: looking for simplicity
Researcher role	A research instrument in itself: he or she is aware of his or her influence and that his or her design can neither be neutral nor perfect; particular skills are needed to collect the data	Particular care not to influence the research process (avoiding biases); no particular skills are needed to collect the data
Explanation	Concerned with in-depth understanding, conceptualization issues and hidden layers of meaning	'Straight' and 'superficial' explanation (excluding anything that cannot be investigated through simple and unambiguous questions or that does not lend itself to quantification)
Intention	A deep understanding of the phenomenon	Control of distribution and generalization issues

The basic distinction of qualitative vs. quantitative approaches can be refined by considering the level of *prominence of the qualitative* element in the research design. Miller and Crabtree (1994) suggest four possible designs: concurrent, nested, sequential and combination. A concurrent design involves both qualitative and quantitative studies being simultaneously but independently performed on the same topic. In the end, one examines to what extent the findings converge. In a nested design, qualitative and quantitative techniques are directly integrated within a single study in a system of checks and balances to ensure validity. The sequential design limits qualitative research to the exploration of key variables (exploratory research) that need quantitative measurement and inference subsequently. In contrast, the qualitative element is prominent in combination or case study designs. Qualitative findings are used as such (conclusive research) in a contextual approach and local theories are developed. Quantitative data only help to get a better understanding of a particular case.

Table 3.3. Checklist for considering qualitative or quantitative approach.

Is the researcher interested in individualized outcomes?

Is the researcher interested in examining the process of research and the context in which it occurs?

Is detailed in-depth information needed in order to understand the phenomena under study?

Is the focus on quality and the meaning of the experiences being studied?

Does the researcher desire to get close to the data providers and immerse in their experiences?

Do no measuring devices exist that will provide reliable and valid data for the topic being studied?

Is the research question likely to change depending upon how the data emerge?

Is it possible that the answer to the research question may yield unexpected results?

Does it make more sense to use grounded theory than existing *a priori* theory in studying the particular phenomena?

Does the researcher wish to get personally involved in the research?

Does the researcher have a philosophical and methodological bias toward the interpretive paradigm and qualitative methods?

Source: Henderson (1991, p. 103).

Complementing Yin (1989), Marshall and Rossman (1995) make a distinction between seven research strategies: experiments, surveys, archival analyses, histories, case studies, field studies (ethnographies) and in-depth interview studies. We could locate those strategies on a continuum ranging from highly quantitative (experiments) to highly qualitative (in-depth interview studies). However, we again stress that the choice of an appropriate research strategy does not depend on the qualitative or quantitative dichotomy but rather on the study's goal and the related research questions. A study can aim to describe, explain, understand and/or predict events and processes (see Table 3.1).

3.1.3. Qualitative research paradigms

Denzin and Lincoln (2000) go further than the traditional trade-off between positivism and interpretivism by distinguishing seven moments, presented as many ways of thinking and performing qualitative inquiry. These moments include different sets of ontological, epistemological and methodological stances, which correspond to a historical evolution. However, all seven moments are still in operation today and are legitimate in various disciplines.

The first moment, 'the traditional period', is one in which 'qualitative researchers wrote "objective", colonializing accounts of field experiences that were reflexive of the positivist scientist paradigm' (Denzin and Lincoln, 2000, p. 12). Qualitative research is limited to content analysis where data are reduced to frequency tables.

The second moment, 'the modernist phase' (post-positivism), is characterized by an attempt to formalize and put more rigour in qualitative research. While creativity is enhanced, canons of 'good' qualitative research are suggested (Becker *et al.*, 1961) and strong methodologies are developed to help the emergence of grounded theories (Glaser and Strauss, 1967).

The third moment of 'blurred genres' (including constructivism and naturalistic inquiry) is where qualitative research reaches maturity and multiplicity: researchers have a full set of paradigms, methods and strategies at their disposal. The focus is on 'thick descriptions' (Geertz, 1973) in order to develop theory that makes sense out of a local situation. The issue of trustworthiness is highlighted and criteria are proposed to evaluate qualitative studies, paralleling the positivistic criteria of validity and reliability.

The fourth moment brings a profound rupture or a 'crisis of representation' in the way of considering qualitative research. The focus is no longer on rigour and the development of systematically constructed theories. Research and writing is made more reflexive and critical. New models of truth, method and representation are sought: 'fieldwork and writing blur into one another' (Denzin and Lincoln, 2000, p. 17). A triple crisis of representation, legitimation and praxis confronts qualitative researchers embedded in the discourses of post-structuralism and postmodernism. The crisis of legitimation involves a serious rethinking of traditional criteria for evaluating qualitative research.

The fifth, sixth and seventh – 'postmodern experimental ethnographic writing', 'post-experimental' and 'the future' – moments struggle to make sense of these crises. New ways of writing and developing theories are developed (narratives, 'tales from the field', more local and small-scale theories), whereas research is more participatory, activist and action-oriented. The representation of the 'other' becomes a key issue and problems of silenced groups are (re)considered.

3.2. Alternative Approaches to Investigate Decision Making

The methods that may be used to study consumer DM are generally categorized in two groups: input–output methods and process-tracing approaches. This distinction parallels the distinction between structural and process approaches that was introduced in Section 2.2. In this section, we will briefly discuss the fundamentals of these two families of methods that are described in more detail by Bettman *et al.* (1991) and Carroll and Johnson (1990). In addition, we suggest a third way to investigate DM – naturalistic qualitative research.

3.2.1. Input–output methods

As previously mentioned, structural DM approaches are primarily concerned with the relationships between inputs and outputs, in order to explain how choices are made on the basis of the information provided about each alternative (Maule and Svenson, 1993). In structural approaches, *theoretical models* are elaborated and expressed in mathematical equations with input variables (e.g. product information, price, social pressure) as independent variables, and output variables (e.g. perception or preference judgements, choice) as dependent variables. These models allow to relate variations in the output judgements or decisions to the variations introduced in the input variables. Simulations or games can then be run based on linear or non-linear, additive or non-additive forms of the models. For example, in the family of expected value or utility models, the value of different alternatives can be calculated by summing the products of the values (monetary worth) and probabilities associated with each outcome:

$$EV = \Sigma \, p_i v_i$$

It is possible to predict which alternative will be chosen on the basis of the assumption that the alternative with the highest expected value is preferred. In the SEU model, objective probability and monetary worth are replaced by subjective probability and utility. Decision trees are often used to graphically represent these relationships between inputs and outputs.

Input–output models may also be tested empirically through *survey or experimental data*. Some of the input variables are manipulated and the result of the process on the output variables is measured. It should be noted that input–output methods are static (a decision is modelled as taking place at a given moment in time) and do not attempt to directly measure the DM process but rather assume an underlying process affected by some factors in a certain way. For example, in Russo's information format study (1977), the 'observed monetary savings by consumers are consistent with the hypothesis that the new unit price format led consumers to process the unit price information to a greater extent' (Bettman *et al.*, 1991, p. 72).

Chronometric analysis is another type of input–output method that has been used in a consumer decision context (e.g. Johnson and Russo, 1978; Sujan, 1985). The basic data collected here are the times taken by the subject to produce a response, usually measured as the time elapsing between the presentation of a stimulus and the response to that stimulus. Different apparatus may be used for this measurement, from stop watches to tachistoscopes (Russo, 1978). Time responses are assumed to directly reflect the amount of processing effort used in completing the task (Bettman *et al.*, 1991), which may lead to better insights into issues such as the level of effort, sequence of responses or decision rules in cognitive processes.

3.2.2. Process-tracing methods

In contrast with structural perspectives, process approaches are not so concerned with the outcomes of the DMP than with how decisions are made and how they evolve over time. The paramount objective is to come to a better understanding of the psychological processes underlying DM. Therefore, process-tracing methods are required since they allow measurement of the ongoing decision process without disturbing it. Three major methods may be considered by the researcher (Bettman *et al.*, 1991; Svenson, 1996): verbal protocols, information display boards and eye movement recordings.

In *verbal protocols* or 'think aloud' technique, the subject is asked to think aloud as he or she is actually performing a required task (e.g. shopping or choosing among alternatives). Data are recorded on tape or written in the form of protocols. This method should not be mistaken for introspection or retrospective reports because the subject is instructed to verbalize thoughts and feelings as they occur in the course of solving a problem and not before or after it. Once collected, protocol data are analysed to develop models of the processes used by consumers in making judgements and choices, or at least to examine aspects of it (e.g. choice criteria, decision rules, goals). Bettman and Park (1980) and Biehal and Chakravarti (1989) have elaborated extensive schemes for coding protocols. Although the method is useful to know more about the mental processes of an individual, it entails severe shortcomings. Data collection and analysis is extremely time-consuming; therefore, sample sizes are often small. Furthermore, the quality of the data can be questioned as subjects' protocols may reflect biases, self-censoring or their inability to verbalize some internal states and processes (Bettman *et al.*, 1991). Finally, there may be experimentation biases in that the process of providing protocols may affect the DMP being carried out.

The objective of information acquisition approaches is to monitor the way and, more precisely, the sequence in which information is acquired. An *information display board* is used, nowadays presented to subjects as a computerized matrix array, often with product alternatives and brands as rows, and attributes as columns. In each cell, some information is available about the value of the particular brand's attribute. The subject is asked to choose an alternative after examining as many cards as desired, one at a time. Data result from the number and sequence of cards that have been selected, as well as from their information content. This technique proves to be a powerful tool for repeated decisions but lacks precision in disentangling specific aspects of the decision process (Svenson, 1996). Actually, the information board method only enables examination of external information-seeking behaviour and not internal psychological processes. Moreover, it is an obtrusive technique, again with possible experimental biases. The presentation format may also bias the decision process because the matrix display helps the subject structure the decision problem and makes the information available both by brands and attributes, which is not similar to real-life situations (e.g. on supermarket shelves) in which information is organized only by brand (Bettman *et al.*, 1991).

Eye movement recordings have also been used to study information acquisition patterns (e.g. van Raaij, 1977; Russo, 1978). Subjects are asked to sit in front of a screen or table displaying the choice objects. The course and sequence of eye movements in examining the objects is then recorded by a special apparatus. The resulting data secure a very detailed trace of the information search process and useful cues about the decision rules that were or were not used during the choice task. The eye movement technique has additional advantages. On the one hand, it is more useful than verbal protocols for studying repeated, routine decision processes that occur rapidly, and it is more difficult for subjects to censor. On the other hand, it requires less effort than retrieving a card on an information board. Obviously, the technique also presents some drawbacks: data collection is time-consuming and expensive; the apparatus may be obtrusive; the choice stimuli are often oversimplified in order for the researcher to precisely localize eye movements. Moreover, eye fixations may be interpreted as information-seeking responses but do not reveal many details about the internal processes of the mind. A middle ground between the eye movement recording and the information board technique is provided by the computerized mouse lab method developed by Johnson *et al.* (1991) and Payne *et al.* (1993). A mouse, which approximates the details of eye movements at a lower cost and effort, is employed to monitor the sequence and timing of information acquisition in different types of task environments.

3.2.3. Naturalistic methods

Both input–output and process-tracing methods are obtrusive. Most often the subject is aware that his or her DMP is being observed or measured, which leads to major biases. In order to limit these, Bettman *et al.* (1991, p. 76) suggest use of different methods at the same time because 'multimethod approaches let us separate the effects of the research method from those associated with the phenomenon under study'. We think there is another solution, which is investigating DM in more natural settings through qualitative techniques. We will briefly discuss three methods: in-depth interviews, participant observation and diaries.

According to Rubin and Rubin (1995, p. 17), *interviewing* is the art of hearing data that requires 'intense listening, a respect and curiosity about what people say and a systematic effort to really hear and understand what people tell you'. Qualitative interviewing is also called 'in-depth interviewing' as contrasted with a structured survey interview. In-depth interviewing goes beyond asking questions and listening to people; it entails sharing social experiences. There are different types of in-depth interviews. The interview guide approach is often referred to as a semi-structured interview. It lists the topics and issues to be covered but does not specify any particular way and order of asking questions.

Informal conversational interviews are unstructured and non-directive interviews, since the questions are not planned but rather emerge from the immediate context and are asked in the natural course of interaction (Henderson, 1991). Cultural interviews focus on 'the norms, values, understandings, and taken-for-granted rules of behavior of a group or society. Topical interviews are more narrowly focused on a particular event or process and are concerned with what happened, when, and why' (Rubin and Rubin, 1995, p. 28). Finally, focus groups consist in gathering six to ten people who are unfamiliar to each other but who share certain characteristics that are relevant to the study problem. The first role of the interviewer is to stimulate discussion and the expression of different opinions. The format is then rather unstructured. The interviewer acts as a moderator by asking questions when necessary to involve everyone in the discussion and to keep the debate focused on the topic.

Participant observation is the most comprehensive qualitative method and is often assimilated with field research. Field research consists in systematically collecting data through the social interaction of the researcher and informants, in the environment of the latter (Taylor and Bogdan, 1984). This includes observation, informal interviews and narratives. It is often used in conjunction with other techniques (e.g. document analysis, introspection). Participant observation is especially appropriate to examine and understand collective phenomena. The method enables catching subtle nuances of attitudes and behaviours and examining social processes over time. This requires the observer to immerse himself or herself in the setting. Much time and effort are needed: he or she must get into the group, participate in its life and become accepted. The researcher benefits from his or her privileged position to get insight and meaning into the problem. At the same time, he or she should keep an objective observing capability. Participant observation is typically unstructured to maximize the discovery or validation of theory (Denzin, 1978). It is useful to investigate DM in its real context, by getting into, and participating in, the daily life and decisions of a travel party.

As to the *diaries technique*, informants are given a notebook and asked to keep it on a regular (usually daily or weekly) basis. They may be instructed to take a few minutes at the end of each day to record all of the decisions that have been made that day. Decisions may involve product alternatives and attributes, choice criteria, information sources, etc. Of course, this technique requires self-discipline, honesty and retrospective abilities from informants, which may entail biases. In conclusion, participant observation and diaries do not seem as efficient as in-depth interviews for investigating consumer DM. On the one hand, participant observation is very difficult to implement due to the limited size and the deep social ties (to say nothing of the blood ties in families) existing in DMUs. The observer may appear to be an intruder. On the other hand, diaries raise the questions of maintenance (how to keep informants involved and assiduous?) and content (it is easier to recall acts and physical behaviours than thoughts, emotions, moods or motivations). In conclusion, participant observation and diaries seem to be more appropriate for tracking decisions during the vacation itself than before it.

3.3. Study Method

3.3.1. Sample

The actual vacation DMP of 25 Belgian (French-speaking) DMUs has been followed for a whole year. Theoretical sampling was used for selecting the DMUs, which means looking for cases that are likely to yield rich and varied information in order to maximize theory development (Strauss and Corbin, 1990). DMUs consisted of four types: six singles (representing tourists who decided on their own), six couples (married or non-married), ten families with children and three groups of friends. Informants were recruited in two stages. The first 12 households responded to a 'call for participation', mailed to a random sample of 240 residents of a small Belgian town. Declaring some intention to go on summer vacation was the only criterion to participate in the study. In the next stage, purposive sampling was used to make the sample more varied on a number of socio-demographic criteria. Missing profiles (i.e. singles and couples, professionals and less educated people) were recruited after a series of door-to-door visits. This quest for both variation and saturation led to the recruitment of 25 DMUs[2] whose profiles are described in Table 3.4.

3.3.2. Data collection

Informants were interviewed in depth before the summer vacation, in such a way that their plans, judgements and DMP could be tracked in time. Previous studies have shown that vacation choices involve a long DMP, which takes place over many months (van Raaij and Francken, 1984; Moutinho, 1987; Dellaert *et al.*, 1998). In those studies it is suggested that vacationers start thinking about their next summer vacation in January or February. For this reason, DMUs were interviewed a number of times before the summer holiday, starting in February. Two-month periods elapsed between interviews, in order to avoid 'contamination' from one interview to the next, while keeping in touch with new evolutions in vacationers' DMPs. As a result, 20 DMUs were interviewed three

---

[2] Actually, 27 DMUs had been recruited and interviewed a first time. However, two DMUs were interviewed only once, as it appeared during the first discussion that they were not really involved in a vacation DM situation. One single person had decided not to go on vacation that year because she intended to build a new house, and one couple was routinely going to their weekend cottage in the 'Ardennes', where they stay each summer.

Table 3.4. Sample description.

	DMU type	Group size	Age range	Educational background	Occupation	Vacation involvement	Number of interviews
1	C	2	61–63	College	Retired	Moderate	4 (Feb., Apr., June, Nov.)
2	F	2	33–40	College	Teacher and nurse	High	4 (Feb., Apr., June, Nov.)
		+2	*0–2*				
3	F	2	56	College and high school	Teacher and housewife	Low	4 (Feb., Apr., June, Nov.)
		+2	*16–21*				
4	GF	2	29–30	College and university	Teacher	Moderate	4 (Feb., Apr., June, Nov.)
5	F	2	42–44	College	Civil servant and housewife	Low	3 (Feb., Apr., Nov.)
		+5	*6–19*				
6	S (F)	1	60	College	Retired	High	4 (Feb., Apr., June, Nov.)
7	F	2	40–41	University	Journalists	High	4 (Feb., Apr., June, Nov.)
		+3	*4–15*				
8	S (M)	1	26	University	Researcher	High	4 (Feb., Apr., June, Nov.)
9	S (F)	1	37	University	Teacher	High	4 (Feb., Apr., June, Nov.)
10	C	2	58–63	University	Judge and housewife	Moderate	4 (Feb., Apr., June, Nov.)
11	S (F)	1	36	College	Employee	Moderate	4 (Feb., Apr., June, Nov.)
12	F	2	40–41	University	Engineer and teacher	Moderate	4 (Feb., Apr., June, Nov.)
		+3	*9–15*				
13	F	2	54–59	University and college	Teacher	High	4 (Feb., Apr., June, Nov.)
		+4	*13–32*				
14	F	2	43–45	University	Attorney and employee	High	3 (Feb., Apr., Nov.)
		+2	*12–16*				
15	C	2	53–59	University	Civil servant and retired	Low	3 (Feb., Apr., June)
16	C	2	52–54	University	Officer and housewife	Moderate	4 (Feb., Apr., June, Nov.)

continued

Table 3.4. *(Continued)* Sample description.

	DMU type	Group size	Age range	Educational background	Occupation	Vacation involvement	Number of interviews
17	F	2 *+2*	38–47 *9–13*	College and university	Teacher and researcher	Moderate	3 (Feb., Apr., Nov.)
18	F	2 *+2*	37–43 *7–10*	College	Manager and employee	High	4 (Feb., Apr., June, Nov.)
19	S (F)	1	56	High school	Volunteer	Low	3 (Feb., Apr., June)
20	S (M)	1	66	High school	Retired	Moderate	4 (Feb., Apr., June, Nov.)
21	F	2 *+3*	35–43 *13–18*	Primary or high school	Disabled and domestic help	Moderate	4 (Feb., Apr., June, Nov.)
22	F	2 *+2*	24–35 *4–6*	Primary or high school	Employees	High	4 (Feb., Apr., June, Nov.)
23	GF	5	25–30	High school	Driver and soldiers	Moderate	4 (Feb., Apr., June, Nov.)
24	GF	6	20–24	College or university	Students, unemployed and employees	Moderate	4 (Feb., Apr., June, Nov.)
25	C	2	25–28	University	Sales rep and employee	High	4 (Feb., Apr., June, Nov.)

Note: S = single (F = female; M = male); C = couple; F = family; GF = group of friends.
Italics involve information about children.

times (in February, April and June), whereas five DMUs were interviewed twice because they had already made their final decision in April. All DMUs were interviewed once again after the vacation (in November) for post-experience thoughts, feelings and evaluations. This longitudinal data collection process is summarized by Fig. 3.1.

During each interview, most members of the DMU were present, including children. Informants could freely and spontaneously talk about three central themes: (i) general vacation and travel behaviour; (ii) expectations and motives; and (iii) current vacation plans and evoked destinations. The real-situation (naturalistic) longitudinal design helped understanding the context, complexities and dynamics of vacation planning. On the one hand, it avoided problems connected with the intention–behaviour discrepancy, because questions were asked about actual instead of intended decisions (Belk, 1985). On the other hand, it avoided problems related to a decision maker's hindsight bias (Curren *et al.*, 1992), which may be self-serving.

All interviews were recorded on tape and fully transcribed. Field notes were also systematically written down during, and immediately after, each interview. These notes describe the setting, relationship with informants, direct interpretation of particular words or sentences, personal feelings about what has been done, said and not said during the interview, critical remarks about the quality of data or the participation of each interviewee. All field notes were compiled in a 'roadbook' and used in the analysis and interpretation process, in addition to the interview transcripts.

We also observed vacationers in settings that are less obtrusive for the decision maker than a discussion at home. Sessions of non-participant observations were held at a vacation trade fair and in two travel agencies (see Fig. 3.2). At the end of March, we made a series of non-participant observations at Brussels vacation trade fair ('Salon des Vacances') during a 4-day period. We followed visitors

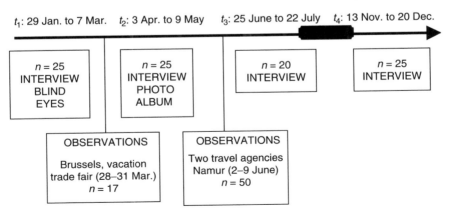

Fig. 3.1.   Data collection process.

in their trade show movements and observed their verbal and non-verbal behaviour (actions, type of information search, etc.). When recruiting visitors, we wanted to have all types of DMUs represented in the sample. Participants were randomly selected and asked whether they minded being followed in their trade show movements. In general, one out of two people accepted. This authorization made note-taking easier and more accurate (especially when participants gathered oral information at specific stands). It also excluded ethical problems. Observations focused on five dominant but not exclusive elements:

1. Setting (place, date, weather, atmosphere in the trade-show hall, etc.).
2. Participant(s) (type and composition of the DMU, socio-demographics, look and mood, etc.).
3. Participants' trade show movements (we indicated their course on a map).
4. Participants' stops at particular stands (how long, why, type of interactions, etc.).
5. Information gathered by the participants (what kind, how much, how detailed, oral or written, etc.).

The observation session was completed when the participant(s) was (were) leaving the trade show hall. We then asked them a few questions (socio-demographics and vacation plans) and offered them a small gift (pocket calculator or photo album).

In addition to these observations at the Brussels trade fair, we also decided to observe people in travel agencies. There was no problem in finding two travel agencies in Namur (one independent and one retailer chain outlet) that were happy to cooperate. A total of 50 different customers was observed during 26 observation sessions spread over 3 days at the beginning of June (Fig. 3.2). Observations were completely non-participant: we were sitting in the back of the agency, discretely writing down everything we could see and hear. An observation guide was used that entailed the following elements:

1. Description of the setting.
2. Description of the observed people.
3. Waiting behaviour of the observed people.
4. Personal interaction of the observed people with the salesman.
5. Post-conversation behaviour.

The observation task finished when there were no more customers in the agency and began again each time a new person came in. All observation notes were transcribed.

3.3.3. Data analysis and interpretation

The analysis and interpretation of the interview and observation transcripts were based on the grounded theory approach (Glaser and Strauss, 1967), which

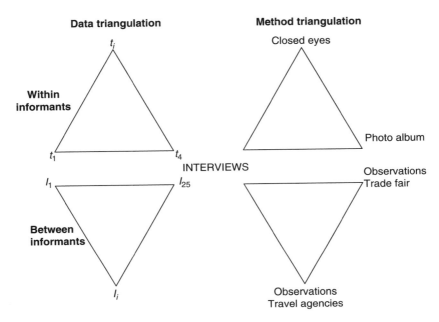

Fig. 3.2. Data, informant and method triangulation.

is 'a qualitative research method that uses a systematic set of procedures to develop an inductively derived grounded theory about a phenomenon' (Strauss and Corbin, 1990, p. 24). These procedures include concurrent collection and analysis of data, enhancement of theoretical sensitivity (in order to interpret the data), and constant comparison of data chunks and emerging interpretations. It should be stressed that grounded theory does not require preconceived theorizing: existing literature is used and integrated 'at the time when the inductive process is largely finished' (Connell and Lowe, 1997, p. 167). Categories, patterns and propositions emerged from the coding process of the data (rather than being imposed beforehand) and were permanently called into question. Memos and diagrams were also used in order to assist with interpretation and establishing connections between concepts. In the following sections we explain how coding, memoing and diagramming were carried out in practice.

The major advantage of grounded theory over other qualitative methods is that it provides guidelines for a rigorous and systematic analysis of data with explicit procedures and research strategies. Other strengths are 'the self-correcting nature of the data collection process, the methods' inherent bent toward theory and the simultaneous turning away from a contextual description, and the emphasis on comparative methods' (Charmaz, 2000, p. 522). However, grounded theory has been attacked for its reduced understanding of informants' experience, its curtailed representation of both the social and the subjective world, the prevailing position of the researcher as the expert and the objectivist procedures on which the analysis rests (Charmaz, 2000). A few authors have used a grounded theory approach to study problems in tourism behaviour (e.g. Teare, 1994; Riley, 1995; Hernandez *et al.*, 1996; Herold *et al.*, 2001). Connell and Lowe (1997) have reviewed the application of inductive methods in tourism and hospitality management research.

Coding

Our approach to analysing and coding data paralleled Strauss and Corbin's (1990) grounded theory procedures, but accommodated the particular type of research we did. In grounded theory, a distinction is made between three types of coding: open, axial and selective. Open coding refers to what is generally accepted as the first level of coding (Huberman and Miles, 1994 call it the descriptive level): the conceptualization and categorization of data. Text chunks are related to concepts, which are given labels and grouped in categories. Axial coding is more inferential: connections between emerging categories are made. The third important step towards building a grounded theory is selective coding. This is not really different to axial coding, in that it also consists of linking and connecting different categories. But in selective coding it is done at a higher, more abstract, level of analysis. A few 'core' categories are selected and systematically related to other categories. After that, the problem is to validate these relationships and to fill in categories that need further development. Two basic procedures support open, axial and selective coding: the permanent asking of questions and the making of comparisons.

Based on these principles, we first established a provisional list of codes on the basis of three interview transcripts, one for each DMU type: single, couple and family. Codes were emerging from the data in a very natural and inductive way. We did not start from a pre-existing list of codes (based on the interview guide or existing literature) in order to avoid 'captivity' due to preconceived ideas and frameworks. Literature was used only after an important category had emerged, in order to develop its possible properties and dimensions (see open coding). Literature was also important when particular relationships and schemes emerged from our data (see axial and selective coding). We thus opted for a constant interplay of analysing data and reading literature, but with data coming first. The initial list of codes evolved as more interviews were being coded. The disadvantage of this is that the first text chunks had very different codes than subsequent ones. Some codes were modified because they did not fit the data, others were even left, whereas, in contrast, new codes appeared. As a consequence, much time and effort were needed to recode everything as soon as a more empirically stable list emerged. Precision was another general principle of our coding procedure. We avoided too many chunks being given the same code, by creating a new code or a new sub-code when a category proved to be too 'voluminous'. Giving an accurate definition to each code and sub-code was another way to escape from ambiguity. In total, 850 codes were finally created from the data.

The three levels of coding proposed in grounded theory can be thought of as a procedure in which theory is abstracted from the data. However, those levels are not always sequential steps but may coincide. The same text chunk can tell something about the concepts (categories) at hand and the relationship between those categories at the same time. For example, in the following quote, we find information at the open coding level about experienced destinations (Finistère, Régastelle), satisfaction, planned destination (Brittany) and regions, and preference. At the axial coding level, there are emerging connections between experienced destinations *and* satisfaction, and between planned destinations *and* preference. Finally, at an even more abstract and interpretive level, a relationship can be established between satisfaction and repeated purchase. This is the selective coding level.

> *Jacqueline:* We went to the Finistère, we liked it. We went in the region of Régastelle, we liked it very much. If we were considering to go to Brittany, we would try to divide it up between the Northern coast and the Southern coast because we like both [23.1].

In the previous example, connections at the axial and selective levels are detected by the researcher. However, it often happens that an informant himself or herself makes a connection between relevant concepts. For example, the father of a large family explains: 'In addition, I have my youngest son who suffers from asthma and that all, I am always afraid that. ... He is little, he is weak. That's why I like finding myself in such a place [i.e. the sea].' In this case, a relationship between health and destination preference is established straight from the interviewee's words.

Memoing

The writing of memos was another technique supporting our interpretation process. Memos represent the written form of the abstract thinking about data (Strauss and Corbin, 1990). We wrote a memo each time it was necessary to interpret, in more depth, what was going on and to explain it consistently at a conceptual level. We had three types of memos:

1. Code memos, which were used for problems related to the categorization of data, relationships between variables and indications of process.
2. Operational memos, which contained emerging thoughts about directions to follow in later interviews, analyses or interpretations (possible interesting comparisons, questions to pay special attention to, ideas to follow up on).
3. Theoretical memos, which pertained to the definition and explanation of important (or potentially important) categories and concepts, with references to relevant literature. This integration materialized the interplay of inductive and deductive thinking.

In total, we had 236 memos that proved to be very helpful for putting some structure into the huge amount of data and for building theoretical propositions.

Diagramming

Last, but not least, a variety of diagrams (flow charts, sets, etc.) helped us synthesize and visualize the logical relationships between categories (properties and dimensions) and their subcategories. For example, provisional within-case-summary matrices were developed to give an overview of the longitudinal process of gathering and analysing information about each vacationer's DMPs. These summary matrices were helpful to follow the evolution of vacation projects and evoked destinations, and could be used as input for questions in later interviews. Moreover, they assisted with the making of comparisons both within and between cases. Conceptual networks were also developed for representing the influence of contextual factors on vacation decisions and DM variables.

Computer assistance

All the previous operations take a lot of time and effort. Until recent years, coding was done by hand, by writing in the left margin of the transcripts, placing slashes between text chunks or underlining quotes with different colours. Cutting, piling and indexing were achieved using scissors and glue. Today, a substantial number of computer software programs help with qualitative data management and analysis. Weitzman and Miles (1995) give a good description of the functionalities of 24 programs. In this research, ATLAS/ti has been used. This program helps with coding text, retrieving and recoding previous chunks when codes are modified or created. ATLAS/ti also enables the integration of memos during the coding process and helps with drawing diagrams (networks and flowcharts). In total, about 35,000 coding operations (i.e. giving a text chunk a code) and 3000 memoing operations (i.e. giving a text chunk a memo) have been performed. However, we preferred to use index cards or sheets to display matrices and diagrams. Note that we did not work with a fixed unit of analysis: a text chunk can be a paragraph, a sentence, a string of words or even a single word.

3.3.4. Trustworthiness of the study

When assessing the influence of the interview process on vacation planning, it appears that being interviewed affected thinking, talking (more interaction within the DMU) and even fantasizing about vacation. For five DMUs, it also sped up the DMP; one informant told us: '[A]fter your interview, we did realize: "well, maybe it is time to think about it if we are to leave".' However, the actual content and motives of vacation decisions and DM variables have not been influenced. In addition, issues of (instrumentation and social) biases, reliability and validity have been addressed through implementing Lincoln and Guba's (1985) criteria of trustworthiness for qualitative studies. *Credibility* was enhanced by the prolonged engagement in the setting, as informants were interviewed three or four times over a 1-year period. At the end of each interview, informants were offered a small gift (chocolates, a photo frame or a world map) to reward them and to keep them involved in the next interview. There was a growing relationship of trust with informants, who became more and more spontaneous and talkative. Moreover, data, categories and concepts were continuously compared and checked against the empirical material in order to make findings and conclusions credible. The issue of *transferability* to other settings is extensively discussed at the end of this book. The description of the sample (Table 3.4), summary tables and the substantial number of interview quotes supporting the theory generation process give readers the opportunity to interpret the data by themselves. Moreover, informants were invited to comment on summary analyses and interpretations provided by the authors during the interviews. These member checks, as well as an auditing process by colleagues, enhanced the *dependability* and the *confirmability* of the findings.

Finally, a set of *triangulation* techniques were used (Decrop 1999a; Fig. 3.2). Informant triangulation was applied in several ways. First, many comparisons were made between the broad range of informants considered in the study. Second, since all members of a DMU were invited to participate in the interviews, multilevel triangulation was possible, which means seeing to which extent individual and group motives, plans and behaviour converged. The credibility and dependability of the findings were further enhanced by longitudinal triangulation. Informants were interviewed up to four times over the year in such a way that the evolution of vacation plans and decisions could be tracked, and information on key variables could be compared at different moments of the DMP. Data triangulation was assured in a variety of ways. Pictures were collected from vacation photo albums (at the end of the second series of interviews). In addition, field notes were written down during and immediately after each interview describing the setting, the relationship with the informants, as well as personal comments about what had been done, said and not said during the interview, etc.

The Context of Vacation Decision Making

4

4.0. Introduction

In this chapter, we investigate the context in which vacation plans and decisions are made. First, the major contextual factors will be described in four categories – environmental, personal, interpersonal and situational – and presented in a general framework. Second, the way these factors may facilitate or inhibit vacation decisions will be interpreted in the light of three emerging dimensions: the persistence of influences in time, their intensity, and the way they are perceived and incorporated into the DMP. The third section will focus on a motivational approach of vacation DM: why the vacationer escapes his or her daily environment for another environment. Finally, contextual influences on vacation DM will be placed in a dynamic perspective. We will present how the vacationer evolves in his or her 'career' by accumulating experience and maturity. But before that, the core concepts of the study are defined, a typology of vacation decision items is presented and the stability of vacation DMUs is discussed. These emerging points are addressed at the outset of this chapter because they are important for a good understanding of the empirical findings that will be described in the following chapters.

Emerging definitions of vacation and travel

Vacation and travel deserve particular attention because these concepts may encompass different realities from one individual to the other. To avoid interpretation biases, each interviewee was asked what vacation, travel and going on vacation meant for him or her. For a large part of the sample, vacation and travel are almost the same: vacation involves travelling (at least ideally) because travel strengthens the vacation feeling. A summer vacation without going away cannot really be called a vacation, and travelling is as such a synonym for vacation. However, the travel-vacation association is stronger than the vacation-travel association. By this we mean that travelling is always connected with vacation (except for people who travel for business), whereas the opposite is not true. On the one hand, travelling and going on vacation are often synonymous, and vacation begins with the journey itself: 'For me, the journey is already part of the vacation: once I step into my car and I leave, it is part of the vacation.' However, for some people, travelling means more than going on vacation: it involves a more active vacation type, moving from one place to another with the major goal of discovering and visiting the destination. In this sense, travel is assimilated with a tour, whereas going on vacation is associated with staying in the same place. On the other hand, vacation does not always include leaving home and, even less, travelling. For many informants, vacation is first of all a state of mind: it implies a break from work and worries, living at his or her own pace and doing activities other than the daily routine. As a consequence, one can feel on vacation at home or when doing particular activities such as reading or gardening. There is no need to go on vacation at any cost. In the same way, vacation is neither a question of duration nor of distance.

In a few words, vacation is a broader concept than travel, which itself is often associated with going on vacation. Vacation is more like a lifestyle, an abstract construct. In contrast, travel is a more concrete goal-oriented object.

A typology of vacation decision items

Travel and vacation being defined, we now look at the *decision items* that may be involved in vacation and travel choices. Besides vacation destinations, which lie at the core of this research, other vacation subdecisions were discussed with informants. Coding resulted in a typology of 16 travel decision items, which are defined in Table 4.1.

The adaptability of vacation decision-making units[1]

While recruiting and interviewing, it was not always easy to categorize informants according to one of the four types of DMUs described in Chapter 3. For example, the mother in a single-parent family first said that she would be going on summer vacation alone that year. She used to go with her two children before but was no longer considering this for the future, unless for short breaks. During the second interview, she was contemplating a proposal to go with friends while having no intention of participating in the DMP. After summer, it turned out that she finally went on vacation alone. This example shows that many vacationers are flexible or adaptable, as they may either go on vacation alone, with children or with friends according to availability, opportunities or passing moods. Since they are involved in more group types at the same time (e.g. parents may

[1] This section has been adopted from Decrop (2005), with permission of JTTM.

Table 4.1. A typology of vacation decision items.

Decision item	Definition
Accommodation	Includes lodging but also the general infrastructure of the place of stay: pool, tennis, disco, etc.
Accompaniment	People with whom one spends one's vacation
Activities	What people do during their vacation time: sports, cultural visits, reading, entertainment, etc.
Attractions	Types of attractions the vacationer visits: museum, cities, monuments, national parks, events, etc.
Budget and expenditures	Amount of money that is spent on vacation and the way it is spent
Destination	Place(s) where the vacation will be spent
Duration	Duration and timing of the vacation
Formula	Global type of vacation: staying in one spot or touring, sea or mountains, city or countryside, etc.
Meals	Eating patterns: what and where one eats for breakfast, lunch, dinner
Organization	The way the vacation is organized and reserved: by oneself, by a travel intermediary, by friends, etc.
Period	Period of the year when one goes on vacation
Purchases	Anything that is purchased and/or taken back home from one's vacation: souvenirs, self-gifts, postcards, photos, etc.
Route	Route that is followed to reach the vacation destination
Tour	Destination area that is visited, and route that is followed for that purpose
Transportation	Transportation modes used to reach the vacation destination and to make excursions there
Vacation style	Vacation lifestyle, which is more particularly characterized by the comfort level of the vacation and the level of integration in local life

go on holiday with their children and on their own; children may have plans with friends in addition to the family vacation), they are forced to adapt their plans. In parties of friends, all members are also involved in other vacation DMUs (family or couple). However, most often, a distinction can be made between the primary DMU, i.e. the type of DMU in which people participate most often, and secondary DMUs, which are more occasional.

In addition, many informants are involved in several vacation projects at the same time (other summer vacations or projects related to winter skiing, short breaks, summer vacation, camps, etc.). Data show that in families and groups of friends, the composition of the DMU is strongly affected by the type of vacation project. Parents will not go on a youth camp with their children; similarly, children will not accompany their parents on a romantic city trip. Married and unmarried couples are much more stable in this respect.

Finally, the DMU must not be defined too narrowly. Sometimes, there are people outside the DMU (i.e. participants in vacation DM and experience) who give the necessary impetus to go on vacation or who influence particular vacation decisions: 'I did not plan to leave, but after talking with my friends, they told me "listen, make an effort, ask your parents for some money, do something, leave a few days".'

4.1. A Descriptive Perspective: What Are the Major Contextual Influences?

A substantial number of contextual factors emerge from our data. Instead of describing the factors one after the other, it is more interesting to see how they can be grouped together. We make a distinction between four types of contextual influences: environmental, personal, interpersonal and situational.

Environmental factors may have a direct or indirect influence on vacation decisions. For example, the legal environment (passports, visas, vaccinations) affects destination choice. Three aspects of the vacationer's environment are more powerful in shaping vacation decisions and DMP: social, cultural and geographical. The social network is a major source of vacation knowledge and may be a reason for the trip itself (i.e. visiting family and friends). Moreover, it lies at the origin of groups of friends and, through this, of many vacation plans. Culture (language, religion, cultural background) influences destination choice as well. For example, some destinations are excluded due to the lack of knowledge of a foreign language. A young single is willing to visit Jerusalem at least once in his life because he or she is a practising Catholic. Finally, geographical or physical factors such as climate and the living or housing conditions have an enduring effect on vacation involvement and destination preferences.

Major influences of *personal factors* on vacation decisions and DM have been discussed extensively in Decrop (1999b). Three important findings need to be remembered. First, data suggest a distinction between primary and secondary personal factors. The former (age, family situation, education and occupation, personality and lifestyles) are the primary roots from which the latter (personal history, vacation experience, personal resources, motives, brand loyalty or variety seeking, and involvement) arise. Our sample is described on these variables in Appendix 2. Second, informants' age and family situation have a substantial influence on vacation DM variables. The family life cycle (i.e. a combination of age and family situation) has received much consideration in tourism literature to discriminate between groups of vacationers (e.g. Gitelson and Kerstetter, 1990; Fodness, 1992). Based on our data, it still seems to be one of the best ways to segment vacationers. The typology of Table 4.2 gives additional insight into the composition of our sample as to this variable.

Table 4.2. A typology of vacationers based on the family life cycle.

Position	Definition
Younger single	From 20 to 40, bachelor ($n = 2$) or divorced (but without children)
Younger couple	From 20 to 40, married or unmarried ($n = 1$) but without children
Younger family	Head of household under 45 with young children (less than 12 years) (unmarried: $n = 1$, recomposed family: $n = 2$)
Mid-life family	Head of household above 40 with (young and) older children (at least one over 12 years), married ($n = 5$) or unmarried ($n = 1$); sometimes, children have left the household while others still participate in vacation decisions ($n = 2$)
Single-parent family	Head of the household is divorced or widowed with children ($n = 1$)
Older couple	Above 50, with no accompanying children because they have left the household ($n = 2$) or because they do not want to go on vacation with their parents any more ($n = 2$)
Older single	Above 50, old bachelor ($n = 1$), widow and no children present ($n = 2$) or divorced
Group of friends	Involves most often younger people (under 40) – a group of younger singles ($n = 2$), a group of younger couples ($n = 1$) or a mixed group (singles, couples and sometimes also a younger family)

Third, four major dimensions emerge from the data coding regarding personality traits and lifestyles:

1. Emotional vs. rational vacationers. Emotional people may be characterized by impulsiveness, instability and improvisation, whereas rational vacationers are rather reserved, stable, organized and mindful. This distinction correlates with the level of risk aversion, so that we could also speak of adventurous vs. careful vacationers.

2. Active vs. passive vacationers. Active vacationers are characterized by a high activity propensity, they cannot keep still ('staying home makes me inert and more tired', 'I leave home for the smallest reason'), whereas passive vacationers usually are 'stay-at-home' types ('I need stability', 'I can enjoy my leisure time at home').

3. Introvert vs. extrovert vacationers. This dimension pertains to how the vacationer interacts with his or her social environment. Introvert vacationers are crowd-averse and limit social contacts to their own DMU. They have a stronger self-image, they are more independent and more moralizing. This continuum could be compared with Plog's (1974) popular typecasting approach of psychocentric vs. allocentric vacationers.

4. Avaricious vs. prodigal vacationers. This last personality type is concerned with vacationers' involvement in money. Avaricious people do not like to spend much, either by constraint ('we live a sacrificed life all through the year'), or by risk aversion ('we do not know what the future of our children will be'). In contrast, prodigal people are Epicurean in the sense that 'it is better to live well today'. They buy something as soon as they long for it. As a consequence, they lack savings.

It should be stressed that the previous typology is hypothetical and not exhaustive. However, findings suggest that personality types have a major influence on vacation destinations, activities, period, style, organization, souvenirs and formulas. For example, the 'stay-at-home' prefers vacationing at the same spot while the 'cannot-keep-still' prefers touring. Extrovert vacationers like to go on vacation when everyone is on vacation while introverts prefer the off-season, when tourist places are not crowded. Careful vacationers avoid such 'dangerous' destinations as Lebanon (political violence) or Madagascar (poor sanitary conditions). Personality types may also impact on other individual variables, like involvement and motives, and on aspects of the DMP like planning, information search, choice criteria, heuristics, decision timing and brand loyalty. For example, adventurous travellers do not book anything beforehand and are looking for ever-new vacation destinations and experiences. Introvert vacationers cast a critical look at mass tourism as they long for authenticity in their vacation experiences.

Interpersonal and situational factors will be described later, as they represent the basic themes of group decision processes (Chapter 8) and structural vs. situational influence (Section 4.2.2), respectively. Following Fig. 4.1, there is an emerging structure operating between the previous four groups of contextual factors. First, environmental influences encompass all other factors. Second, primary personal factors influence other (secondary) personal factors. Third, individual personal factors are the input for group DM where interpersonal factors intervene. Fourth, situational factors may appear when the vacationer enters a real decision situation. This conceptualization should not be understood as a rigid sequence of contextual influences. As illustrated by the downward arrows, personal, interpersonal and situational factors may have a direct influence on vacation decisions and DM variables.

To some extent, our typology of contextual influences is in line with Crawford *et al.*'s (1991) hierarchy of constraints in the context of leisure participation. Three levels are described: intrapersonal, interpersonal and structural. These different types affect the DMP in different ways: interpersonal constraints involve individual psychological variables that interact with leisure preferences; interpersonal constraints stem from the interaction between individuals and raise questions of compatibility and coordination in DM; structural constraints, such as economic barriers or time availability, intervene between leisure preferences and participation. Crawford *et al.*

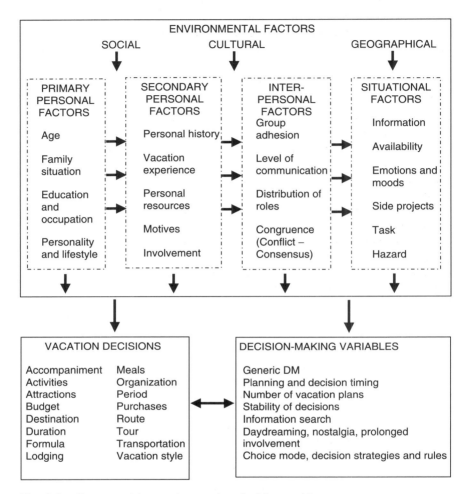

Fig. 4.1. Contextual factors in vacation decision making.

(1991) assume that the constraining process is hierarchical: psychological factors (e.g. stress, religiosity, perceived self-skill) may prevent individuals from facing higher-level constraints. In the same way, interpersonal constraints have to be overcome before the individual may get affected by structural constraints. However, the authors point out that most people frequently respond to constraints actively, by negotiation, rather than passively resigning to non-participation (Jackson *et al.*, 1993).

4.2. An Interpretive Perspective: How Does Context Influence Vacation Decisions?

Emerging from our coding process, three major dimensions may account for the influence of context on the vacation DMP (Fig. 4.2): the first distinguishes whether facilitators or inhibitors have an enduring structural or momentary situational influence; the second pertains to the extent to which DMUs are constrained by their structural or situational context; and the third is about the way those constraints are perceived and considered in making decisions.

4.2.1. Persistence of constraints: structural vs. situational

On the one hand, situational factors relate to conditions that influence the current vacation DMP, or did influence it at particular points in the past. They involve a decision situation that is well determined in time and space (see section 1.2.3). On the other hand, structural factors relate to the general context, to the conditions that influence, or may influence, vacation DM in an enduring way. These conditions are not peculiar to a well-defined decision situation (i.e. the current summer vacation) but pertain to any vacation decision in broad time and space horizons:

> *Joel* (M, 35, family): No, the family situation does not change any way, it is always [the same]. Obviously with the children, well for the airplane (as I have explained),

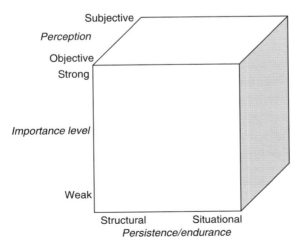

Fig. 4.2. Types of influences in vacation decision making.

that is too much. ... To pay four seats, obviously it costs you double to go on vacation. ... Thus this is a limitation. [Q4.1]

To make the distinction even clearer, one could argue that structural factors have a continuous influence on vacation decisions while situational factors only have a discrete influence.

Related to this structural–situational continuum, most factors listed in Fig. 4.1 can have both an enduring and a more specific situational influence on vacation decisions and DM. For example, the economic situation and occupation are enduring conditions, whereas budget and vacation job have a situational influence. In the same way, climate may be both structural and situational. It has an enduring impact on vacation involvement and destination preferences (e.g. Belgians show a higher vacation involvement than Italians on average, partly due to their poorer climate). In the same way, our informants prefer southern, warm and sunny destinations: 'Well, let's say that since we live in a very humid and drab country, we need to get some sunlight and hot weather.' However, climate also has a situational influence. Weather conditions may result in temporary moods, which may increase or decrease the desire to go on vacation and/or to choose a warm and sunny destination. Going to closer destinations also depends on home weather, since the weather is likely to be the same there. This results in vague vacation timing and in very late generic DM: 'We are going to stay two weeks at the sea if the weather is good – one or two weeks at the sea if the weather is good, but we'll wait the last minute because we can't decide right away.'

Involvement is another typical example of the structural–situational continuum. There is a distinction between: (i) involvement in the generic decision domain (travel and vacation in general); (ii) involvement in a specific decision item (destinations, accommodation, transportation); and (iii) brand-choice involvement (Greece, Turkey). In the data, the level of vacation involvement is more stable over time and less dependent upon the environment than destination involvement, which itself is more stable than the involvement for a particular destination. This is in line with the enduring vs. situational involvement dichotomy (Rothschild, 1979). However, vacation involvement may also be situational. For example, the desire to go away may be stronger in the summertime or when the weather is bad than during the rest of the year or when the weather is sunny. In general, findings suggest that situational factors affect the predictability or external validity of choices, whereas this is not the case with structural factors. Moreover, situational factors may become structural factors when repeated in more decision situations. For example, social opportunities (invitation by family and friends) may be recurrent. This is either by tradition (all family members gather in the family cottage for the summer) or because strong social ties exist, so that the vacationer feels like having a permanent address for vacation, a kind of second home.

However, some factors are either structural or situational by nature. Environmental factors and the family situation affect vacation decisions in an

enduring way, while hazard, mood states, school results, availability, side projects, task and news are only situational as they pertain to consumption situations bounded in time and space. Finally, it should be noted that informants
neglect the influence of their structural context while, in contrast, they often
overemphasize the situational constraints. For example, budget as a situational
variable comes across more frequently than the economic situation as a structural variable. This is because people are much more aware of their financial
limitations when they are confronted with a real, well-defined decision situation. The intervention of an unexpected event (losing one's job) is another, but
lesser, reason.

4.2.2. Importance level of constraints: strong vs. weak

The level of dependence on context strongly varies across informants and DMUs.
Overall, couples are the least dependent upon context and situation, while groups
of friends are the most dependent. Singles and families lie in between.

Informants who show *weak* contextual influences on vacation choices justify
this by their structural context: they are young or retired, no (longer have a) child
to take care of and benefit from material facilitators (e.g. a mobile home). The
absence of strong constraints favours the flexibility and unpredictability of choices
with respect to period, destination, preparation and decision timing. As they are
'free as a bird', those vacationers can respond to sudden desires or impulses:

> *Georges* (M, 66, single): It is possible that in a month from now, I will say: 'I want
> to leave, well. … ' I no longer have ties . … that is, to stay home. … [If] I want
> to leave, I leave. … I'm not going to say that I will leave during vacation time,
> I leave whenever I want. [Q4.2]

In contrast, informants who are *strongly* dependent upon context explain this by situational factors rather than by their structural context. The lack of interpersonal
congruence is also an important inhibitor (Chapter 8, this volume). Of course,
constraints differ from one type of DMU to the other. Single DMUs do not have
interpersonal constraints because they decide alone to go on vacation, when,
where and to do what they want. However, being a single entails the disadvantage
that one has to organize and manage everything on one's own. This affects vacation decisions such as organization (it is more difficult to go by one's own), budget
(being a single means higher accommodation prices), purchases (one has to buy
larger quantities than what is actually needed), destination ('civilized' and well-
known destinations are preferred), formula (a club or an organized tour will be
preferred in order to meet other people), preparation and information search
(information is more detailed and more practical). Singles show stronger levels of
anxiety and risk aversion, not because of their personality but because they have
to travel alone.

Interpersonal constraints, however, prevail in the other types of DMUs. Maybe the biggest problem in groups is to reconcile all idiosyncratic expectations and constraints. Data show that the interpersonal constraint has either a structural or situational influence. It is an enduring structural factor for vacationers who always decide, and go, on vacation with the same people. This is the case with married couples or families where links are legally and morally strong. The interpersonal constraint is more situational for groups of friends, newly made families and pairs of lovers, as these DMUs are not so stable. Participation in the group evolves over time with changing friends, partners and personal resources. A major consequence is that even if a vacation plan exists, the final decision to go or not is often shelved. Thinking about vacation, preparation and information search are intentionally inhibited in order to avoid disappointment and disillusion. In the same way, these informants try to contain fantasy and emotional drives in order to avoid frustration:

Anne (F, 41, family): And I try to think less about it! Otherwise I have stomach ache! Actually, one whole Easter week we had everything to leave and we did not leave! Thus, I try to think less about it, so I am not frustrated. My oldest daughter told me: 'I prefer that we say that we do not leave but then we leave in the end than the opposite!' She just told me that two days ago! The desire is always intimately present! I am always sensitive to everything that happens in the regions we like. I continue to read, to dream. ... My daughter gave me a tape about Romania, about tourist Romania precisely: a document that lasts thirty minutes. But I take it especially in ethnological terms. ... It is very interesting, because the people that watched it always want to go visit Romania! We have been there several times! Thus some kind of feeling still remains, which we try to escape from because we should not have too strong illusions! [Q4.3]

The three groups of friends we interviewed also showed specific constraints. In contrast to the other types of DMUs, structural and situational factors may significantly vary across the members. Constraints are even more serious in younger groups of friends where some members may not make final decisions without their parents' authorization, or have an uncertain occupational status (some are still in school, and going on vacation depends on the school results, whereas others are looking for, or starting, a first job), both factors resulting in limited financial autonomy. Finally, members of parties of friends are also involved in other DMU types (families, couples), which are often prioritized. The decision alchemy consists in reconciling all these idiosyncratic constraints, which proves to be a very difficult task. That is why groups of friends are very unstable DMUs. When asked why they finally gave up their summer vacation projects, the speaker of a young group of friends typically answered:

Annaïg (F, 20, group of friends): We cannot say that we took. ... even a weekend or short vacations, we did not take them because everyone was not available at the same time.
Interviewer: When you say that everyone was not available at the same time, are there some things in particular that did prevent you from going on vacation?

Annaïg: Well yes, for example, some people decided to leave for a certain period ... either with their boyfriend or girlfriend and ... or then family vacations, thus this causes immediately. ... We were never able to have a weekend with everybody. Finally, we were always only two or three or there was no agreement. In fact, everybody had something or on Sunday, there was something to do, thus we were not able to leave during the weekend. The problem among friends is that we can never bring everybody together or only for a short period: for two hours, one day. To bring everybody together, everybody for vacations. ... If for a weekend it is already difficult, imagine how it would be for vacations! [Q4.4]

4.2.3. Perception of constraints: objective vs. subjective

After the structural–situational and weak–strong dichotomies, our data suggest a third interpretation of the formal influence of context on vacation decisions and DM. Most factors of Fig. 4.1 may have both an objective and a subjective influence. For example, many vacation trade-offs (Chapter 5, this volume) do not only result from the objective economic situation (a low income), but are also influenced by more subjective factors such as risk aversion, money perception and vacation involvement. This is illustrated by a woman who could afford to buy new lounge chairs and to go on vacation, but who was urged into the trade-off just because she did not want to put her future in danger. The family situation also involves a lot of constraints that can be divided into objective (e.g. babies and younger children require more care and attention, so parents often decide not to go on vacation) and subjective (e.g. parents do not accept to improvise and live as adventurous vacationers when their travel plans involve young children) constraints.

This objective–subjective dichotomy could be paralleled with the distinction between actual and potential contextual influence. Two phenomena illustrate this parallelism: daydreaming and anticipation. Optimism or prospectivism sometimes leads to forgetting actual contextual and/or situational factors: some informants may be mentally unconstrained even when they are confronted with objective inhibitors. In other words, they are fantasizing or *daydreaming*. For them, projects will be carried out in the future if not this year; dreams are not unreachable. Others are comforted by considering a potential, while hardly probable, opportunity (invitation by friends). In contrast, for yet others, context is taken into account when making vacation plans, as informants speak of dreams or projects that will never be fulfilled:

Pierre (M, 43, family): For Sweden, it will be necessary to take the children into consideration. Thus the children are the ones who will direct vacations, of course; then for me, for not being disappointed ... because it is very simple: I do not dream too much of projects that will not be carried out and ... because it is necessary to take it into account, I think that taking the children with us is not worthwhile because I do not want them to come back disappointed. [Q4.5]

Anticipation is another phenomenon related to the subjective perception of contextual factors. Anticipating inhibitors or facilitators directs the vacation

choices of many informants. Vacation decisions may be delayed when informants anticipate a favourable modification of their personal context in the
future. Emerging from the coding process, major anticipated facilitators
involve modifications in the family life cycle (no more children) or in the occupational status (retirement), hazard and future opportunities (invitation by family or friends), which result in increasing the probability of going on vacation.
In contrast, major anticipated inhibitors pertain to ageing and health most of
the time. This results in a higher travel involvement for younger people ('it is
better to travel when one is fit and well', 'staying at home will be for my old
days'), more active vacation types, and more distant or less touristy destinations ('one shouldn't consider Indonesia after the age of 70'). Anticipated constraints may also be related to an evolution in the family life cycle (marriage
and having children) or in occupation (from student to working life). Finally,
the anticipation of changes in destination attributes (i.e. cost of living or
authenticity) is another reason for visiting that destination without delay. In all
the previous situations, informants are willing to make it now, as later might be
too late: it is now or never. There is a rationalization process going on, in
which the anticipation of future potential constraints is stronger than the desire
to go on vacation itself:

> *Marie* (F, 60, single): In my mind, I tell myself 'you are more than 60 years old, if
> you don't move now, it's possible that one day you will not be able to move any-
> more'. There are inevitable things. Sometimes, you have hikes which are well
> done: if it's too difficult, they are going to tell you 'there is a lodge, a refuge at 11
> km'. And climbing up 11 km a day is more than enough. If later, I can only do 8
> km, I will not be able to do those things anymore. Because I will not have a place
> to stay or, I would have to carry my material on my back. I also tell myself that I
> have to hurry up. It's also probably that which influences me each time I want to
> leave, I forget that we do not feel like doing it. [Q4.6]

Personality often is an indicator of daydreaming and anticipation. While daydreamers and informants invoking anticipated facilitators could be considered as
optimistic (i.e. they convince themselves that a vacation is still possible even
though their current context and situation are uncertain), idealist or indecisive
(i.e. they postpone decisions even when they are able to make these decisions
now), interviewees mentioning anticipated inhibitors show a rather pessimistic,
risk-aversive, realistic and decisive nature.

Daydreaming and anticipation are a clear indication of prospectivism:
informants are rather future-oriented as far as vacation contextual influences
are concerned. However, the past is also important in shaping vacation decisions and DM variables. For example, destination preferences may be
affected by emotional states like fear (the wife of an older couple does not
want to visit destinations where there are too many Germans because of
frightening war memories), sadness (an old widow avoids places where she
went with her deceased husband because then she feels weak and sad) and
nostalgia:

Jean-Pierre (M, 42, family): Yes, the sun is something that we miss [general acquiescence]. The nostalgia or … my wife and I, we were both born in Africa also and we used to live with the sun, that means, I do not know if it is … we feel this need of sunlight and hot weather. [Q4.7]

Findings indicate that personal history has a deep impact on vacation definitions and motives, and destination preferences as well. For two households, destination choice was driven by the desire to go back to roots, as some members were born or had spent a substantial part of their life over there.

In conclusion, daydreaming, anticipation and nostalgia are major phenomena in vacation DM. Campbell (1987) considers them as features of modern patterns of consumption that have their origins in sentimentalism and romanticism. Urry (1990) further highlights that daydreaming and anticipation of intense pleasures are major reasons for tourist satisfaction. According to Graburn and Moore (1994, p. 236), nostalgia is closely related to authenticity, since it may be seen as an 'evidence of dissatisfaction with modern life and of the search for simpler and more morally uplifting qualities in other places, times, or cultures'.

4.3. A Motivational Perspective: Push Factors in Vacation Decision Making

The question of what drives consumers to behave as they do is of paramount importance to understanding vacation decisions and DMP. When asked why she considered a particular vacation formula, an old widow answered: 'There is also the social contact: meeting people. But is this the result of the type of vacation I take or, additionally, of the person I am?' In this question, the person unwillingly introduced the distinction between push and pull factors. The former are considered socio-psychological forces that predispose the individual to go on vacation. The latter represent the product attributes that attract the individual towards a particular vacation alternative.

The concepts of *push* and *pull* factors (see Section 1.3.2) have been adapted to tourism by Dann (1977). This view has been widely used in order to explain tourist motivation. Push factors are 'internally generated drives causing the tourist to search for signs in objects, situations, and events that contain the promise of reducing prevalent drives' whereas pull factors are 'generated by the knowledge about goal attributes the tourist holds' (Gnoth, 1997, pp. 290–291). To put it in simpler words, push factors are deep-rooted motivations, whereas pull factors refer to the mental images individuals hold of the real world (Kent, 1990). Dann (1977) argues that push factors pertain to the desire to travel while pull factors are concerned with destination choice, the latter being consequent on the former. For Gnoth (1997), push and pull factors can be seen as two types of motivators that he connects with works by Murray (1938) and Tolman (1932) in behavioural psychology. On the one hand, Murray makes a distinction between *need* (an enduring personal disposition) and *press* (a temporal mental representation of stimuli), which combine to form a 'thema' or an 'equivalent group of behavioral situations'. On the other hand, Tolman hints at 'a dichotomy of internal and external motivators containing drive-based emotions and cognitions' (Gnoth, 1997, p. 290). In the two cases, the distinction inside (push factors) vs. outside (pull factors) the person prevails. Gnoth extends this dichotomy to the difference between lasting motives and situational motivations. It should be noted that in this book, push and pull factors are used specifically and not as an overall explanation of vacation DM. Push and pull factors refer respectively to personal drives or motives and to the product's attraction power. As such, these terms proved to be appropriate to reflect some emerging findings.

Findings brought to light one basic push factor that drives informants to leave their daily life for a vacation life, i.e. the need to break from routine or to get away (a change of scenery). This need to get away is further refined into a temporal and spatial escape.

4.3.1. Escape in time

For a large part of the sample, the temporal escape pertains to getting away from everyday life. Leaving the pace and stress related to ordinary occupational or household activities is the primary motivation. There is a transition from everyday-life time, which is associated with stress, hurry, a tight schedule, to vacation time, which is connected with rest, relaxation and living at one's own pace. Vacation lifestyle is affected as one takes one's time and simple pleasures are rediscovered:

> *Claude* (F, 38, family): After all we learn to enjoy everything: I mean we go in the morning to the market. ... It takes me sometimes two hours to go to the market and then we realize 'it took us ...', but it does not matter. Actually, we did not lack time, we enjoyed looking [at] what was there. At Re's Island, since we didn't really like the beach, we took the time to go to the markets, to see a little ... therefore, I mean, for example, we cook by ourselves ...
> *Jean* (M, 47): To choose some olives.
> *Claude*: Oh yes, we were going to choose our olives, to taste them and everything that was there. After all, that's all which fills a day because finally ... [Q4.8]

The previous quote shows that vacation time is characterized by hedonic consumption as well. Emotional drives get stronger than during everyday-life time. Reason is temporarily overridden by dreams, favourable atmospheres or moods: 'Oh, we feel good, we will not do without that.' In the same way, financial behaviour may be different on vacation than during the year: 'Money gets more easily from one's pocket.' Vacation also allows to spend more time with the other members of the DMUs: there is more room for discussion, for participating in joint activities (Chapter 8, this volume). Finally, those informants can feel on vacation at home (at least as far as they are not disturbed by daily tasks) and want to avoid excessive disorientation due to travelling to faraway countries. This escape in time has already been highlighted in the anthropological work of Graburn (1983, 1989) that is based on the processual approach (see Section 1.3.2). Life is seen as an alternating sequence of mundane (profane) and special (sacred, ritualized) time periods where 'the latter mark a break from the former while adding special meaning to life' (Graburn and Moore, 1994, p. 234). Vacation and tourism are a typical example of such special breaks.

4.3.2. Escape in space

For other interviewees, an escape in space is more important than an escape in time; there is a need to leave home to really feel on vacation. They argue that even during the holiday, one tends to continue the daily routine or, even worse, to work more than during the year. The break is not sharp enough. This drive towards another spatial environment for vacation strongly depends on gender, occupation and the housing conditions.

First, there is a *gender-occupational* differentiation of the spatial transition from daily to vacation life. For working informants (most often males), vacation primarily means not going to work. Motives are connected with rest, leaving the stress and the (boring) tasks of daily work, or spending more time with the family. An escape in time is enough. In contrast, for non-working informants (most often females), vacation definitely means leaving home, travelling and choosing accommodation where the household tasks will be minimized (so hotels instead of campsites). They are motivated by a more active vacation type, including discovering new things and meeting other people. This gender-based working–non-working dichotomy is a reflection of the Belgian society, which is still characterized by a strong patriarchy: the man is the *pater familias* who provides for the household's needs, whereas the woman cares for the children, shopping and the household tasks (Gijsbrechts *et al.*, 1995). Note that this gender-occupational differentiation of vacation motives remains after retirement. In contradiction with women, men consider (or anticipate) the period following retirement as 'continuous vacation', confirming the yin-yang of the concept: vacation exists just because work exists. For working interviewees, the nature of the job also affects vacation involvement and motives. For instance, going away is the only means for professional people to escape their work environment since they work at home.

Second, the *living and housing conditions* affect vacation experience, involvement and the choice of a particular destination environment. Informants who are lodgers, living in apartments or in cities, have a stronger desire to go on vacation and to escape their home surroundings for a totally different environment. Vacationers living in 'better' conditions (e.g. the owner of a big house with a garden) do not have that kind of expectation as they imagine enjoyable vacation activities (e.g. bricolage or gardening) while staying at home. When asked whether vacation ideally means going away or staying at home, a (single) mother in her forties answered:

> *Brigitte* (F, 37, single): Maybe I would also say, if there was a beautiful house in the countryside and if I'd work in the city and if I'd have – I don't know – a swimming pool, and well then if … if there is a good weather, I stay at home. It's clear that I never take advantage of the countryside beauty. … It [i.e. the preference for going away] could be related to this. Related to my domicile, to the environment. … Yes, it's certainly that. [Q4.9]

For some informants, escaping the home environment is not enough; they need to get away from Belgium because travelling in Belgium does not really give a vacation feeling. In addition to geographical distance, escape may be connected with the simple (psychological) fact of crossing a border, with experience (which causes weariness), the duration of the stay (shorter if in Belgium), or the change in climate and cultural environment. It should be noted that the vacationer is attracted both by cultural similarities and dissimilarities. Some informants are not willing to visit a destination that is too different from their western Belgian cultural environment. This is explained by risk aversion and, more precisely, by the fear of the unfamiliar and the cultural shock:

> *Christian* (M, 59, couple): However, there are some countries where we feel ourselves, I would say, lost somehow. We don't intend, for example, to go to Japan which is a country …
> *Marie-France* (F, 53): Oh no, a money matter …
> *Christian*: It's not a money matter, but it's a totally different culture. [Q4.10]

There are more informants who, in contrast, are attracted by cultural differences with their home environment. This attraction is motivated by discovery, knowledge and social contacts (see Section 4.3.3). For those people, language is not a real obstacle to learning new things, or sharing experiences with the local. Gibbering, gesturing and even smiling help to establish the cultural contact. This motivation may even lead to the desire to learn the destination language.

It should be pointed out that a few interviewees are motivated by an escape in both time and space. Some want to relive experiences and revive memories by going to certain places. Others wish to change their mind after painful events (e.g. the partner's death), to escape dark memories by just leaving home for another environment, or by avoiding particular destinations associated with those memories. Another remark is that the change of place may alter time perception: 'Time is not the same when one is on … when one stays at home as when one leaves. Time is elastic, definitely.' Finally, the transition from daily to vacation life appears to be recursive: a few informants declare that they like to go away but also to come back. This phenomenon results from a saturation or from homesickness and seems to be peculiar to the vacation phenomenon.

4.3.3. More specific motives

In addition to the basic temporal and spatial escape, a number of more specific, goal-directed motives are found in the data. These refine the idea of transition from everyday to vacation life. They vary (in importance and combination) from one individual (or DMU) to the other. Six categories emerge from the coding process:

1. Discovering new things and visiting the destination in order to acquire knowledge. There is often a well-defined goal: e.g. seeing how other people (the locals) live, discovering other cultures or visiting sites that are historically or currently important. Vacationers want to come back with something learned from the vacation. This motive is often contrasted with the relaxation motive, which is associated with beach and tanning and is not considered a profitable vacation.

2. Resting and relaxing in order to take breath and eliminate stress. This is being out of one's element in the broad sense of breaking with routine and habit. The lust for sun is often associated with this motive. Vacation has a utilitarian function: people look for long-term benefits such as a better mood, working better or recovering health. Vacation is like a therapy: it creates necessary conditions for forgetting daily problems or for solving them through recovered clear-mindedness.

3. Looking for people in order to share social experiences (be it with the locals, other vacationers or travel partners). This motive is particularly strong for single DMUs, which leads to the following proposition: being a single decision maker does not mean a trip alone. This motive may be paralleled with Dann's adaptation (1977) of the concept of anomie[2]. He suggests that anomie results in a human need for social interaction that can only be fulfilled away from the home environment, e.g. on vacation.

4. Doing exciting activities and having fun in order to take a big bite out of life and forget everything just for a few days. Excitement and fun are related to particular leisure (most often sport) activities, social togetherness or romantic experiences. Vacation plays a hedonic function: one is looking for emotional benefits from consumption experiences. Following Dann (1977, p. 188), fantasy is an important dimension of travel motivation. It is related to anomie and ego-enhancement, since the fantasy world of travel helps to overcome the normlessness and meaninglessness of everyday life and presents the vacationer with the opportunity to boost his or her ego 'in acting out an alien personality'.

5. Looking for personal values (e.g. prestige, richness, knowledge) in the vacation experience in order to impress others ('I was there!') or to go back to roots

---

[2] Anomie refers to 'a society whose norms governing interaction have lost their integrative force and where lawlessness and meaninglessness prevail' (Dann, 1977, p. 186). The term originates from Durkheim (1952).

('My family has lived in Africa for a long time'). Vacation is an opportunity to develop self-image and ego-enhancement. This need of being socially recognized is considered by Dann (1977) as the second major reason (in addition to anomie) to explain what makes people travel.

6. Going to 'true' places in order to experience an authentic environment that has not been corrupted by vacationers. Both tourist traps and 'staged authenticity' (MacCannell, 1973) must be avoided:

> *Pierre* (M, 43, family): I accept to go to India but I will go by my own to discover the true face of the country and not the artificial face. We have other friends who travelled to Thailand. … They went to the south of Thailand to see the giraffe women and they say that it is artificial; they advise us not to go seeing that because they are people who only live from tourism, it's awful! If you want to take a picture of a child, you have to pay. … There is nothing natural anymore. [Q4.11]

Meeting and living the life of the locals, going off the beaten track and bringing preconceived ideas or information into reality are other authenticity motives emerging from the data. The lack of authenticity sometimes lies at the origin of post-experience satisfaction, dissatisfaction or regret when the vacationer realizes that he or she could not really integrate in the local way of life and was forced into distant observation. Two different cultural worlds coexist: that of the vacationer and that of the local. On the one hand, the vacationer is unwillingly prevented from leaving his or her environmental bubble (Boorstin, 1964) because of the tour operator's control (organized trip), or cultural (language) or personal (being introvert) differences. On the other hand, there is a much more intentional reason for avoiding this confrontation. Many informants have a moralizing discourse on destination choice. They argue that they would never go to destinations where they would face excessive poverty and human misery because they would not be able to bear it ('I would be ill at ease') or because they would find it indecent:

> *Peter* (M, 40, family): But it's true that in the very first place, both of us think that there is something indecent in going to show off a certain occidental wealth (it is necessary to name it like that) in countries where it lacks everything, where it governs a dirty misery and where it governs a shocking poverty level. [Q4.12]

In the same way, they refuse to participate in the tourism exploitation of those people ('landing as colonizers') and to support authoritarian political governments.

4.4. A Dynamic Perspective: the Vacationer's Career

Contextual influences are not the same during a vacationer's whole life. The fact that context should be considered dynamically is a major conclusion of this chapter. Findings suggest that vacationers go through a series of periods, which are characterized by different levels and types of contextual influences on vacation choices and DM. These periods are based on the individual's position in his or her life cycle (age and family situation) and occupation:

> *Brigitte* (F, 37, single): It's true that it is also a function of the life's stages somehow. There was a period where the children were little and I did not leave or I used to go to the sea with them some days. But there is also the fact of not being at home, eventually, in a special family pension where there is nothing to do. Now, the children are older. There is also another thing: I lived for a long time in Italy. Thus, then, when it's possible, we try to go back over there and to go to say hello to some friends. Thus, it became an objective to me: when I have money and when I can go over there and ... thus, I will be more attracted by things like that than by opening a catalogue and tell myself 'Well, I will go one week over there or over there', like that. You are always somehow connected with ... well now there is Italy where I want to go back each year. There was a period where vacations were with my grandparents because both of them were in Dordogne, thus we used to visit them. Thus it's always related to a context, it is never only to buy a trip and leave. [Q4.13]

This quote may be interpreted according to the concept of the vacationer's career developed by Pearce (1988), based on Hughes (1937). It is defined as 'the moving perspective in which the person sees his life as whole and interprets the meaning of his various attributes, and things that happen to him' (Pearce, 1988, p. 27).

4.4.1. Transition moments

In the data, transition moments can be identified between what has been done *before* and what will be done *after*. However, this is not to say that what has been done before will again not be possible in a later period of life. Transition moments do not define a linear evolution of contextual influences. Four types of transition moments emerge from our analyses:

1. The modification of the family structure: switching from being a single to a couple, the birth of a baby, children leaving the household or the death of the travel partner are events that bring drastic changes in the family structure and thereby in the DMU. One's everyday and consumer life are affected as well as one's vacation behaviour and DMP. For example, the death of a family member either strengthens ('I cannot spend my leisure time at home anymore') or weakens ('since I am alone, I became stay-at-home') travel involvement.

2. The modification of the occupational status, like the passage from a student life to the professional life, or retirement, has an enduring effect on time and income. Getting retired opens new vacation perspectives (period, destination, preparation and decision timing) as time management becomes less stringent. The vacation period, which is often dictated by professional requirements, becomes a real choice when one retires. The transition from being unemployed to employed also facilitates vacation as it implies financial improvement and an increased vacation budget. As a consequence, new destinations or formulas may be (re)considered.

3. Ageing and health problems may result in a deep modification of one's vacation behaviour and DM. For example, a single might completely reconsider his or her travel behaviour just because he or she cannot benefit from discounts for youth travel by train any more. This is related to price discrimination.

4. The modification of the spatial environment: the house is the reason for many travel lapses in a vacationer's career. Buying, building or maintaining a house asks for trade-offs (Chapter 5, this volume) and financial sacrifices so that vacationers cannot afford a trip for a few years.

Periods with heavy contextual constraints may result in the accumulation of frustrated feelings for highly involved vacationers. Those feelings often prepare the way for catch-up effects once these particular constraints have disappeared. For example, an older couple desires to make up for lost time now that they have more money again, since all their children have left the household. Finally, different periods in the vacationer's career may be marked off by special vacation events such as a honeymoon trip and major-occupational-change breaks. These may be paralleled with 'rites de passage' (van Gennep, 1909) or intermittent pilgrimages (Turner and Turner, 1978; Smith, 1992).

4.4.2. Growing experience: brand loyalty vs. variety seeking

The vacationer's career is characterized by a growing vacation experience. However, there is an emerging distinction between: (i) the absolute number of trips and vacations in the past; and (ii) the experience (in variety and intensity) of each vacation subdecision and, in particular, vacation destinations. These two dimensions do not always come together although there often is a correlation. A few households often go on vacation, but always to the same place. Of course, experience grows as far as vacationers evolve in their life cycle. However, the relevant distinction is not weak vs. strong experience but rather brand loyalists vs. variety seekers (Chapter 7, this volume). This dichotomy could be interpreted as quality vs. quantity, or deep vs. broad knowledge. On the one hand, brand loyalists are interested by the quality of their vacation experiences. On the other hand, variety seekers long to accumulate and pile up different vacation experiences. This difference may be illustrated by the discovery and knowledge motive (see Section 4.3.3). Both brand loyalists and variety seekers are concerned with that motive. However, perspectives differ. For brand loyalists, discovery and knowledge acquisition are still possible when visiting the same place several times. Loyalty does not mean a boring repetition but rather further exploration and deeper knowledge:

Damien (M, 21, family): But doing the same things is not only true for travel (and there I get out a little bit of what we were talking); it's not only for travel that we redo things. I take a domain that I know pretty well, it is the musical domain. The fact that I listen three times, four times to the same CD or that I watch three, four times the same concert, it does not bother me at all, because anyway, each time I discover some things that I have never [heard or] seen during the first listening or the first visions. It does not bother me at all to repeat them, things like that. And for travelling, it's the same thing. [Q4.14]

In contrast, variety seekers argue that discovery and knowledge cannot really be achieved when returning to the same place. This is related to the lassitude of well-known destinations and the resulting willingness to innovate. Innovation and curiosity are necessary vacation ingredients, as novelty gives rise to enjoyable emotional states such as the attraction of something new, being surprised and filled with wonder (Unger and Kernan, 1983; Graillot, 1997), and to broader knowledge. It should be pointed out that the vacationer's brand loyalty or variety-seeking behaviour has implications on the type of DM model that is operative (Chapter 9, this volume). Always going to the same place involves routine problem solving and a habitual DMP. In contrast, variety seeking implies a more extended problem solving, since a new destination must be chosen each time.

4.4.3. Shift in motives and expectation level

The vacationer's career is further characterized by a shift in motives and expectation level due to maturity and experience. This is in line with Pearce's argument (1988) that the vacationer's career takes a form of progression he parallels with Maslow's hierarchy of needs. Although Maslow is not found as such in our data, there are more indications that *vacation definitions and motives* are changing and are determining more periods in the vacationers' career. When asked about vacation motives, the parents of a full-nest family point out:

Michèle (F, 43, family): But quietness is the general rule.
Patrick (M, 45): And then when we are sick and tired, well, we find ourselves on calm. ... In playa de Aro. It is because there, we go out at night very late.
Michèle: We were much younger also.
Patrick: Yes, but [pff] I tell myself: I do not see myself anymore in the same context at our present age, wondering when the band of the first floor was going to stop, the cars were going to stop horning. And then, when we are almost asleep, it is the garbage bus that comes and picks up everything. We knew that, he! And we used to like that also, but now, I tell myself: 'how come we used to like that?' [Q4.15]

Older vacationers are characterized by a growing maturity. Involvement weakens ('As I grow older, I think I attach more and more importance to the quality of my everyday life than to 15 days, which would be more enjoyable'), cultural discovery and knowledge acquisition become major travel motives and destination preferences are given more easily (one realizes that some dreams will never be fulfilled so that priorities are given).

The family situation also influences this evolution of vacation motives and involvement. As children grow older, parents become either stronger or lesser involved in going on vacation. Involvement may get stronger because destinations, formulas and activities match parents' expectations to a greater extent. In contrast, involvement may weaken because children are not enthusiastic any more about going on vacation with their parents, or because they have left the DMU. In the same way, vacation definitions and motives change: with young children, vacation is seen as a period of rest, relaxation and play. There is no need to go far away to spend a nice vacation; staying at home is even considered as an alternative. In contrast, parents with older children are primarily motivated by sharing social experiences (they complain: 'we do not see our children during the year') and acquiring knowledge. When children have left, there is more room for culture, learning and discoveries.

The importance given to decision criteria may change as well in a vacationer's career. For example, a couple acknowledges that climate is no longer a major attribute in destination choice now that they have retired, because they will have enough time to go to a sunnier destination if they previously experienced bad weather. Finally, an upward shift in the general *expectation level* characterizes a lot of informants. Experience strengthens involvement and makes the vacationer more demanding in quantity and/or quality: 'I did already travel a lot and see many things but I would like to see still more and be dazzled.' People who do not travel do not realize what they are missing. After going on vacation abroad for the first time, a young girl admits: 'I have now given a real meaning to the word vacation.' Moreover, satisfying alternatives in the past may no longer be enough in the future. This shift in the expectation level may pertain to particular vacation decision items (like accommodation) or vacation in general. When asked what he expected from his next summer vacation, the father of a large family replied:

Jacques (M, 43, family): The good weather and the entire happiness. When I say entire, it is something like … that they are a little … let's talk about the past, that they are better than last year. You understand, that's what I want to say. It's necessary that always one vacation – or some vacations or a vacation day – be always better than the day before. It's like when one … it's like when a fisherman, when he goes to fish, it is necessary that what he fishes, if he returns tomorrow, needs to be better than the day before that he went. Well, it's the same thing with me: the vacations, it's necessary that I tell myself: 'well if we are going to go there … if tomorrow, we leave 'the day before, what did we do?' Ah well 'we did that' and well tomorrow, it has to be better; it has to be better because if it's not better, that's not worth it.' [Q4.16]

This quote highlights a kind of enduring search for amelioration, which could be paralleled with incrementalism in the 'muddling through' DM paradigm (Lindblom, 1959; Chapter 1, this volume). Lindblom asserts that people do not optimize or satisfice but try to solve problems along the way in order to continue their intended way of behaviour or to reach intended goals. This shift in the expectation level may be interpreted as a consequence to continue the intended vacation behaviour. A choice is made only if the new alternative is better than the status quo, which is determined by the previous vacation experience.

Vacation Planning and Decision-making Processes

5

5.0. Introduction

This chapter presents the major findings regarding the overall vacation DMP (including the generic decision to go or not to go), whereas Chapter 6 will focus on destination decisions. First, we examine global aspects of DMPs: when and which decisions are made? This refers to decision timing and vacation plans. When dealing with complex products, consumers use plan their decisions (Bettman, 1979; Park and Lutz, 1982), i.e. they select from among alternatives of a specific course of action in anticipation of particular needs or problems (Walters and Bergiel, 1989). Plans are more formally defined as 'those specific procedures or actions taken to achieve a goal' (Miller *et al.*, 1960, quoted in Bettman, 1979, p. 47). Next, we will consider the criteria and strategies that are used in making vacation decisions and choices. We will see that vacationers explicitly or, most of the time, implicitly use a variety of strategies pertaining to how they handle decision goals and criteria in making a decision. The final section is devoted to information collection. The wording information *collection* is preferred to information *search* because information is an ongoing process: it is not as actively and purposefully searched as traditionally assumed.

Multiple levels in vacation decision making

Before going into the questions of when and which decisions are made, it is worth mentioning that vacation DM involves a lot of decisions and subdecisions. In Fig. 5.1, three levels of decisions are distinguished: generic decisions to go or not to go; modal decisions pertaining to the types of vacation; and specific decisions such as destination, transportation and accommodation. These levels should be regarded as conceptual and not as hierarchical or sequential. The findings presented in this chapter will show that the generic decision to go on vacation is not always considered first; nor is the destination decision considered in the last instance. The generic level involves non-comparable choices (Johnson, 1984, 1986), e.g. spending time on a vacation or repairing the house, whereas each vacation item at the level of specific decisions entails comparable alternatives. Comparability is defined as the degree to which alternatives are described or represented by the same attributes. Non-comparable alternatives have few attributes in common, while comparable alternatives share the same attribute background. The level of modal decisions lies somewhere in between, since some decision items are considered in any vacation type (e.g. destination, transportation, accommodation, activities), whereas others are particular to one type and are not comparable with the other vacation types (e.g. ski material, tour). The difference between the first two and the third levels in Fig. 5.1 is that generic and modal decisions involve exclusive, substitutable or independent alternatives, whereas vacation decisions bear on inclusive, complementary or dependent alternatives. It should be noted that the level of modal decisions is not analysed in this book since our study focused on the *summer* vacation.

5.1. Decision Timing

5.1.1. The generic decision to go or not to go

Most models postulate that the generic decision to go or not to go is the first the vacationer makes before going into more specific subdecisions (van Raaij and Francken, 1984; Um and Crompton, 1990; Mansfeld, 1994). Data show that this is not always the case. Before participating in the study, all informants had

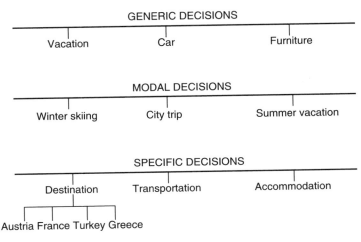

Fig. 5.1.   Decision levels in vacation decision making.

some intention to go on summer vacation, but this is not to say that they had made an ultimate decision about going or not. Among the 25 DMUs, a distinction emerged between three groups. For the first group ($n = 7$), the problem of generic DM was not relevant, as going on vacation is routine and does not really involve a decision. Interviewees who are holidaying each year do not wonder 'do we go on vacation?' but go straight to the more specific questions: 'when do we go?', 'where do we go?', 'how do we go there?', 'where do we stay, once there?' Being adaptable also helps not having to take any generic decision:

> *Thierry* (M, 28, couple): And actually I think that in the end, when you have a 'spare wheel' [i.e. going somewhere by car without any reservation], you don't really worry about whether you are going to leave or not, because you say to yourself, we know we will definitely be going there at some stage, and we always have that 'spare wheel!' [Q5.1]

For the second group ($n = 7$), the decision to go was taken early (i.e. before the first series of interviews) before specific vacation decisions. An early generic decision is typical of a rational DMP, where the decision to go is the first 'logical' step before going to more specific aspects. Early decisions and booking are motivated by four major reasons:

1. Bargain-hunting: benefit from lower prices due to early booking.
2. Availability: the vacationer makes early decisions in order to be able to choose what he or she really likes.
3. Accompaniment: making sure that all members of the DMU will join the travel party.
4. Risk aversion: earlier DM involves earlier trip preparation, which is necessary for particular destinations and which avoids missing major places of interest.

In contrast, for the third group of informants ($n = 13$), the generic decision came later than some subdecisions because of external constraints. For example, a younger family had two alternative plans. Transportation (car), accommodation (camping), activities (beach and visits) and organization (by oneself) were already determined. However, in April they still did not know whether they would or would not go on vacation:

> *Anne* (F, 41, family): Actually, it's not up to us to decide. There are administrative factors that stand in the way at the moment, and it is clear that if we're looking for a job, and he [her husband] finds a job starting on June 15th, it's not entirely appropriate to ask for holidays for the entire month of August! It would be a bit stupid to refuse a job on the grounds that you cannot go away on vacation this year. It is the second year where we do not have control over anything! [Q5.2]

The previous quotation shows the need to make a distinction between generic intention (initially this family estimated the chance of going on a summer vacation at 100%) and actual generic decision. Where there is a will, there is not always a way.

Late generic DM is one of the most surprising findings of this study. The reasons for this lateness vary widely:

1. Dissonance avoidance: early decisions risk being regretted because of the intervention of situational variables (a sick child) or missed opportunities (invitation by a friend).

2. Expectancy: vacationers may be waiting for a last-minute offer or more information on particular situational variables (e.g. children's own vacation plans, school results, employment situation, the birth of a baby, the development of an illness).

3. Loyalty: vacationers who repeat previous vacation experiences do not feel it necessary to make early decisions.

4. Transportation or accommodation vacancies: informants argue that these are always available. For other vacationers (e.g. those travelling by mobile home or going by car to a family cottage), no reservation is necessary, so why hurry up?

5. Personality: the passive and day-to-day traits of some vacationers result in short-term planning.

These reasons show that late decisions mainly stem from pragmatic considerations and not from emotional or impulsive drives, as could have been expected. Some interviewees regretted that they were not in a position to make earlier decisions, which resulted in some alternatives never being chosen. Destination choice seems to be particularly contingent upon decision timing. When realizing that it is too late to go to a particular (newer or further) destination, DMUs fall back on better-known or closer destinations:

> *Joel* (M, 35, family): I already missed the chance to go to Italy last year but we did not have the time. Neither to look into everything we could ... where we could book, the places we should go to, because I do not know Italy all that well. All things considered, I said to myself: 'If I start looking into it now, I'll be at it for two weeks. It's too late, I'm already on holiday, that's that, there's no time left.' [Q5.3]

5.1.2. Specific vacation decisions

Before going into interpretation, we first describe which and when decisions were made based on the three series of interviews carried out before the summer vacation. The case-by-case evolution of DM is summarized in Appendix 3. In the *first series of interviews*, about one DMU out of two ($n = 13$) spoke about concrete vacation plans. One group of friends and one older couple had even taken a final decision on most vacation items (i.e. destination, accompaniment, duration, formula, transportation, activities, organization). However, none had already made a booking. Most often, those informants had thought about their future vacation based on personal vacation experience, general knowledge or incidental information gathering (through reading, relatives or friends). Purposeful information search was very rare (see Section 5.5.2). A second group of DMUs ($n = 9$) also started to consider their future vacation but not in concrete terms. They had a few, but very vague, ideas. No final decision on specific vacation aspects had been made. They did not commit to active information search. The last group ($n = 5$) contradicts expectations from literature and commercial practice, as these DMUs had not thought about their summer vacation yet and, all the more so, did not have any vacation plan. For those informants, the first interview came too early: the summer vacation appeared to be still so far from actual preoccupations ('I have much work', 'we are just coming back from winter vacation', 'I consider building a house'); they strongly depended upon situational factors, like the children's own vacation plans, or they were willing to benefit from potential opportunities or a last-minute ticket. The case of an older couple is even more extreme: a vacation decision is not necessary, since they have a vacation cottage where they spend the summer period each year.

The initial situation in t_1 is not a good predictor of the speed of the evolution of decisions. In the *second series of interviews*, three of the five DMUs who made a final decision (confirmed by booking) had hardly thought about their summer vacation in t_1. Most other DMUs are characterized by status quo: plans have not really evolved. This is due to the intervention of situational variables, or just because these vacationers are not strongly involved in vacation. However, some leads (informants prefer this word to 'projects') appear and a few vacation subdecisions are taken (period!). For a few informants, projects are reconsidered in more depth: some projects disappear while totally new projects arise. Finally, one single DMU has given up the idea of going on vacation because she will be busy with building her house.

There is more evolution in the *third series of interviews*. Among the DMUs who did not make a final decision in t_2 ($n = 20$), seven reached a final decision on most vacation items, whereas three made smaller steps forwards in their plans. In addition to this evolution in the main projects, new side projects appear. However, for seven other DMUs, status quo still prevails: only slight changes or one additional decision is made (Appendix 3). For the three remaining DMUs, projects have even 'receded' or been given up.

Table 5.1 summarizes the emergence of the different vacation decision items over time.[1] Destination is not included in the table because there is a comparison problem. Since it was the focus of our study, more questions were asked about destinations than about any other vacation item. As a result, text chunks involving destinations are more numerous. Therefore, it is very difficult

---

[1] It should be noted that most result tables of the empirical chapters of this book consist of numbers of occurrences in the data. Each occurrence represents a text chunk of a varying size (a word, string of words, sentence or paragraph) that has been given one particular code. Those numbers serve to give an idea of the importance of codes but should not be used for statistical analyses.

to get a precise idea of the relative importance of destination in comparison with the other vacation decision items.

One may conclude from Table 5.1 and Appendix 3 that transportation, accompaniment, organization, formula and vacation style are the first decisions to be made (January to February). Later on (March to April), destination and period are considered to a large extent. As summertime approaches, more practical decisions are made about accommodation, activities, duration, meals and attractions. Route and tour are the last aspects to enter the DMP. This partly confirms and contradicts empirical findings by Jeng and Fesenmaier (1997) and Dellaert *et al.* (1998). The first group of authors make a distinction between core, secondary and en route decisions. Core decisions are planned in detail well in advance of the trip: they include the date, location of overnight stay, travel route, members of the travel party and choice of a primary destination. Secondary decisions (i.e. attractions to visit, activities, secondary destinations) are considered prior to the trip but are largely flexible to accommodate the possibility of changes. En route decisions are generally activated only when the trip has actually started: only then will travellers think about alternatives as to where to eat and shop, where to stop and rest, and what to purchase.

Emerging findings also suggest that vacation DM is an ongoing process that does not cease once a particular choice is made. When explicitly asked when they actually started thinking about their summer vacation, a few informants typically answered: 'Since the previous vacation'. In the data, many plans appear to stem from a previous experience:

Table 5.1. Evolution of the emergence of vacation subdecisions (number of occurrences in the interview transcripts).

Vacation subdecision	t_1	t_2	t_3	Total
Accommodation	59	66	34	159
Activities	49	60	36	145
Period	52	54	39	145
Transportation	64	50	29	143
Accompaniment	55	39	30	124
Duration	33	44	42	119
Tour	22	27	27	76
Route	18	28	28	74
Attractions	21	23	20	64
Budget and expenses	18	27	15	60
Meals	18	27	15	60
Organization	25	16	13	54
Purchases	14	18	16	48
Formula	21	10	11	42
Vacation style	7	3	3	13

Martine (F, 37, single): Denmark, a rucksack, the Faeroe Islands – I've been thinking about it ever since I went to Iceland. I looked into the history, and I said to my self 'the Faeroe Island must be similar'. Now I've been thinking about it for a whole year but maybe it will not happen. [Q5.4]

Previous experience can date back to several years. Holiday time also seems to be a privileged period for thinking about one's next project. The time just after vacation is favourable as well: (good) memories are still in mind and satisfaction leads to considering new plans. For other interviewees, thinking about vacation grew in the period just after Christmas and New Year celebrations, or was triggered off by incidental information collection or opportunities (invitation by friends). In Section 5.5, we will show that information collection is an ongoing process. Finally, phenomena such as daydreaming, nostalgia (Chapter 4, this volume) or cognitive dissonance (Chapter 7, this volume) are other indications of the timelessness of DM.

5.2. Plans and Decision Outcomes

5.2.1. Number of plans

Data show that most informants were involved in more vacation plans at the same time. This aspect has been neglected in the literature so far, which focuses on single-purchase situations. Multiple plans more often involved sequential projects (one *after* the other) than alternative projects (one *or* the other). Multiple plans not only involved the primary DMU (i.e. the DMU in which the person makes most of his or her decisions) but also other DMUs. For example, in addition to going on family vacation, some parents were considering making a weekend city trip by themselves. There were a lot of such 'mixed' DMUs, wherein some members had additional vacation plans with 'outsiders'. This urges informants to time the different projects or to make trade-offs that may result in conflicts between members. However, in this chapter we only consider the summer vacation plans of the primary DMU. Other plans are treated as 'side plans' or situational factors (see Section 4.2.1).

In Appendix 4, the evolution of the number of summer vacation plans (in the sequential meaning) is given for each DMU. A first group ($n = 13$) showed that most DMUs start, and keep up, with only one summer vacation plan. A second group ($n = 6$) is characterized by a growing number of projects. In contrast, a third group ($n = 8$) demonstrated that the number is decreasing (sometimes not to go on summer vacation at all). The number of summer plans always ranges from zero to two, with a mean of 1.07 in t_1 and 1.2 in t_2. In t_3, four DMUs no longer have a summer plan. Two other DMUs have already gone on vacation. The remaining 21 households have one or two projects, resulting in a mean of 1.12 projects per DMU.

After the summer vacation, it appears that 16 DMUs actually did accomplish their unique summer project. Three households experienced two holidays, in conformity with their plans. In contrast, four DMUs achieved only one of the two projects they had before the summer. The second project had been left out because of health problems (in an older couple), poor school results and retirement (in an older family), money resource and lack of interpersonal congruence (in a single-parent family). The four remaining DMUs did not go on vacation at all, while having one (two DMUs) or two projects (one DMU). This is explained by the intervention of situational variables (i.e. moving house, the illness of a member of a large family, health problems of an inviting parent of an older single) or by the impossibility to combine individual contingencies (i.e. a group of friends). It is interesting to see that the type of DMU does not affect the external validity of plans, and that most of the previous inhibiting factors had been mentioned in earlier interviews.

5.2.2. Evolution of vacation plans

When looking at the evolution of the content of vacation plans, one notices that most subdecisions are quite stable over time. Decisions regarding transportation, accommodation, activities, organization, attraction choices and purchases are the more stable over time. In contrast, destination, period, duration and accompaniment are far less stable because these aspects strongly depend on situational variables. As summer approaches, plans move from fantasy to reality. This evolution can be interpreted as a growing commitment to choice, as fantasy pertains to an ideal, uncommitted vacation while reality relates to 'making it happen'. More precisely, the first series of interviews often involved no precise plan but rather vacation ideals:

> *Marie* (F, 60, single): Well, for example, I dream of going back to Reunion Island but I know very well I won't be going back during the hurricane season (it is unreasonable to go into the mountains when the weather is bad). But one day, when I'll retire, one of my dreams is to spend three or four months in the mountains at the Reunion. [Q5.5]

In the second series of interviews, plans became more concrete and realistic. This shift towards reality was even more pronounced in the third series of interviews. It also happened here that expected vacation aspects were replaced by second-choice or 'spare' solutions. The objective intervention or the subjective awareness of contextual factors was the major reason for this shift. This is in line with Um's conclusion (1990) that facilitators are more important in the early stage of the DMP while inhibitors are more important in the later stage of making an actual choice. According to the findings, it is only when the consumption situation approaches that plans incorporate more 'reasonable' and more available elements. Two simple counts make the shift from a fantasized to a real vacation more apparent: first, dreamlike words were much more frequent in the first series compared to the second and third series; second, informants mentioned spare plans much more often in the second and third series than in the first.

This shift from fantasy to reality is comparable to Mansfeld's (1994) adaptation of the 'value stretch' concept (Rodman, 1963). Three levels of values are distinguished regarding various activities in which the individual is likely to be involved: preference, expectation and tolerance. The preference level pertains to ideal vacation values that are not necessarily available. The expectation level is concerned with what the vacationer expects to find in his or her next vacation experience. The tolerance level involves a vacation plan with minimum values on some aspects. As summertime approached, many DMUs were forced into trade-offs and were ready to make the necessary 'sacrifices' to go on vacation. Some expected aspects were written off: vacationers realized that there was a discrepancy between what they expected to do and what the situation allowed them to do. Through this awareness, a threshold of minimal satisfaction arose, under which the prospect of going on vacation was no longer attractive:

> *Pierre* (M, 43, family): We go to the Belgian coast some weekends just to please them [i.e. the children] but my wife and I tell ourselves that we would be hard pressed to stay there for eight days. That would be a real sacrifice for the sake of the children! [Q5.6]

The FCB[2] grid (Vaughn, 1980; Ratchford, 1987; Rossiter *et al.*, 1991) may also be used in order to interpret this shift from dream to reality. In this grid, products and consumers' attitudes are classified into four quadrants in terms of two dimensions. The vertical dimension represents the level of involvement, whereas the horizontal axis pertains to the degree of thinking vs. feeling that consumers have for the product. From the data, we could say that many DMUs follow a 'feel-learn-do' sequence in their vacation choices. This decisional sequence characterizes purchase decisions where involvement is high and feeling is most involved (Vaughn, 1980). Indeed, it has just been said that vacationers first dream and fantasize about their next vacation (they feel about it); next, contextual contingencies are taken into account while more practical information is gathered (they learn about it); finally, vacation choices are made (they do it). Of course, the feel-learn-do model is not applicable to all cases, and other types of sequences are found in the data. In particular, the feel-do-learn sequence characterizes a substantial part of informants who are deciding upon an initial feeling without much thoughtful deliberation and who are searching for more information (learning) about the destination only after the purchase of the product, i.e. during or after the vacation experience (see Section 5.5).

Finally, it should be pointed out that the shift from dream to reality has implications on the type of DMP that is operative (Chapter 9, this volume).

---

[2] FCB stands for Foote Cone & Belding, a major US advertising agency.

Data show that the growing realism of vacation plans and the feel-learn-do sequence is typical of hedonistic and, to a lesser extent, adaptable vacationers. Hedonistic vacationers are first emotionally driven towards dream vacations and destinations, but are later forced into practical considerations and more 'reasonable' choices. Adaptable vacationers find it easier to adapt to vacation plans according to structural and situational contingencies. They switch from one value level to the other without too much frustration. In contrast, the feel-do-learn sequence is much in line with opportunistic DM, whereas the learn-feel-do is typical of rational vacationers.

5.3. Vacation Decision Criteria

Emerging vacation decision criteria can be discussed following the classical four *P*s of the marketing mix. In Appendix 5, those criteria are presented according to their emerging importance and are detailed for each DMU of our sample. Note that the recourse to one choice criterion does not exclude the other. There are more indications that choice criteria are used in combination or depending on the situation: 'We choose based on the availability, special offers and also ... our desires.'

When going through the data, it is evident that *price* is one of the major aspects in vacation decisions and choices. For 19 out of 26 DMUs, we find more than three occurrences of price as a choice criterion. A large part of these (9/19) are even hypersensitive to price in vacation matters: 'Anything is good, be it free.' Price is related to the destination in general[3]: '[I]f it is a destination which does not work out to be too expensive, that is not bad either.' This implicitly refers to the package that the tour operator sells to the tourist or that the vacationer composes on his or her own. Price also often pertains to particular vacation subdecisions. Organization ('it is cheaper to go by our own' or 'when I go on vacation, I compare the prices of several travel agencies') and period ('if we could, we would travel during the off season because prices are much cheaper') are very sensitive to price. Informants also pay attention to the price of accommodation and transportation. Formula, food, activities and purchases are more marginal in this respect.

Product decision criteria often come across in the data. The vacation product should be understood as consisting of the various components listed in Table 4.1. However, the relative importance of destination as a choice criterion is again difficult to assess in an objective way for the reasons explained in Section 5.1.2. Nevertheless, it can be shown that destination is not always important in vacation choices. This is an interesting result for the tourism

---

[3] This should not be confused with the cost of living at the destination, which is a destination choice criteria (see below).

industry, which is in contradiction with most vacation DM models, where destination is presented as the key decision (e.g. Woodside and Lysonski, 1989; Um and Crompton, 1990; Mansfeld, 1994). In Appendix 5, one can see that DMUs for which it is an important choice criterion are hardly more numerous than DMUs for which it is not (ten vs. nine). For the latter, criteria such as accommodation, accompaniment, budget or period are much more relevant (see Table 5.2).

Moreover, other marketing variables may get more attention than destination. Findings also indicate that the state of mind, breaking with the stress of everyday life, may get the priority on the destination itself: 'No, because in my eyes, vacation is a bit like paradise, it is a sweet and quiet harmony, no matter the place where it is spent.' For informants with a high vacation involvement, 'anything is worthwhile': the destination is not as important as travelling or being on vacation.

A third group of DMUs considers destination as an important choice criterion (they are not willing to go anywhere), but it is secondary in comparison with more fundamental decision items, like accommodation, transportation or accompaniment (Appendix 5). Here, vacationers first decide on these aspects before going to destination choice:

> *Brigitte* (F, 37, single): Now it will be linked to what my friends will choose. Obviously if it's in Italy, that's great, but …
> *Interviewer*: So if they tell you that they are going to Spain or another country … ?
> *Brigitte*: Yes, I will definitely go, alright.
> *Interviewer*: So you go more for your friends than for the country?
> *Brigitte*: Yes, yes. But obviously, if they were going on vacation to a Northern country with no sun, maybe I would be less attracted to it. [Q5.7]

Table 5.2. Major vacation decision criteria.

Criteria	Number of DMUs for which it is a major criteria
Destination	10
Accommodation	10
Period	8
Transportation	6
Activities	4
Budget	4
Accompaniment	3
Duration	3

Note: Only the criteria related to the vacation product (see Fig. 4.1) are considered in this table. The assessment of whether a vacation decision item is a major choice criterion for a DMU is based on the answers to questions about the usual vacation DMP. It is also based on informants' indications such as 'in general, we choose our vacation according to …', 'what's important for us is …', 'in the broad lines … is what everyone wishes'.

There is one last thing to mention about destination as a choice criterion. About half of our informants (see Appendix 5) show a lot of affection (if not love) for a particular destination. This depends neither on their general vacation involvement, nor on the importance of destination as a choice criterion. This affection may stem either from personal history (informants who have lived for a long time in Italy or Africa or who have close friends in France), from a wonderful vacation memory of the place, or from enduring daydreaming and fantasies ('I always dreamt about going to Egypt'). A hate relationship with a particular destination is also possible, but it occurs less often in the data. In these cases, the particular beloved (abhorred) destination may be used as a choice criterion. This is not to say that destination in general is a choice criterion. Destination is not important as such; underlying motives are much more relevant.

In addition to price and product, other marketing variables are important in leading vacationers' choices. Promotion and place are the major ones (see Appendix 5). Through the coding process, it appears that *promotion* is mainly concerned with sales promotion and personal selling. A substantial part of informants choose their vacation or at least elements of it, according to price discrimination related to temporary discounts (off-season, early booking or last-minute), rebates for having special characteristics (a single used to travel by train all over Europe because of a special package price for people younger than 26), and even prizes (contests): 'But let us make the point: we always worked it like that, we do things at the last minute because we are always hoping to get a super deal at the very last minute.' Other informants mention personal selling (advice from travel agents) or (outdoor, display) advertising as major factors affecting their choices. Non-commercial communication (advice from parents and friends) is also very relevant for many DMUs. Finally, *place* or, more precisely, availability, is another important marketing variable: 'And the final place [i.e. the destination] depends more on the agency in the end, the agency or the possibilities offered by the agency.'

5.4. Vacation Decision Strategies

5.4.1. The generic decision to go or not to go

At the level of generic decisions, it appears from the data that decision strategies do not bear on particular choice criteria, but rather involve the allocation of discretionary time and income. This is in line with Bettman and Sujan's contention (1987, p. 142) that 'consumers, regardless of their levels of expertise with the individual options, are unlikely to have well-formed criteria for initial choices among non-comparable alternatives'. Besides travel and vacation, informants consider buying major items such as house (maintenance, reparations or housing), health, leisure, clothes, furnishing, car and books. This leads to generic (most often financial) trade-offs, which are influenced by the objective personal resources resulting from the economic and occupational situation, and by more subjective factors such as vacation involvement (position of travel and vacation in the household's hierarchy of values), perception of money and risk aversion (Chapter 4, this volume).

Many DMUs declare they are careful: they do not want to use up savings or to upset the family budget by going on vacation. As a consequence, they are not ready to sacrifice anything for vacation. In contrast, vacations are often given up for other items such as house maintenance and new furnishings. These informants go on vacation only when they can afford it or if they have an opportunity to go for free (invitation by family or friends, winning a contest). Even if they can afford it, they may anticipate future inhibitors (see Section 4.2.3). However, the generic decision does not always lead to a complete renunciation of vacation for other items, but to an adaptation of vacation decisions. Data also reveal an asymmetrical income elasticity: 'If there is not enough money, the first item to be sacrificed is vacation. However, if there is money, this is not to say that I will go on vacation immediately.' In contrast, there are DMUs who spend a lot (sometimes everything they have) on vacation and travel. Some of them have no problem doing this because they can financially afford it. Others have to make sacrifices (no more smoking, no more 'caprices') and keep resulting savings for vacations. Let us point out that these sacrifices sometimes occur *after* the vacation experience. Finally, the generic decision of going vs. not going on vacation may be considered from the opportunity cost[4] point of view:

> *Joel* (M, 35, family): So you see, you stay there for ten days or here in Belgium doing 40 kilometers each day, that's 10,000 francs gone. So, with 10,000 I can pay for my vacation, I already have petrol for going and coming back. So in the end, I prefer to go. [Q5.8]

5.4.2. Specific vacation decisions

It has already been pointed out that going on vacation involves a lot of decision items (see Table 4.1). Those vacation decision items should not be seen as independent elements but rather as complementary items, since going on vacation means the choice of a destination *and* a means of transportation *and* a type of accommodation (possibly plus other items) at the same time. Therefore the relevant questions regarding vacation decision strategies pertain to which vacation

---

[4] The opportunity cost is a basic microeconomic principle. It is based on the idea that limited resources should be allocated in an optimal way. But even in that case, there is an opportunity cost, i.e. 'the value of what the resources could have produced if they had been used in the best alternative way' (Mansfield, 1989, pp. 10–11).

decision items are considered, what is their relative importance (are they major decision criteria?) and in what sequence they are considered. The discussion about whether strategies are based on alternatives or attributes is not relevant here because, as it has been said before, non-comparable alternatives are involved.

Some informants do not use any well-defined strategy in making their vacation decisions. They insist that 'it is not really planned, nor reasoned'. On the one hand, these vacationers are adaptable: vacation DM that year may not be the same as vacation DM the next year. On the other hand, they are opportunistic: they leave it to hazard, events and opportunities to decide for them (Chapter 9, this volume). DM is unforeseen, almost unwilling. A need arousal seems to be related to a choice solution just because of temporal proximity:

> *Danièle* (F, 44, family): Sometimes, we still want to go somewhere, and then the opportunity arises. Our parents tell us 'Oh, we are going to Spain, would you like to join us?' and we say 'Why not?' and off we go. The times when we have gone away with *Intersoc* [i.e. the travel branch of a mutual insurance company] as monitors, it was also because your brother-in-law said: 'Don't you really want to go? You know, I need leaders.' And that's how it was decided! Six months earlier we wouldn't have known we were going there. [Q5.9]

No comparison with other alternatives is made; DM is spontaneous. This is an indication of the 'garbage can' DMP (Cohen *et al.*, 1972) described in Chapter 1. Almost any vacation solution can be associated with any problem, provided they are evoked at the same time.

Most informants use more choice criteria in making vacation decisions. Most of the time, they occur in a sequential or hierarchical way. It has been pointed out (see Section 5.2.2) that vacation items are generally considered in a particular temporal sequence because some decisions condition others: 'I think at that moment, from the moment that our period of vacation will be fixed, during the preceding months we will pay attention to the travel agencies, seeing what kind of last minute departures they are offering.' More particularly, destination choices will have a major impact on transportation, organization, duration, period and preparation decisions. When speaking of their decision planning with respect to Brittany or Burgundy, the father of a younger family explains:

> *Claude* (M, 40, family): It is not like leaving from one country to the other opposite side of the world, where it is necessary to reserve in advance, where a minimum of precautions at the health level is necessary (to make some vaccinations, etc.). Well, here, it is ... we leave. Eventually, tomorrow we can leave and it's fine. [Q5.10]

Decision criteria may also be considered in a hierarchical way, in a decreasing order of importance. For example, an unmarried couple first determines the destination, before considering period, accommodation and budget criteria. In this case, the first criterion is less likely to be reconsidered after a decision has been made: 'We had already decided to go there, it was really just a question of dates and … of a well-defined apartment. But the destination was not really anymore … it was not called into doubt again.'

Other informants base their decision strategy on choice criteria in a compensatory way, in that a weakness on one vacation aspect is compensated by a strength on the other. In most cases, we could also speak of trade-off strategies (Park and Lutz, 1982). Vacation trade-offs result either from financial constraints or a fixed budget (the DMU is not willing to spend more than a certain amount of money). The comfort level (accommodation, transportation, meals) or the content (destination, activities, visited attractions) of the vacation is often sacrificed for other vacation items (duration, destination). For other interviewees, spending money well is the major objective, which translates in a good quality/price ratio, or less expectedly, positive climate/price, destination/price or time/price ratios. Time or a limited amount of vacation days also leads to tricky choices: this excursion (attraction) instead of the other? that destination or the other?

According to findings, vacation trade-offs often bear on the number of vacations that will be taken. Travelling more often but for shorter periods or on smaller budgets is considered. In contrast, other informants prefer 'to keep a higher budget for going once rather than a few times spread out'. Some vacationers are not willing to spend too much in terms of money or days off on their summer vacation, in order to keep enough reserves for other projects (winter skiing, vacation with another DMU type, projects for future years). In the same way, the side plans of some family members may lead to financial trade-offs. For example, in a mixed DMU, parents refuse to spend too much on a trip with friends in order not to cut down on the family vacation; in other DMUs, parents sacrifice the family vacation for their children's own vacation plans.

Most of the time, compensatory decision strategies involve qualitative reasoning. However, a more quantitative processing based on a kind of weighted additive rule is also encountered. For example, in a group of adult friends:

> *Patrick* (M, 45, family/group of friends): We did that, we handed out a kind of table with a few criteria which had to be rated saying: 'That is something that is important for me, the comfort of the accommodation, the food, the climate, the price.' We established parameters. And in relation to these parameters, we saw for example that budget was rated the highest. … And there are other criteria. … We saw, for example, that comfort or the quality of food were not important criteria. [Q5.11]

Finally, a few informants only use one choice criterion to direct their decisions. They are not compromising on that paramount criterion: the alternatives that do not exceed a particular threshold are eliminated. The generic decision to go on vacation is even put into question if an expected value on the criterion is not reached. For example, an old widow will not leave if she is to travel alone. Other informants do not compromise about comfort: 'One goes well or one does not go at all.' In contrast, those DMUs pay less attention to, and have greater improvization on, other criteria.

5.5. Information Collection

In our sample, vacation preparation is concerned with two major activities: information collection and practical preparation (getting ready). The latter pertains to visas, foreign currencies, car verification, shopping for food, clothes and more particular items, doing the wash, packing one's cases and bags. Most of these preparations occur in the very last days before leaving home. Moreover, all but two DMUs do not have a strict planning in terms of what will be done (activities, attractions to be visited, tour and itineraries) during the vacation before departure. Instead, they prefer day-by-day planning at the vacation spot, or even total improvisation according to local opportunities, climate or moods. In the same way, they are adaptable as they are ready to change vacation plans (Chapter 9, this volume). In this section, the focus is on information collection. First, major sources of vacation information are listed. Next, the extent and the evolution of information collection are discussed.

5.5.1. Information sources

In Table 5.3, the major information sources emerging from the coding process are listed in decreasing order of importance. Findings confirm the preponderance of social and commercial sources of vacation information (Nolan, 1976; Francken and van Raaij, 1979; Gitelson and Crompton, 1983). More surprising is that informants consider their social network as a less important information source, although they often mention it. Paradoxically, they trust friends and relatives more than any other source of information. Only one's own experience is valued higher. This is in contradiction with Nolan's (1976) conclusion that informal sources rank lowest in credibility. In our data, commercial sources of information are particularly distrusted or, at least, suspicious:

> *Vincent* (M, 26, group of friends): Looking even at a guidebook is not necessarily the same as what you are going to see by yourself.
> *Interviewer:* So you're not really interested then in looking up guidebooks?
> *Vincent:* No, they hardly ever tell the truth. [Q5.12]

In many situations, the source of information is not identified. Data contain a substantial number of vague sentences such as 'the rumour has it that', 'one is generally told that', 'people are talking so much about it'. Rumour or the fact that one repeatedly has heard something lies at the origin of many stereotypes (Chapter 6, this volume), which are particularly powerful in shaping a destination image and reputation: 'I would not stay at the Côte d'Azur. And, going

Table 5.3. List of major information sources.

Type of information source	Definition	Number of occurrences
Social	Social network: acquaintances, parents, friends, colleagues, neighbours, local population, people met by chance	415
Commercial	Information coming from commercial networks in the broad sense: tour operators' brochures, travel agencies (display, personal selling), tourist organizations, tourist offices, consulates and embassies	319
Guides	Guide books, geographical maps and travel books	199
Media	Media: cinema, radio, television, written press, posters, discs, videos, CD-ROMs	172
Readings	Written sources in a larger sense: novels, comics, dictionaries, documents (except guide and travel books)	110
Experience	Personal experiences: 'I know it because I have already been there' or 'because I have already passed by it'	83
DMU	The source of information is a particular person from the DMU (e.g. who has already experienced the destination)	31
Internal	Not well-defined internal sources: 'we know lots of things ourselves'; 'we hear about it a lot', general culture and personal interests	25
Courses	School classes or courses with an educational goal	11
News	Mention of recent events and news	8

back to that question, people talk so much about how expensive it is. Prices are so exorbitant at the Côte d'Azur that it's better to be sure.' The travel diary is still a unique source of information that is used by three informants. They use it before the trip, to write the route, the list and description of sights to be visited, as well as practical information. The travel diary is a kind of road-book used as a complement to the traveller's guide. The travel diary is also used during the trip to keep a record of activities, emotions, anecdotes of the day, emerging reflections, etc.

5.5.2. Extent of information collection

A distinction can be made between low and high information searchers, based on the amount of information gathered and the time devoted to it. Of course, the boundary between those two categories is not set, as the extent of information search not only depends on individual characteristics (e.g. personality, time resources and the nature of occupation), but also on a number of situational factors. One of these situational factors is accompaniment, based on the type of DMU. For example, a family prepares a trip in more depth when children accompany than when parents go on their own. Other factors are the destination and duration of the trip (going on a long trip to a distant place requires more detailed and earlier preparation than going for a short and nearby trip). A last factor is the organization. When the trip is organized for you, you do not need to worry about preparation and information search. This is not true when the vacationer is going by his or her own initiative, and definitely not true when he or she is organizing the trip on behalf of others.

Low information searchers

Most informants in this sample ($n = 15$) only collected a limited amount of information. This is in opposition with most models described in the literature that present vacationers as high information searchers, due to the perceived risk involved in vacation choices (Mathieson and Wall, 1982; Mansfeld, 1992; Mäser and Weiermair, 1998). Information acquisition was incidental rather than purposeful, except during the very last days before the departure or reservation. This is confirmed by our observations at Brussels' Vacation Fair, where most visitors did not search for well-defined information but were wandering around, 'shopping' for information at more destination stands. Low information searchers also tended to have precise plans quite early, but postponed final decisions in order to stay free for potential facilitating or inhibiting situational variables. Finally, low information searchers did not prepare their trip in much depth and long beforehand, as they preferred discovery and the unexpected. When asked in June whether they were already informed about Tenerife, the speaker of a young group of friends answered:

Vincent (M, 26, group of friends): No, it's on the spot. That's better unplanned, to decide on the day: 'We'll go and visit this, we'll go and visit that', it's ... planning everything in advance is a bit annoying.

Interviewer: So you prefer the unexpected and to organize everything once you arrive?

Vincent: Yes, it's better ... to say already, to see the images and everything. When you arrive, you no longer see it in the same way. You pass it by and you even do not inquire about it because you have read about it, you are ... it's better to go without having seen anything. You go, you discover and you're more amazed because you're discovering that ... [Q5.13]

High information searchers

High searchers (*n* = 10) are characterized by intensive preparation and active information collection from diverse sources (with a predominance of the personal experience of relatives, general readings and the more specific travel literature). The major emerging reason for searching so much information is high vacation involvement (Gitelson and Crompton, 1983; Fesenmaier and Johnson, 1989) rather than demographic indicators such as being female or a higher education level (Francken and van Raaij, 1979). Risk reduction is one specific aspect of involvement (Laurent and Kapferer, 1985) that also seems to explain higher information collection, corroborating Mansfeld (1992). For those informants, information is a key factor in vacation success that helps them avoid missing major places of interest of the region or misinterpreting the destination:

> *Gilles* (M, 18, family): In the end, to really make the most of it. ... Without the books, the people who go to Mycenae say: 'Well, in Mycenae there are stones everywhere, but really it's a bit dull.' Whereas when you revive all the characters who were there and all that used to happen in Mycenae, it's just like it was. ... Even in Rome, there are certain things like that where without books, you do not know.
> *Jacqueline* (F, 54): If you do not have books, you do not know how to revive the past.
> *Gilles*: It's not an instant satisfaction as much as it is a ... well, you need the whole experience. [Q5.14]

Moreover, the level of information collection may be influenced by the amount of discretionary time and the nature of occupation (Chapter 4, this volume). This is particularly obvious when looking at the profile of the visitors at the Brussels Vacation Fair: a large majority of visitors were either aged 15–20 years or over 50. It also appears from the data that high information searchers tend to be high information providers. As they are willing to share vacation passion and knowledge, they proselytize and represent reliable information sources for their relatives:

> *Anne* (F, 41, family): And for example in Hungary, I tried to send a number of friends there: I am a bit contagious like that.
> *Peter* (M, 40): Proselytizer.

Anne: Proselytizer, yes. When there is a place I like (and I like all the places I go), I like telling other people to go there. [Q5.15]

5.5.3. Functions of information: collection, daydreaming and 'reconnaissance'

Three findings need to be mentioned about the functions of information search. First, gathering information is not the same as integrating or memorizing it. Brochures, guides, articles from magazines and newspapers can be stored in a more or less systematic way. This is not to say that this information is read (Wilson and Wilson, 1988). During our observation sessions in two travel agencies and at the Brussels Vacation Fair, many informants were collecting huge amounts of information (brochures, booklets, maps), but will they really use and read it? The interview data suggest that a kind of archive accumulates over the years, from which the vacationer draws when necessary. This archive must be looked at as a material information store, in addition to the individual's immaterial mental store (memory). This distinction introduces another emerging dichotomy: intermediary vs. terminal information. Terminal information is concerned with the actual content of searched information (destination attributes, transportation price), whereas intermediary information pertains to how and where to find the terminal information. Formal sources (books, guides, brochures, photos, films, maps) contain terminal information while informal sources (social network) give heuristic knowledge.

Second, information collection seems to be a good indicator of preferences but a weak predictor of actual choice. Although she had gathered a lot of information about Brittany, a woman in her forties finally chose another destination (Jura), about which she knew hardly anything:

Anne (F, 41, family): Yes, but I've not been to Brittany. I went to Jura, about which I had little knowledge. You see it's a bit like that: I had loads of information on the Ardèche region but I did not go there either … because obviously we went to Jura. [Q5.16]

Situational variables and emotional factors are the major emerging reasons for this discrepancy between information search and actual decisions. Information collection clearly supports daydreaming. The vacationer may fantasize and imagine about dreamt vacations while browsing through brochures and books. Texts and pictures already provide a taste of the trip.

Third, comparing known information (expectations) with reality may be an important motive for travelling. For four DMUs, information collection was no longer a means to an end but rather a goal in itself. After reading novels by two Italian authors, an informant wanted to see what the two cities (Sienna and Florence) depicted in those novels looked like. Other interviewees were characterized by 'reconnaissance' information search since gathering information was the major purpose of their trip, such as suggested by the three following examples. A teacher wanted to gather first-hand information about Turkey in order to prepare a future school trip in that country. A young single was willing to visit as many different countries as he could in order to be able to choose *the* country for his intended honeymoon trip. A couple was visiting friends in Geneva to get their feedback on, and addresses in, Vietnam – a country they were considering for their next summer vacation.

5.5.4. Evolution of information collection

The timelessness of informants' information search is in line with the ongoing character of DM discussed above. In this study, the extent of information collection was quite stable over time and did not grow as summer approached. No sequential steps were found from little to more information, from a broad to deep or from a passive to a more active information collection process. In contrast, a lot of quotes indicate that information was gathered incidentally and *à la carte*, i.e. when the tourist really needed it. In the very last days before a trip was booked or experienced, most informants had a heuristic knowledge (they knew how and where to find the effective information) but lacked a precise knowledge of the destination.

Incidentally, however, information collection was heavier. First, information search was more extensive during the vacation experience itself. Most informants discussed their trip and went through their documentation day after day, during breakfast or after dinner. They consulted the information sources they brought with them or went to local tourist offices. Second, information search was higher just after a decision or booking had been made, and just after the vacation. In these instances, the reduction of cognitive dissonance may come into play: one wants to make sure that the right choice has been made, or that one has lived a worthwhile vacation. Both pre- and post-experience dissonance requires new information (Walters and Bergiel, 1989). On the one hand, pre-experience dissonance leads to information that confirms the decision:

> *Peter* (M, 40, family): If we go to Italy, we will go to see Christine because she's an Italian teacher and a friend of our best friend. She's been going to Italy for the last 15 years, so it's sure we'll go [i.e. visit Christine]. … If we go there [i.e. Italy], of course. [Q5.17]

On the other hand, informants' post-experience dissonance often results in an active search of supportive evidence that the right (wrong) choice has been made (Chapter 7, this volume).

However, there was a shift from internal to external sources of information over the three periods of interviews. During the first period, information about the destination was found in previous experience and general knowledge. During the second and third periods, external sources became more important.

Social and, a little later, commercial information was being gathered. There was also much more discussion and information exchange within the DMU. This is in line with Francken and van Raaij's (1979) findings that social information sources are consulted increasingly throughout the vacation sequence. However, these authors rather speak of a shift from mass media (advertising, brochures) to personal media (salesperson, friends, personal advice), which is not supported by our data.

This evolution from internal to external sources goes along with another phenomenon emerging from the data, i.e. 'snowball' information search. By this, we mean that information accumulates naturally, growing from one source of information to the other, without much searching effort. Most often, social contacts (including members of the DMU) lie at the origin of the snowball effect. The information given by parents, relatives or friends proves to be intermediary rather than terminal, and calls for more information search:

> *Danièle* (F, 44, family): Yes, because my mother-in-law said to me that we would find all that we needed at the house, that she had left a Michelin guide there and that the woman, the owner of the house, had also prepared some stuff. And actually, there were a few books, of which two or three were about hiking and walking in the region. [Q5.18]

Findings show that snowball information collection also involves an evolution from general (destination) to more specific (practical) information:

> *Pierre* (M, 43, family/couple): We go step by step: we took general information, we read a lot, now we have seen slides, i.e. much more detailed slide shows; so we start to circle the places that you have to avoid, which are not worth seeing, and the places that you should stop off at more; we start to find out about modes of transport in the country. By all of that kind of things, we move nearer. The next step is to meet Vietnamese living in Belgium or in France in order to get more precise information and also addresses. So, we go deeper and deeper and I think that when we will go, it will still be a big adventure because you never know what is going to happen on the day, but at least we know we won't lose too much time. [Q5.19]

Destination Perception, Evaluation and Choice

6

6.0. Introduction

This chapter will focus on destination judgements and decisions. More precisely, we will consider the way vacation destinations are perceived, evaluated and chosen. These three aspects are in line with the classical distinction between cognitive, affective and conative consumer responses in DM models (e.g. hierarchy of effects models). There are two possible perspectives to investigate those aspects: the alternative perspective, which is concerned with the different destinations that are considered in the DMP; and the attribute perspective, which focuses on the characteristics of the destinations that are used to form judgements and decisions. In Fig. 5.1, it has been pointed out that, in contrast to generic and vacation decisions, destination decisions involve one or more comparable alternatives as choice is based on a common set of attributes.

6.1. Destination Alternatives

The concept of consideration set[1] (CS), or the set of the different destination alternatives that come to the consumer's mind for his or her summer vacation, is of particular interest in this research. Through the longitudinal aspect of the study, the evolution of considered destinations could be followed. Most informants

---

[1] The concept is used in the general meaning. We do not assimilate it with the concept of evoked set, as other authors do.

spontaneously mentioned a number of destinations while talking about their summer travel plans. Moreover, more particular questions were asked such as:

1. Have you considered particular travel destinations yet? Which destination(s)? Why that (those) destination(s)?
2. Are these destinations available to you? Why?
3. [If more destinations] Which destination do you prefer, or are you most likely to go to?
4. Are there some destinations where you will never go?

6.1.1. Types of consideration sets

Six types of CS emerged from the coding process that are described in Table 6.1. This typology, which incorporates contextual factors, may be paralleled with the typologies of Um and Crompton (1990) and Woodside and Lysonski (1989) (see Section 2.2.1). To some extent, it can also be compared with traditional conceptualizations by Howard (1963, 1977), Narayana and Markin (1975) and Brisoux and Laroche (1980). Following the latter authors, all existing brands are first classified in either the awareness or the unawareness set. The former is divided into a processed set and a foggy set, depending on the mental processing of salient attributes. Brands that have been processed either fall into the evoked (acceptable purchase alternatives), the rejected (unacceptable) or the hold (brands not considered as primary purchase alternatives) set. First choice is made from the evoked set of brands.

Each set of the empirical typology of Table 6.1 contains no, one or more destinations. These sets are not exclusive (a destination may switch from one set to the other) or exhaustive (the interviews were not aimed at counting and listing all the destinations in each set). When looking at the relative importance of each set (in terms of how often the informant mentioned destinations), the evoked set proves to be the most important in the interview data. The excluded and unavailable sets are also important, although to a lesser extent. In contrast, the alternative and awareness sets are marginal.

Over time, we see that the unavailable set becomes much more important than the excluded set. This trend is in line with the evolution of plans from dream to reality (see Section 5.2.2) and helps differentiating these two types of CS. On the one hand, the excluded set contains destinations that are rejected by the vacationer in a definite and *willing* way. Most of the time this is the result of a general lack of interest ('New York does not interest me at all') or an excessive weakness of the destination on particular attributes (climate, nature, culture), which are highlighted by informants. Motives and activities may also be the reason for excluding particular destinations (e.g. a few informants avoid any 'beach' destination, like Spain). Variety seeking and emotional factors also come into play (see Section 7.3). Note that the excluded set may vary according to

Table 6.1. Types of consideration sets in vacationers' decision-making processes.

Type of consideration set	Emerging definition
Evoked set	Destinations considered spontaneously (i.e. without probing) by the vacationer for future (i.e. not especially the next) summer vacation. These are the expected destinations
Excluded set	Destinations definitely rejected by the vacationer ('I would never stay there')
Alternative set	Destinations not considered by the vacationer in the first instance: these are either spare destinations (not a priority destination, but 'one never knows') or opportunistic destinations (sudden awareness of a previously unconsidered destination)
Unavailable set	Destinations considered by the vacationer but that are temporarily unavailable because of particular situational constraints (Chapter 4, this volume)
Dream set	Destinations considered as ideal places for travelling or vacationing, but that are permanently unavailable because of enduring structural inhibitors (Chapter 4, this volume)
Awareness set	Destinations the vacationer knows but does not express any affection with: this reveals knowledge but not intention

vacation motives and definitions. The following quote illustrates how destinations like Poland and Russia are excluded for vacationing (relaxing) but would not be rejected for travelling (visiting):

> *Michèle* (F, 43, family): But I would never want to go to Poland or … even Russia.
> *Patrick* (M, 45): Yes maybe because if we go there, it's more to visit, so we tend to fall back on the first case [i.e. travel and not vacation].
> *Michèle*: Yes, that's what we call traveling, it's not a vacation. [Q6.1]

In contrast to the excluded set, the unavailable set is composed of *temporarily* and *unwillingly* rejected destinations. Findings show that this set strongly depends on situational factors, which are concerned with a particular decision situation and become more important when the summer vacation approaches. Time (related to occupation), money and children are the major inhibitors. It is not surprising that the unavailable set is less stable than the excluded set. It also proves to be far less stable than the dream set. The difference between the unavailable and the dream sets is a reflection of the difference that has been introduced between situational and structural influences (see Section 4.2.1).

6.1.2. Evolution of destination evoked sets

The evolution of the number of spontaneously evoked destinations is illustrated by Appendix 4. The evoked set is either composed of alternative destinations (one *or* the other) or of combined destinations (a combination of more destinations in the same vacation plan). In the data, the number of evoked destinations ranges from zero to four. Most of the time, only one or two destinations are evoked. It never happens that the informant spontaneously gives more than four alternative destinations. This is in line with empirical findings by Woodside and Sherrell (1977), Thompson and Cooper (1979) and Woodside and Lysonski (1989), who respectively report average evoked sets of 3.4, 2.7 and 4.2 destinations. Bronner and De Hoog (1985) support Woodside and Sherrell's (1977) proposition that vacationers make the effort to evaluate only a few (four ± two) alternatives among a much larger set of available choices. There are two emerging explanations to the limited size of destination evoked sets: first, destination is not always the major vacation choice criterion (Chapter 5, this volume), so that informants do not process that item in much depth; and second, it proves to be a hypercomplex product. Belonax and Mittelstaedt (1978) show that having more choice criteria leads to larger evaluation costs and hence to smaller CSs. When being asked whether they had thought of destinations other than three evoked places (Turkey, Prague and Saint Petersburg), the parents of a large family answered:

> *Louis* (M, 59, family): No, it's already complicated enough to think about three. I don't think we thought about another one.
> *Jacqueline* (F, 54, family): It's already complicated enough! And after all, we don't have any other desires: it's always the same ones that come back. Prague, we will go there too, but maybe one time at Easter, for a week or ... we realize that maybe there are less tourists if we go in the off-peak season, outside the main summer vacation time. It's easier, it's closer. No, we haven't thought of other things. [Q 6.2]

Other destinations are mentioned but these fall into the other sets described above. However, we should say that these other sets are smaller than the evoked set. This confirms that 'the average size of the respondents' consideration [i.e. evoked] sets was significantly greater than the average number of countries mentioned in the respondents' inert, unavailable, and inept sets' (Woodside and Lysonski, 1989, pp. 12–13).

When looking at the evolution of the evoked set over time, there is a relative stability between the first (1.93 destinations/DMU or 1.62/plan[2]) and second (1.96/DMU or 1.58/plan) series, and a slight reduction in the third series of interviews (1.72/DMU or 1.29/plan). Four groups can be distinguished (see Appendix 4):

---

[2] It should be recalled that DMUs may have more than one summer vacation plan (see Appendix 4).

1. DMUs with a large evoked set (three or four destinations), which is diminishing over time ($n = 6$). These are highly involved vacationers, with less personal constraints (singles, couples or older families), but they make their decisions very late (less than one month before departure). The content of plans also shows less stability: newer plans or destinations often appear over time.

2. DMUs with an initially small (one or two) evoked set, decreasing to zero or one destination in t_2 or t_3 ($n = 7$). This group is characterized by early DM (a destination is definitely chosen or the decision not to go on vacation is taken). These are rather highly involved and older single vacationers.

3. DMUs with an initially (t_1) small but then (t_2) expanding number of vacation destinations, and then (t_3) decreasing again ($n = 5$). These informants show little stability regarding the content of their vacation plans, most of the time because of children (either as a structural or a personal constraint). The final decision is taken very late, or is never made.

4. DMUs with a low (zero or one) and stable number of evoked destination alternatives ($n = 7$). This group is characterized by low vacation involvement, a lot of constraints, early (or last minute) DM and loyalty (people going to the same place).

The timelessness of a CS is a last noticeable finding, which confirms the proposition that vacation DM is an ongoing process. The vacation destinations or projects that are currently evoked by interviewees sometimes stem from an earlier CS. Those destinations or projects were previously abandoned or postponed due to personal or structural constraints, or higher preferences for other alternatives. Now they are coming back to the surface again. Further, most informants do not only have vacation ideas and plans for the summer vacation, but also for other periods of the year. In the same way, plans and destinations do not always pertain to the current year (i.e. 1996) but also to the coming years. More projects, which are in different states of progress, coexist in the vacationer's mind. Instead of speaking of different CSs, data suggest that it is preferable to speak of one 'macro' CS with a temporal dimension. Indeed, the different alternatives included in one CS do not pertain to one and the same consumption situation (or purchase decision) bounded in time and space. As far as destinations are concerned, the CS should be defined as a set of alternatives that are all possible in the near future. We think this is quite peculiar to vacation and travel services, whose decisions are recurrent but still highly variable. This allows the consumer to solve trade-off problems more easily and not to give up desirable alternatives forever: 'If it is not this year, it will be for next year.' In contrast, a few DMUs consider only one vacation project at a time. These vacationers 'work' in a sequential way: they do really start thinking to the next vacation only once the previous experience has ended:

> *Marie-France* (F, 53, couple): Personally I don't do very much planning. I have friends who plan a lot in advance: 'Trips next year and then in two years, we'll put a bit of money aside, so we can go to such a place … '. But I don't do that at all:

the vacation comes and I plan a bit beforehand but these are not precise projects. I don't live in the hope of realizing ... [Q6.3]

The last emerging interpretation about the CS is related to what has already been said in Section 5.2.2. For most DMUs, the final chosen destination has little to do with the destinations that were initially mentioned. There are two major explanations for this. On the one hand, there is a growing reality of plans. In t_1, informants used to dream aloud when mentioning possible summer vacation destinations. While aware of actual and potential constraints, they tried to convince themselves that 'it is yet possible'. That dream dimension is much less present in the two following series of interviews. Considered destinations become more 'realistic', in the sense that contextual inhibitors are taken into account to a large extent. As far as the evoked set of destinations is decreasing to a singleton (see Appendix 4), the unavailable set becomes larger than the dream set. This finding is in line with Um and Crompton's (1990) two-stage conceptualization, where destination choice evolves over time from the awareness set ('all the preferred destinations of your dreams') to an evoked set, which only includes the 'reasonable' alternatives once situational constraints have been taken into account. Moreover, opportunities such as an invitation by relatives or a special offer that is advertised (Chapter 9, this volume) may occur. This results in the sudden awareness of previously unconsidered destinations. These new alternatives may finally be preferred and chosen over the other alternatives.

Based on previous findings, the conceptualization of Fig. 6.1 is proposed. First, there is the perceptual stage: the vacationer is either aware or not of existing destinations. Next, destinations in the awareness set are evaluated. If evaluation is positive, destinations fall into the evoked set (more preferred) or the alternative set (less preferred). If it is negative, they result in the excluded set. In the evoked set, destinations may be classified into one of three sets depending on contextual influences: if contextual inhibitors are enduring, they end up in the dream set; if they are situational, they fall into the unavailable set; if there is no contextual inhibitor, one speaks of the available set. The final choice is made either from the available, alternative or awareness set. In the alternative set, we find spare destinations. A spare destination is chosen when the available set decreases to no alternative at all (due to particular constraints).

It also happens in the data that destinations, which were not considered in the first instance, are suddenly proposed to the vacationer (see the dotted arrow from the unawareness to the awareness set in Fig. 6.1). The latter may finally choose one of those opportunistic destinations rather than one of the alternatives in the available and alternative sets (see the dotted arrow from the awareness set to choice). This straight recourse of the awareness set highlights that evaluation is not always necessary for choice. Nedungadi (1990) offers another explanation. He focuses on the stage of CS formation prior to evaluation and choice. He (1990, p. 273) provides empirical evidence that brand choice is 'significantly altered outside the traditional evaluation-based route, through variation in the

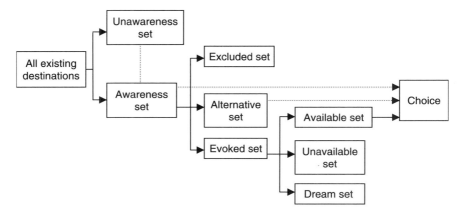

Fig. 6.1. Conceptualization of destination consideration sets.

retrieval and consideration of brands'. He suggests a memory-based choice depending on brand accessibility: for a brand to be included in the CS, the consumer must recall that brand and fail to recall other brands that might otherwise be preferred.

6.2. Destination Attributes

This section no longer focuses on alternatives but on the attribute background of destination judgements. While interviewing, a lot of judgements came about incidentally and spontaneously, as an open-ended discussion format had been chosen. However, two major perception and evaluation questions were asked in a systematic way each time a DMU was being interviewed, in such a way that judgements and attributes could be compared both between DMUs and within the same DMU over the three or four series of interviews:

1. 'Imagine that I do not know … [one destination spontaneously evoked by the informant], could you tell me about that destination?'
2. 'What are the three most attractive aspects of this destination to you?'

The former question stands for perception (the informant is asked to describe or draw a portrait of the destination), whereas the latter represents evaluation, as a ranking or sorting is explicitly required. Probing ('what do you mean by …?') was used to clarify the meaning of some aspects. From the data, it is obvious that destination judgements are based on product attributes to a large extent, i.e. they involve an analytical mental processing of vacation destinations. However, we also come across more global or holistic judgements. In this section, the conditions that influence a holistic rather than analytical type of judgement are first explained. Further, major destination attributes are listed and grouped together in broader dimensions. Finally, the evolution of the attribute background of judgements over time is discussed.

6.2.1. Mental processing: analytical vs. holistic judgements

MacInnis and Price (1987) have suggested that any product is perceived in terms of pieces of information about particular attributes and more gestalt-like or holistic impressions. As to evaluation, Mantel and Kardes (1999) refer to attribute-based vs. attitude-based judgements. Echtner and Ritchie (1993) present this attribute–holistic continuum as the third component of destination image. An *analytical* judgement means that the destination is described in detail, that more attributes are given. In the following quote, a young single talks about South America, a destination he is considering for the summer vacation:

> *Jean-Benoit* (M, 26, single): Among the classical destinations, it's one of the destinations which grab your attention: it's far away, it's very different from Europe. There are a lot of things to see, other cultures to discover. And a priori I would say that it's still relatively well-organized on the spot, there are still amenities. … There are still a lot of people who go to visit these countries, so it's not as if you find yourself in the middle of nowhere, except for a bus which passes every three days and things like that. [Q6.4]

In this quote, we find five different attributes: distance, visits, culture, infrastructure and crowds. There is also an explicit comparison with the home environment (Europe), and an implicit comparison with other destinations. All this indicates a more analytical type of judgement. In contrast, a *holistic* judgement involves a vague and very general description of the destination. As a consequence, less can be said about underlying attributes because there are less of them. A holistic judgement limits the attribute space, as illustrated by these typical examples from the data:

1. 'China definitely is something extraordinary.'
2. 'It's a fabulous country.'
3. 'It is different and moreover, that's Switzerland. Admittedly, I do not know: that's something else.'
4. 'But Buenos Aires and Argentina is something beautiful too, but that's a whole expedition, Argentina.'

Findings indicate that the level of holism is influenced by the type of judgement, by destination knowledge and by the informant's personality. First, evaluation judgements are presented in a more holistic form, whereas perception judgements tend to be more analytical. To some extent, this confirms Creusen and Schoormans' (1997) findings that image attributes (which are usually processed in a more holistic way) are more important in preference judgements, whereas characteristic attributes (which are generally processed in a more analytical way) are more important in similarity (perception) judgements. This is also in line with the contention that for experience products, preferences are not the outcome of the extensive information processing of separate attributes. Preferences are formed readily and via some holistic processing instead (Zajonc and Markus, 1982). Mittal (1988) proposes the concept of 'affective choice mode' to capture this mode of preference formation. Destinations that are better known also call for more analytical judgements. This phenomenon has already been supported by Creusen (1998) and Bettman and Sujan (1987). The latter authors show that experts are more inclined towards analytical judgements (which are based on concrete rather than abstract attributes), whereas novices tend to process products in a more holistic way (i.e. they give overall product evaluations). Further, a large number of studies (see Mantel and Kardes, 1999 for a review) show that individuals process information more thoroughly, i.e. they engage in analytical judgements, with higher levels of involvement. Finally, the individual's personality and eloquence is at play. A few informants find it hard to explain things in detail and use very global ways of expression:

> *Interviewer:* But you still like to go back to the same place?
> *Georges* (M, 66, single): I like going back there because I like it, especially on that beach in Playa America. I absolutely love it there.
> *Interviewer:* What does particularly attract you in Playa America?
> *Georges*: That's not easy to say. I am happy there because the weather is great and everything … and I watch the world go by around me. [Q6.5]

This could be paralleled with the need for cognition of the vacationer, i.e. the extent to which he or she engages in, and enjoys, thinking (Cacioppo and Petty, 1982). Vacationers with a high need for cognition have a propensity to make analytical judgements (which is effortful), whereas vacationers with a low need for cognition will rather give holistic judgements (which is effortless). Mantel and Kardes (1999, p. 337) suggest that 'high need for cognition individuals make more carefully thought-out and specific detail-oriented judgments'.

6.2.2. List of emerging attributes

Open coding resulted in about 50 different destination attributes (see Appendix 6). For convenience, these were grouped in four categories:

1. People: anything that has to do with the local people (number, friendliness, mentalities, habits, language, ethnicity) or other tourists (number, type).
2. Geography: geo-physical (climate, space, localization, nature) or geo-human (socio-economic and political situation, housing and living conditions) characteristics of the destination.

3. Culture: any attribute related to the set of social, artistic, religious or intellectual expressions, which define the local society. It also includes references to the written or immaterial past (history), and monumental or material past (architecture and ruins) of the destination, popular culture (folklore) and handicraft.

4. Vacation: attributes connected with experiencing the destination, i.e. particular attractions (be it museums, historic sites, cities, parks, sport or cultural events), comfort level, food, tourist infrastructure, cleanliness, safety, visits, ambience, liveliness, conviviality, change of scenery (exoticism).

The first three categories are more related to the general characteristics of the destination, while the last category is about the benefits of using the destination for a vacation. Of course, these four categories are not completely independent from each other. For instance, it happens in the data that an attribute like food is used to describe the local people ('in France, they eat a lot of meat') rather than being a benefit to the vacationer.

Clichés are often used by informants as destination attributes (Table 6.2). These are generally accepted concepts ('everyone knows that …') or stereotypical images of the destination. This finding confirms results of several studies (e.g. Chapman and Chapman, 1967; Pechmann and Ratneshwar, 1992), which have shown that people have a tendency to rely on their prior beliefs, *stereotypes* or expectations (i.e. to be theory-driven) rather than on the actual data (i.e. to be data-driven) for their judgements. A memory-based processing is used more often by interviewees than a stimulus-based processing. Those stereotypes are often used as a basis of covariation judgements, in order to infer the value of other attributes. For example, going to Switzerland suggests that one will experience a clean and well-organized country. Our analyses brought to light that clichés are often cultural and involve human and material destination attributes.

6.2.3. Dimensions of destination attributes

In addition to the descriptive typology of the previous section, destination attributes can be categorized in a more abstract and interpretive way. Four major dimensions result from our analyses (Fig. 6.2). These must be interpreted as continuums with numerous possible positions between two opposite poles.

The first dimension is related to the physical–human dichotomy discussed in the descriptive typology in the 'geography' category. On the one hand, we have physical destination attributes, like climate, space, localization or nature (animals, plants, earth). On the other hand, we find human destination characteristics (socio-economic and political situation, housing and living conditions). This includes the 'people' and 'culture' categories. Vacation attributes also have either a more physical (attractions, infrastructure) or a more human nature (safety, liveliness).

Table 6.2. Stereotypes in destination judgements.

Type of stereotype	Example from the data
The type of vacationers one meets at the location, often connected with a negative vision of the country of origin	'Buses of Japanese tourists'; 'the Dutch people with their cans'; 'the full-of-money paunchy German tourists'
The mentality and way of life of the local people	The good-life Italian, the well-organized Swiss, the cold but clean Scandinavian, the dog-eating Chinese, the left-driving Englishman
The general (natural) environment of the destination	Canadian wide spaces, Australian kangaroos, Dutch windmills and tulips, African jungles, Greek blue
The safety environment of the destination	Thai brothels, drugs in Amsterdam, Russian maffia in Saint Petersburg
The recreational environment of the destination	Spanish 'playas', Scottish pubs, Brazilian samba, North Sea 'cuistax'[a]
Particular products that are associated with the country or the region: food products or handicrafts	Cuban cigars, Portuguese Porto, Breton pancakes, Italian Chianti, Provence herbs, Turkish carpets
Particular well-known persons or characters, stars	Strauss and Lehar in Vienna, Celine Dion in Canada, Bob Marley in Jamaica, Mickey Mouse in Euro-Disney
Historical and cultural highlights of the country	Maltese knights, Sri Lankan buddhas, Egyptian sphynx, Breton menhirs and dolmens, Scottish castles
Recent news	English mad cow disease

[a]A cuistax is a four-wheeled pedal go-kart that one can rent on the Belgian coastline.

The second emerging dimension builds on the uniqueness of the attribute to the destination. It results from the following questions: 'To what extent is this attribute unique or typical for the destination?' 'Is this a unique attribute or a shared characteristic of many destinations?' Echtner and Ritchie (1993) have identified this dimension as a major component of destination image and have paralleled the unique part of the destination with Pearce's symbols (1988) and MacCannell's (1989) 'markers' or must-see sights. For Tversky (1977), the distinction between unique and shared attributes is crucial in understanding comparison processes of brands. Further, a connection could be established between this dimension and the diagnosticity[3] construct (Pechmann and Ratneshwar,

[3] Diagnosticity refers to 'the extent to which an individual's mental representations of the data (at the point of judgment) are informative with regard to the objective differences among the stimulus brands on each of the target attributes' (Pechmann

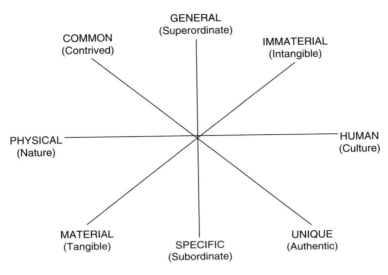

Fig. 6.2.   Dimensions of destination judgements.

1992). Finally, informants often use unique attributes in a positive inferential way: unique means better. A unique attribute is often synonymous with authenticity, whereas common has the negative connotation of contrived:

> *Claude* (F, 38, family): [speaking about Brittany] It's very well portrayed, I mean typical. There are some pretty things: we would stop on the road and we would see a little chapel which is extremely old and there you go, it's a bit … it's not something completely new as we'd say: there are vacation villages dumped there just like that, a village built because they found the place to be suitable. Nothing is typical in it, they were just implanted. … So there is not the case; these are vacations which still fit the Breton culture, which is … [Q6.6]

The third dimension is materiality or tangibility. It is usually argued that tourism services have an intangible nature (Chapter 1, this volume). The reality of the data is much more subtle. On the one hand, there are vacation attributes that refer to a material reality, to tangible, or more broadly, sensory items (particular attractions, tourist infrastructure, climate, nature, socio-economic situation, housing, but also smells and luminosity). On the other hand, attributes like ambience, liveliness, exoticism or friendliness encompass very immaterial or intangible realities that cannot be sensed or touched (Flipo, 1988; Burton, 1990).

and Ratneshwar, 1992, p. 374). Note that 'diagnosticity' is more appropriate than 'ambiguity' (Hoch and Ha, 1986), as it is the result of the consumer's subjective perception of products, while ambiguity pertains to the actual distinctiveness of products.

The former attributes underlie judgements related to a physiological experience of the vacation destination, whereas the latter translate a psychological experience. The dichotomy of functional vs. psychological characteristics is used by Echtner and Ritchie (1993) according to whether these characteristics are observable and measurable or not. Moreover, findings indicate that this distinction has much to do with the difference between search qualities, i.e. attributes of the product that the consumer can evaluate before purchase, and experience qualities, i.e. attributes that the consumer can only evaluate after purchase and/or consumption. Zeithaml (1981) positions the vacation product as high in experience qualities in the same way as restaurant meals or haircuts.

The fourth emerging continuum is about the generality of attributes: specific vs. general. For example, when asked for the three aspects that attract her the most in Denmark, a young single woman simply answers: 'It attracts me because it is another people to see.' In contrast, the father of a large family replies: 'It's the French-speaking part of Switzerland too, we understand the people, we can already talk to them.' These two quotations show how the same underlying attribute (i.e. people) is presented at a general or a specific level. This dimension may be related to the hierarchy in categorization theory (Rosch *et al.*, 1976; Rosch, 1978) between subordinate, basic and superordinate categories. For example, 'needle-like peaks' is a subcategory of 'mountains', which itself is a subcategory of 'landscape'. The literature argues that basic categories carry the most information and are the first categorizations made during the perception of the environment in childhood (Rosch *et al.*, 1976). Note that this fourth dimension could be considered as a subdimension of the material–immaterial continuum, as tangible attributes tend to be more specific, whereas intangible attributes are more general. This is in line with conceptualizations (Dubé-Rioux *et al.*, 1990; Breivik *et al.*, 1998) that present intangibility as a two-dimensional construct (i.e. abstractness or inaccessibility to the senses, and generality).

In the data, there are different kinds of attribute combinations along the four previous dimensions. For example, this description of Madagascar combines natural, material, unique and specific attributes:

> *Chantal* (F, 35, family): Yes, the nature, definitely. In Madagascar, there is a special forest which you can only find there. With the tigers and the little chimps and all that, the special mountains in peaks where you need to wear special soles on your shoes because it's as sharp as knives. [Q6.7]

Overall, physical attributes appear to be more salient in judgements than human attributes (see Appendix 6). In the same way, unique and general attributes are more frequent than common and specific attributes. Finally, material attributes slightly outdo immaterial ones. However, it seems that immaterial (image, friendliness) attributes are relatively more important in vacation destinations than they usually are in other products. This finding is in line with the contention that 'feel products are considered by consumers primarily in terms of non-verbal images and emotional factors such as psychological benefits and values' (Evans *et al.*, 1996, p. 316).

6.2.4. Evolution of the attribute background of judgements over time

Findings suggest that the attribute background of judgements is quite stable over time.[4] By this, we mean that almost the same attributes were used to describe or evaluate the same destination in the successive interviews before the summer vacation. However, these were seldom elicited in the same order and in the same words. In perception judgements, there is a mean of 2.7 (ranging from zero to six) identical attributes between the first and the second (or third) series of interviews (see Appendix 7). For evaluation judgements, the mean is 1.58 (ranging from zero to three). The vacation experience makes the attribute background still more stable for perception than for evaluation judgements.[5] On average, 3.06 (ranging from zero to six) and 1.56 (ranging from zero to four) identical attributes are used before and after the vacation experience to respectively describe and evaluate the same destination. When taking all series of interviews into account, i.e. the two before and the one after the summer vacation, this results in 1.21 common perception and 0.5 common evaluation attributes.

Material and physical attributes, which describe characteristics that are found at the destination (nature, surroundings, economy), are the most stable in the data (see Appendix 6). One of the possible reasons for this is that these are also more general: superordinate attributes like landscapes, the environment or the sun are more stable because they are retrieved more easily from memory than subordinate attributes, like the name of particular attractions or food (see Rosch *et al.*, 1976). Stapel *et al.* (1997) suggest that abstract traits (used for identification) are given more easily than concrete attributes (used for comparison).

The stability of informants' judgements seems to be affected by destination knowledge and involvement: the more knowledgeable and involved the vacationer is, the more stable his or her judgements are. Moreover, the attribute background appears to be more stable for perception than evaluation judgements (see Appendix 7). Finally, it is interesting to observe that those very informants who do not show stable judgements over time are also the ones who show very little similarity between perception and evaluation judgements.

6.3. Destination Choice Criteria

In contrast with vacation decision criteria (see Section 5.3), the major destination choice criteria do not bear on the four *P*s of the marketing mix. Rather, they involve the relative importance given to product attributes. Destination choice

---

[4] 17 DMUs are considered in this analysis, i.e. DMUs who answered the perception and evaluation questions about the same evoked destination in t_1 and in t_2 or t_3, in such a way that a comparison was possible.
[5] Only the DMUs ($n = 16$) that actually went to the same destination as the one evoked (and then described and evaluated) before the vacation are considered here.

criteria are listed in Table 6.3 according to their importance (decreasing number of related quotations) in the text material. From the table, it can be seen that climate is of paramount importance in destination choice. Belgium is a wet and rather cold country. This has a considerable influence on informants' mood. They show an overall desire to leave the Belgian climate for sunnier and warmer skies. Therefore, southern destinations (France, Spain, Italy, Greece, Turkey, the Mediterranean and Canary islands) are much more popular than northern regions. To a lesser extent, interviewees are also looking for places that are not too crowded, with a nice geo-natural environment (sea, beach, mountains, or, in a more holistic way, landscape and contact with nature) and appropriate tourist installations (which make the stay more comfortable and particular activities possible). Visits and the change of scenery are other major criteria guiding destination choice. The other criteria listed in Table 6.3 prove to be more marginal. According to the attribute dimensions described in Section 6.2, physical and material attributes prevail in destination choices. Human and immaterial attributes are less important.

Destination criteria are not related to a particular destination but have an enduring influence on destination choice. The number of decision criteria that are considered by DMUs ranges from one to ten, with a mean of 5.32. However, most of the time, DMUs focus on one or two major criteria. Findings also indicate that criteria are evolving over time: new criteria appear whereas others are no longer mentioned. This is in line with Park and Lutz (1982, p. 108): 'decision criteria, alternatives, and preferences vary and evolve over time, with new inputs of information and with changes in the psychological states of the decision maker'. However, this is not the case for the major criteria, which are much more stable over time.

6.4. Destination Decision Strategies

In contrast with the other decision levels discussed at the outset of Chapter 5, destination decisions involve *comparable* alternatives because they bear on the same set of underlying attributes. Data highlight four major decision strategies: attribute-based, alternative-based, constraint-based and opportunistic strategies.

In the data, *attribute-based strategies* are used most widely. In these strategies, 'the values of several alternatives on a single attribute are processed before information about a second attribute is processed' (Bettman *et al.*, 1991, p. 60). Often (*n* = 5), one attribute was put forward and the informant tried to find the best alternative on that criterion; sometimes a second important attribute was also taken into account. This is an indication of the lexicographic heuristic where the alternative with the best value on the most important attribute is selected:

Table 6.3. Destination choice criteria.

Attribute	Number of occurrences	Attribute	Number of occurrences
Climate	93	Friendliness	3
Crowded/deserted	23	Language	3
Nature: geology	22	Mentality	3
Infrastructure	20	Nature: holiday	3
Visits	14	Economy	2
Change of scenery	13	Holistic	2
Quietness	8	Localization	2
Cost	8	Nature: fauna	2
Surroundings	7	Security	2
Space	7	Social	2
Comfort	6	Social intervention	2
Monuments	6	Ambience	1
Authenticity	5	Cleanliness	1
Culture	5	Image	1
Attractions	4	Light	1
Food	4	Nature: flora	1
History	4	Smells	1

Jacqueline (F, 52, couple): My husband said: 'Why not going to a Bed and Breakfast?' We agreed, but on condition that it reflects the region. So we looked for an area where there would still be a certain authenticity. Only that. Therefore, maybe the Breton countryside, but I love the sea so much … I will not resist. My husband looked at Limousin, but I don't know, that didn't grab me, I don't know why. You see, when you go down towards Provence (which I love, I love Provence), I wonder where there is authenticity yet. We went to Dignes, it was really good, but we did see that they had constructed a kind of fake Roman city for tourists. It was very [much] like a fake Pompeii. It was hideous, horrible! And all the tourists are parked in there. For me, it's not going to Dignes; you should go and stay with people if they would like that.

Interviewer: So that's why you thought of Auvergne?

Jacqueline: Well there, every time we went to Auvergne I said to myself there is a certain charm. [Q6.8]

Other DMUs (*n* = 3) excluded unacceptable alternatives based on one or more criteria. This can be paralleled with the elimination by aspect heuristic, where a cut-off level for the most important attribute is determined, and all alternatives with attribute values below the cut-off level are eliminated:

Claude (F, 38, family): I'd like to say that among my criteria are places that are not too frequented by tourists. So there are a lot of places that we are never going to see, such as the *Côte d'Azur* or the Belgian coast (because we don't like the Belgian coast very much). Therefore, there are places where quietness will be the criterion, that's one thing already.

In *alternative-based strategies*, 'multiple attributes of a single alternative are considered before information about a second alternative is processed' (Bettman *et al.*, 1991, p. 60). In the data, compensatory strategies appear to be used most frequently. A few decision criteria are taken into account and weighted. Each alternative is then evaluated on these criteria, which results in a ranking. The alternative with the highest overall 'score' is chosen, provided the contextual factors allow it. As a consequence, although it is preferred for particular attributes, a destination may be rejected because of a weakness on another, more important, attribute:

> *Christian* (M, 59, couple): Brittany, you've been there already, and I would love to go, it is there to be discovered. But sure the problem is the weather: it rains a lot in Brittany, you have to be lucky. Therefore, we went to Provence a couple of times because we are assured of a certain amount of sun. Moreover, there was a time when I was very interested in the Massif Central: Auvergne and all its volcanoes. But there again, the weather is still uncertain; that's why we did not go at the end. [Q6.9]

For a lot of DMUs ($n = 9$), the destination decision strategy has little to do with attributes and alternatives, but is instead ruled by elements external to the product itself. These elements are constraints, motives, hazards (Chapter 4, this volume) or decision criteria of a higher (vacation) level. However, for the sake of simplicity, we will speak of *constraint-based strategies*. This is in line with Um's (1990, p. 9) contention that 'destination choice is a satisfying behavior which is constraints-driven, rather than an optimizing behavior which is attribute-driven'. In constraints-driven strategies, destination is not a real choice, but is the consequence of expected constraints or unexpected events. Major contextual constraints are limited financial resources, poor health conditions, lack of product availability and interpersonal conflicts ('you first have to find common ground'). For a few DMUs, destination is not a major vacation decision criterion (see above). On the one hand, destination choice is ruled by motives like rest, recovering health or variety seeking ('I do not like going twice to the same place'). On the other hand, destination choice is the result of other dominant vacation decision criteria, such as price, transportation and accommodation:

> *Patrick* (M, 45, family): There are budgetary matters which can intervene. As regards distance, we choose vacations which are accessible by car, we look for regions where there is an organized system of renting accommodation. [Q6.10]

Finally, a number of informants are characterized by *opportunistic decision strategies*. They do not use any well-defined strategy in making their vacation decisions but insist that it is not very planned or reasoned. Generic and specific decisions, like those for destination, depend on opportunities (e.g. special offers, proposition by a friend), hazard, temporary moods and desires. This makes DM impulsive, unforeseen, almost unwilling as illustrated by quote

Q5.9. Needs are recognized when opportunities arise and no effort is made to compare choice alternatives. This is an indication of a 'garbage can' DMP (Cohen *et al.*, 1972). Almost any solution can be associated with any problem, provided they are evoked at the same time. Opportunistic strategies require vacationers to be highly adaptable: they do not have well-defined decision criteria and destination preferences, and are open to many alternatives. They use spare solutions when opportunities do not arise. In groups of friends, hazard facilitates DM. This is illustrated by the particular example of a group of young friends where the annual destination choice resulted from a draw: 'In the end, we had many potential destinations, everyone stated their preferred destination and randomly, we drew out of a hat and decided to go to Spain.'

The four previous types of decision strategies are not exclusive. In the data, there are more indications that choice heuristics are used in combination. For example, a full-nest family chose their destination after the elimination of alternatives based on quietness, climate and visits; then a more pragmatic criterion, i.e. availability, was taken into account. Here is another example of such a mixed strategy:

> *Michèle* (F, 41, family): First of all, you should ...
> *André* (M, 40): At the moment, we are looking for ideas.
> *Michèle*: Looking for common ground. And afterwards, it's true that there will still be a route to decide on. You also have to look at your budget because with five people ...
> *André*: It could also be a place that is not far away but something more particular.
> [Q6.11]

When looking at the data with more scrutiny, mixed strategies may be interpreted in terms of means-to-an-end structures where alternatives (destinations) are the means, attributes (destination decision criteria), the consequences and motives or higher-order decision criteria (price, quality) the ends. Alternatives and attributes are used in an instrumental way: 'When I was with Mum, normally we used to decide "ok, we'll go there" but for the last few years, we just went to the Canaries where it is hot. We went there to relax.'

Post-experience Processes[1]　　　**7**

7.0. Introduction

This chapter focuses on vacationers' (dis)satisfaction processes. Many researchers in consumer behaviour have stressed the importance of considering post-purchase assessment: DM does not cease with the purchase. Product evaluation takes place during and after the consumption experience, and this reinforces further behaviour. This has obvious implications for marketing strategy. It is not surprising then that (dis)satisfaction has grown to be one of the most popular topics in the marketing literature. The systematic study of tourist (dis)satisfaction is a more recent endeavour that still entails some grey areas. Ritchie (1994, p. 11) points out the need for 'research related to post-experience feelings and behaviour with a view to understanding the impact of previous travel experience on future choice behavior'. In this chapter, vacationers' post-experience processes are revisited from an interpretive perspective. We respectively deal with their antecedents, i.e. how they come about, and their consequences, i.e. what they result in. This double focus of interest is both theoretically and practically relevant: 'First, to improve the understanding of satisfaction judgments, it is important to identify the causes and correlates of consumer satisfaction or dissatisfaction. Second, to improve predictions and managerial decisions, it is critical to consider various post-choice behaviors, such as complaint behavior and repeat vacation' (Mazursky, 1989, p. 333). It should be noted that the thrust of the findings presented here emerged from the last (post-experience) series of interviews. Before going into the findings, the specific literature about tourist (dis)satisfaction is summarized.

---

[1] This chapter is an adapted version of Decrop (2001), with permission of CAB International.

©A. Decrop 2006. *Vacation Decision Making* (A. Decrop)

7.1. Literature Review

In addition to the general DM models described in Chapter 2, a few authors have focused their research on the formation of tourist (dis)satisfaction. (Dis)satisfaction was first described as an attributional problem. Following equity theory, Francken and van Raaij (1981, p. 110) postulated that 'the attribution of inequality is an important factor in determining dissatisfaction'. This means that the service offered by the provider should sufficiently justify the amount of money that was paid for the service. If not, this will lead to dissatisfaction. The implication is that dissatisfaction should arise only if negative feelings about the vacation are attributed to factors external to the vacationer (supply variables such as accommodation, transportation and food), not if they are seen as the result of internal factors (such as attitudes, expectations and intrinsic rewards). This theory has further been developed (van Raaij and Francken, 1984; Zalatan, 1994) and empirically supported (Gitelson and Crompton, 1984; Lounsbury and Hoopes, 1985; Botterill, 1987).

Other authors refer to the classical disconfirmation theory when studying post-experience travel evaluation. Pizam *et al.* (1978) were the first to conceptualize tourist satisfaction as the result of the interaction between a tourist's experience at a destination area and his or her prior expectations. Chon (1989, p. 5) further explained that tourist satisfaction depends upon 'the goodness of fit between his/her expectation about the destination and the perceived evaluative outcome of the experience at the destination'. Expectation is made of the traveller's previous images of the destination. These images are compared against what he or she actually sees, feels and achieves during his or her stay at the destination. In later studies (Chon, 1990, 1992; Chon *et al.*, 1994), Chon adapted the classical expectancy disconfirmation model using Sirgy's evaluative congruity theory and brought empirical support for it. Four mental states, or evaluative congruities, are distinguished, resulting from the comparison process between the perceived image of the destination and its perceived reality. Each state is translated into a degree of tourist (dis)satisfaction. Mazursky (1989) somewhat qualified the disconfirmation theory by showing that past experience (reflected by norms) is determinant in shaping satisfaction and hence future tourism decisions. He further argued that norms form another baseline standard, which does not necessarily coincide with the expectational baseline.

It is remarkable that this disconfirmation paradigm has been dominating satisfaction research for the past 15 years (Schofield, 1999). Research by Duke and Persia (1996a,b), Ryan and Cliff (1997) and Weiermair and Fuchs (1999) are all within this tradition. In addition, the comparison between expectation and actual product performance has been extensively used for measurement. In importance–performance analysis (Martilla and James, 1977), the relative importance of various attributes and the performance of the firm in providing those attributes are combined for strategic analysis and planning, i.e. to identify areas for service quality improvements (see Hudson and Shephard, 1998). In

SERVQUAL models (Parasuraman *et al.*, 1988), a measure of service quality is obtained for each attribute by deducting the expectation rating from the perception rating for that attribute (see Ryan and Cliff, 1997; Weiermair and Fuchs, 1999). Finally, pre- and post-purchase and experience measurement of judgements is used in image modification studies (e.g. Pearce, 1982; Phelps, 1986; Chon, 1987; Sussmann and Unel, 1999). The omnipresence of the disconfirmation model has been challenged in the past few years. Among other authors, Ryan (1999, p. 267) warned that 'the apparent ease of [satisfaction] measurement makes us blind to the real nature of the experience tourists seek and often find'. In the same way, for Fournier and Mick (1999, p. 5), 'the reliance on a single paradigm or method may pose serious limitations for any marketing phenomenon'. Therefore, they decided to distance themselves from the disconfirmation model and revisit satisfaction research in more depth. Based on lengthy and unstructured in-house interviews about consumers' ownership experiences with technological products, they proposed a more holistic, context-dependent and dynamic process of satisfaction. This chapter may be seen as a similar attempt to step back from the dominant disconfirmation paradigm to redirect tourism satisfaction research along new emergent lines.

7.2. The Antecedents of (Dis)satisfaction

When identifying the antecedents of informants' (dis)satisfaction judgements, three major explanations emerge from the data. First, there is a comparison process between the just-lived vacation or destination and previous vacation or destination experiences. Relative performances are compared with kinds of norms resulting from previous experience. This comparison may have some bearing on the destination in general or on specific attributes of it, such as illustrated by the two following quotes:

> *Paul* (M, 63, couple): I am personally satisfied but I would not start it over again, I would not start again. I will never go to Malta again, that's certain, whereas I would be happy to return to Greece. I don't know whether you grasp the distinction. [Q7.1]

> *Paul* (M, 63, couple): The only reproach I would make: I found that there were not many big unusual sights in Cyprus in comparison with Sicily, Crete, etc. where actually there were much more things to see. At least regarding monuments, I did not see anything. … There are a few churches but these are not … [Q7.2]

The previous finding is related to experienced-based norms theory (Woodruff *et al.*, 1983; Cadotte *et al.*, 1987), which suggests that consumers are comparing actual product performances against performance norms. Performance norms are based on experience and may take the form of another product brand (e.g. the preferred brand or the standard brand). Besides performance norms, Woodruff *et al.* propose two other experienced-based standards of comparison:

brand attitudes and expectations. This introduces the second emerging finding about the antecedents of satisfaction.

Satisfaction may result from a direct comparison process between expectation (based on previous experience or other sources of information) and performance on specific attributes. The level of expectation, and the matching probability that post-experience assessment results in (dis)satisfaction, is very dependent on the destination itself:

> *Michèle* (F, 41, family): To some extent, having rain in Ireland is less serious than having rain at the Côte d'Azur because you don't go there for ... you go there for ... but I personally know some people ... for example, it seems that in some southern destinations, in Spain or in Provence, the weather was not that nice this summer; even cloudier and rainier than here. Actually those people were extremely disappointed and others even shortened their vacation wondering 'What did we come here for?' [laugh]. In Ireland, you will not pack up and go just because it rains. Because actually, I guess one knows it, it is risky... [Q7.3]

Based on this comparison process, there are three possible resulting moods:

1. Disappointment: vacationers are dissatisfied because (some of) their expectations have not been met.
2. Surprise: vacationers are satisfied because destination performance goes beyond expectations; enjoyable, unexpected things have occurred.
3. Indifference: vacationers are neither satisfied nor dissatisfied, since (positive or negative) expected aspects were found in the real vacation experience.

This is in line with the classical expectancy disconfirmation model (Oliver, 1980; Churchill and Surprenant, 1982), which postulates that consumers enter into purchase with expectations of how the product will actually perform. Once the product is purchased and used, outcomes (actual product performances) are compared against those expectations. This comparison process results in either confirmation (performance equals expectations) or disconfirmation (positive if performance is better than expected; negative if it is worse). Positive disconfirmation leads to satisfaction while negative disconfirmation results in dissatisfaction. Simple confirmation implies a more neutral response; however, there are indications in the data that vacationers are more likely to be satisfied in this case. As it has already been pointed out, disconfirmation theory has been widely used to explain tourist (dis)satisfaction (e.g. Chon's studies).

Finally, it is worth noting that informants often simply mention the difference between vacation expectations and performances, without any evaluation. This is interpreted as post-experience beliefs or perception judgements, and leads to the proposition that the comparison process between expected and actual performance is not a sufficient condition for (dis)satisfaction. This is not even a necessary condition since (dis)satisfaction does not always result from the product itself, but may be the consequence of an attributional process. By this we mean that, in certain situations, informants locate the origin of their (dis)satisfaction in other factors than the product and the experience itself. 'It's my fault', 'It's his fault' are typical replies. In the first case, we could speak of internal attribution or *mea culpa* behaviour. The vacationer is (dis)satisfied simply because of his or her own decisions and behaviour. In the following quote, the father of a family explains that his family is dissatisfied about their last vacation in Brittany just because they lacked knowledge of the destination:

> *Jean* (M, 47, family): We are still happy with our agency. They did not make any mistake or whatever. No, that was all right. But maybe we made an unwise choice regarding the geographical location. Because one always starts with some lack of knowledge. [Q7.4]

In the second case, we may speak of external attribution. Possible sources of external attribution for (dis)satisfaction are people (tourist intermediaries, friends and relatives, even some members of the DMU), hazard (e.g. an unexpected truck strike has caused big traffic jams) or information sources (guides, brochures, travel agents). The distribution of attribution is asymmetrical: external attribution is more frequent in satisfaction judgements, whereas internal attribution occurs more frequently in dissatisfaction judgements. To some extent, this phenomenon, which is interpreted as dissonance or altruism, is in contradiction with van Raaij and Francken (1984). These authors postulate that vacationers who attribute their dissatisfaction to external factors are more dissatisfied than vacationers who attribute their dissatisfaction to themselves. This emerging attributional framework may be related to the attribution theory perspective on consumer (dis)satisfaction (Folkes, 1984). Attribution theory postulates that consumers use three bases to classify and understand why a product does not perform as expected: stability (are the causes temporary or permanent?); locus (are the causes consumer- or marketeer-related?); and controllability (are the causes under volitional control or are they constrained by external factors?). The latter two conditions are found in our data (see Q7.4).

The previous emerging explanations of vacationer (dis)satisfaction share the same utilitarian view. In contrast, some chunks in the data show that (dis)satisfaction may have a more hedonistic and emotional background. Mental states like post-vacation depression, the joy of coming back home (because of homesickness or risk aversion), or the pride of having broken with the past are not directly related to the destination itself and utilities to the vacationers. It suggests that post-experience feelings and emotions should be added to the cognitive approach to consumer (dis)satisfaction. This affective perspective is supported by Westbrook (1980, 1987) and Westbrook and Oliver (1991). Our data give empirical evidence to Westbrook's proposition (1980) that (dis)satisfaction partly results from personality traits or enduring attitudes (an optimistic vacationer is more likely to be satisfied than a pessimistic vacationer, whatever the destination performance), and momentary moods such as joy, depression or harmony.

There is a last aspect that needs to be mentioned about the antecedents of (dis)satisfaction. Vacation (dis)satisfaction is seldom equally distributed among the different members of the DMU. This is particularly the case in families where parents may be satisfied with a vacation decision, whereas children are dissatisfied, and vice versa. The mother of a recomposed family evaluates their camping experience as follows:

> *Anne* (F, 41, family): Oh yes, the children like it: it's much funnier. Moreover it is a closed-in place where they can do whatever they want: it's safe. It's definitely less comfortable for the parents but for them, it is a dream vacation. As soon as they arrive, the kids, the girls make up a group of friends because it's rather a family, at least in the summertime, family [camping]. And the little boy too: he has found a little neighbor… [Q7.5]

Distribution conflict is a major emerging aspect of group DM (see Section 8.4) that may be connected with equity theory (see above).[2] A vacationer will be dissatisfied if he or she perceives inequalities in the distribution of the costs and benefits of the vacation experience. In contrast, he or she will be satisfied if the exchange is fair or in his or her favour. This is in line with literature by Oliver and Swan (1989) and Francken and van Raaij (1981).

The previous findings suggest different explanations of vacationers' (dis)satisfaction. These are combined in Fig. 7.1. Theories are presented following a continuum on the left side, which represents the individual vs. social nature of the explanation. Emotions lie on the individual side because they are person-related. Experience-based norms theory and the classical disconfirmation approach also basically involve the individual but pertain to the product, whereas attribution and distribution of costs–benefits theories are rather concerned with the group.

7.3. The Consequences of (Dis)satisfaction

After the antecedents, the consequences of (dis)satisfaction judgements are now considered. Different situations emerge from the data. First, experience leads through (dis)satisfaction to perceptual and attitudinal change. On the one hand, experience contributes to changing perception judgements, to breaking down preconceived ideas about particular destination attributes. For example, after several visits to Spain, someone realizes that 'they [i.e. the Spanish people] become a little bit more friendly'. In the same way, a teacher of history is completely reconsidering her lectures after visiting countries (Turkey, Morocco or Italy) that are often associated with negative clichés. On the other hand, one

---

[2] However, it should be noted that equity theory has first been used in a B-B framework (i.e. relationships between sellers and buyers) and not in a B-C context (i.e. the family DM unit).

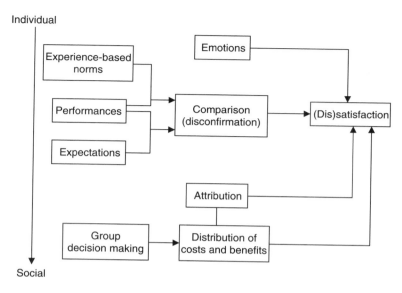

Fig. 7.1. The antecedents of vacationers' (dis)satisfaction.

comes across attitudinal or behavioural change. As a result of dissatisfaction, most vacationers are willing to change destination, i.e. they exclude the just-visited destination from future consideration sets ('You will never get me there again'). Repeated dissatisfaction resulting from several missed vacation experiences reinforces the willingness to change radically (e.g. summer vacation is left out for winter ski vacation). Attitudinal or behavioural change does not always stem from dissatisfaction but may also arise when vacationers are satisfied. This may be explained either by the desire to break with routine or by emotional factors. For example, although she is satisfied with her last vacation, an old widow does not want to go on vacation any more because she felt even more depressed after the vacation experience. Variety seeking is another major explanation.

   Findings indicate that discovering new things or acquiring broader knowledge is one of the major reasons for variety seeking. Another reason is the fear of being disappointed by a second experience at a place that is connected with (very) good memories. Experience causes an upward shift in the expectation level, which results in a higher risk of not being as satisfied as before. Westbrook and Newman (1978) suggested that high levels of satisfaction with a previously owned brand are often accompanied by some dissatisfaction following repurchase. This is in line with Oliver's (1980) expectancy disconfirmation model. A rise in the expectation level means that negative disconfirmation (i.e. product performance is worse than expected) is more likely to occur. Avoiding painful memories associated with particular destinations is also mentioned: 'I systematically refuse the destinations where I went with my husband in the past because I think that's useless to torture oneself just for fun.' Further, personal factors come into play: variety seeking is an expression of status; it is used to reveal an adventurous, unstable or prospective nature, and to enhance self-image. Finally, some variety seekers have no other justification than a question of principle, a rule of thumb: 'And then we have a principle, never go twice to the same place. No, because the world is too small ... actually too big to waste our time going twice to the same place.'

While dissatisfaction most of the time leads to attitudinal and behavioural change, satisfaction results in brand loyalty and repeat purchase. When satisfied, the vacationer is loyal ('We must go back there'), he or she desires to go back to the same destination and to live the same vacation experiences again. The father of a full-nest family declares that they will return to the same destination (France) until they are no longer satisfied or happy with it:

> *Patrick* (M, 45, family): But we did already tell you: we like to go back to places which we enjoyed. It is about the same as when people are going to a restaurant because they enjoy being there and because it is usually good. And then it happens once that they are less well served and they don't go there anymore. And I personally think it's about what happens: you have good memories and you want to go back there. Maybe you will go there again in another context and you will say 'Well, we now did go round it'. And actually it is not because you did go round it, it's simply because parameters would not have been as enjoyable or positive as before, and then you will go somewhere else. [Q7.6]

For a few 'masochists', dissatisfaction also results in brand loyalty. This is explained by the following reasons:

1. Destination evaluation happens in a compensatory way: attributes are given different weights, and the weakness of one attribute can be offset by the strength of (an)other, more determinant, attribute(s). For instance, a mother is dissatisfied with her last vacation in Switzerland because of the climate, but she is nevertheless ready to go back there because her satisfaction with other attributes (i.e. the tourist infrastructure and the Swiss mentality) is higher.
2. The vacationer is resigned, as there is no real alternative to the chosen way. For example, dissatisfaction about a crowded destination or organized tours (which allow too little time to visit) results in repeated behaviour because those vacationers cannot afford to visit that destination in the off-season, or by themselves.
3. The informant realizes that he or she is dissatisfied because he or she has missed important aspects of the destination: 'And while coming back in the airplane, I was even saying to myself "Well, I'd like to go back again, just to make the [day] trips I did not make".'
4. Other informants themselves find it hard to explain why they are likely to repeat their behaviour while being dissatisfied. Emotional drives towards the destination seem to prevail over rational considerations: 'And even the first time

I went to the Vatican, I found it too big. I was crushed. However, just after it, I wanted to return there; that's very strange.'

Another important consequence of vacationers' (dis)satisfaction is information giving and, more particularly, word of mouth. A feeling of satisfaction results in advising relatives to visit the destination ('You must go there'), and giving a lot of information about its attributes. For a few informants, this kind of proselytism is very pronounced:

> *Anne* (F, 41, family): And for example in Hungary, I tried to send a number of friends there: I am a bit contagious like that.
> *Peter* (M, 40): Converter.
> *Anne*: Converter, yes. When I find a place I like (and I like everywhere that I go), I like telling other people to go there. [Q7.7]

In contrast, dissatisfaction leads to negative word of mouth to relatives and friends. This is rather holistic (less detailed information is given) or focuses on only one attribute: 'Take care of your money if you are going to France'. An even more severe response to dissatisfaction is complaint behaviour. For example, an older single woman wrote a letter to the local tourism office, while another made a phone call to the travel agent. Complaints may also occur while in the vacation spot (an older female widow succeeded in moving hotel after complaining to the tour operator's representative). However, data show that only a small minority of unsatisfied vacationers start active complaining behaviour after the vacation experience. This is in line with empirical findings by Andreasen and Best (1977). The set of previous emerging propositions regarding the consequences of vacationers' (dis)satisfaction is summarized in Fig. 7.2. A distinction is made between psychological responses, which occur inside the person, and overt responses, which are the observable consequences in the outside world.

7.4. Related Phenomena

In addition to the antecedents and consequences of tourist (dis)satisfaction, four related phenomena deserve close attention. First, *cognitive dissonance* (Festinger, 1957) occurs very often. Informants put some decisions and choices into question, and express post-decision or post-experience regret: 'And also when I think about it again, I say "Well, we should have gone to see that".' As a consequence, vacationers make efforts to reduce those dissonant elements by justifying that they actually made the good choice ('I do not regret it at all'), that they wanted to avoid saturation ('It's like when eating pastry, there is a time when it does not taste anymore'), that the good choice is only postponed or that, although it was not a good choice, there was no alternative solution. Informants are looking to having good conscience. It is much less likely that they acknowledge

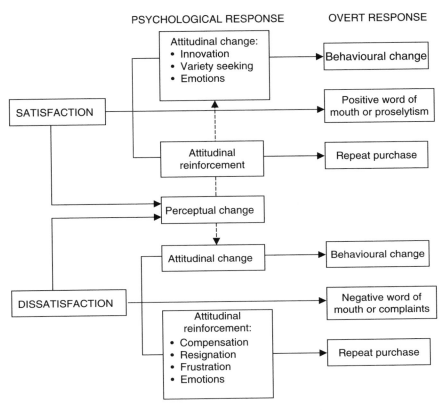

Fig. 7.2. The consequences of vacationers' (dis)satisfaction.

having made an unwise decision. Attribution (see Section 7.2) is another dimension of cognitive dissonance, although it occurs less often. Finally, it is worth noting that dissonance results in information collection. Most of the time in our data, post-experience dissonance results in an active search of supportive evidence that the right (wrong) choice has been made. After coming back home, a dissatisfied informant looks for – and gets – confirmation from several information sources that he or she indeed made a poor financial choice. Most often, post-experience information is related to price and product performance, but it may also pertain to the number or perceived performance of rejected alternatives. After realizing that they missed interesting spots in Paris due to a lack of information, an older couple bought two guides for 'the next time'. This may be interpreted as a kind of information catch-up effect. A last finding indicates that the vacation experience itself constitutes new information, as thoughts and conversations that occurr during the trip may be the source of dissonance.

Prolonged involvement is a second emerging interpretation of post-experience information collection. After visiting a particular destination, there seems to be a growing sensitivity to any information regarding that destination. There is a voluntary search or a more or less automatic bias in selective perception. When listening to the news, the informant's ears are pricking up as the destination region or country is mentioned:

> *Roger* (M, 63, couple): In 1964, we went there and we came back in love with the place. It was magical. As a result, one of our main interests is Turkey or anything to do with Turkey. We will read a book about Turkey much more easily than we would read a book about Peru. If we see a programme on the television or hear one on the radio, we will always be attentive to it. Why? Because there is a little place in our hearts which is Turkish. Because it truly was …
>
> *Jacqueline* (F, 58): An enchantment. [Q7.8]

This phenomenon is confirmed by the observation data of Brussels Vacation Fair. Visitors were automatically attracted by the information stands of destinations that they had experienced before. Prolonged involvement is also related to hedonic consumption. Post-experience information search prolongs and extends the emotions and moods triggered by the vacation experience:

> *Anne* (F, 41, family): Yes, it is very nice to get to know a bit of the town and then to read a novel about the place in which, for example, someone discovers the town after us. Of course, Denis [i.e. a French writer] wrote a novel before we had read it, but it has been translated just a few years ago. And then we can feel again the same way the author did about the place. [Q7.9]

Third, reading through the interview transcripts creates the impression that informants are generally much *more satisfied than dissatisfied*. This is in line with the results of many academic, government and business surveys, which show that the overall level of consumer satisfaction is high (Wilkie, 1990). However, this impression should be balanced. Overall satisfaction[3] indeed occurs more often than overall dissatisfaction (83:13 quotes). However, positive evaluations no longer prevail when considering the destination in particular: about equal numbers (170:155 quotes) of satisfaction and dissatisfaction judgements are observed.

Finally, there is a clear tendency to evaluate the destination in a global way. Informants evaluate the destination as being good, and then it is good for all aspects, or as being not good, and then it is not good for any aspect. This phenomenon may be interpreted as a *halo effect*. A positive halo is much more

---

[3] Is concerned with the overall evaluation of the vacation experience. Typical text chunks are: 'We liked it very much', 'It was a nice vacation', 'Going away did me good'.

frequent than a negative halo. It is characterized by those typical sentences: 'Everything is beautiful there', 'It seems that everything matches there', 'I dislike nothing in this destination'. Again, this may be explained by the natural human tendency towards optimism and by cognitive dissonance (if everything is good, there is no dissonant element).

Group Processes in
Vacation Decision Making[1]

8.0. Introduction

The thrust of the findings presented so far involve the vacationer at the individual level. However, vacation decisions are generally considered as joint or syncretic (i.e. they involve all members of the household), since tourism activities are intensively group-based (Chapter 1, this volume). Few papers have been devoted to the social dynamics of vacation DM. Many studies have focused on the distribution of roles within the household but other major aspects, such as group cohesiveness and interaction, conflicts and power relationships, have been neglected so far. In this chapter, we investigate those variables and processes involved in group DM for the summer vacation: how plans and choices are made within the group, which role(s) each member plays, how conflicts are solved, etc. This information came about quite spontaneously in the interviews; for roles, more specific questions have been asked. Three group types are contrasted here: couples, families and parties of friends. Filiatrault and Ritchie (1980) were the first to consider different vacation DMUs in a comparative perspective (i.e. married couples and families of varying compositions). In this study, groups of friends are included as well because it is now a major DMU type for leisure and holiday activities. Couples and families may be considered primary formal groups, whereas a party of friends is more like a primary or secondary informal group (see Section 1.2.3). A group of friends is defined as a set of people who share 'a voluntary, personal relationship, typically providing intimacy and assistance, in which the two [or more] parties like each other and seek each other's company' (Price and Arnould, 1999, p. 39). The more specific

[1] This chapter is an adapted version of Decrop (2005), with permission of JTTM.

literature about group processes in vacation DM is presented in the first section of this chapter. Findings will then be summarized along four major themes: group cohesiveness, distribution of roles within the DMU, issue of conflicts and consensus in DM and two phenomena that are typical of this sample's groups of friends–delegation and group-think. Before going into the findings, the issue of stability of vacation DMUs is briefly discussed.

The stability of vacation DMUs

The problem of the adaptability of vacation DMUs discussed in Chapter 4 leads to three questions about the stability of the DMU. The first is about stability over time: do vacationers always decide, and go, on vacation with the same people? The second is about stability over vacation types: do vacationers decide, and go, on vacation with the same people whatever the nature of the project? These two questions have been addressed at the outset of Chapter 4; we have shown that informants could be involved in more vacation DMUs and more projects at the same time. A more subtle dimension of stability should be considered as well, i.e. the stability over the different vacation decision items. Are they the same people who participate in all subdecisions? Findings suggest that the composition of the DMU may vary. For example, in a full-nest family the two children do not participate in the generic decision to go on vacation or in the destination decision. However, they have their sayings about accompaniment and activities. In contrast, couples are less affected by this, although the wife or the husband may dominate particular vacation subdecisions. Jenkins (1978) provides empirical indications about this. It would be interesting to examine to what extent each decision item involves the participation of each member of the DMU. However, our data do not allow this kind of investigation. Most logically, the interpersonal constraint is growing as the size of the DMU increases (Chapter 4, this volume). So, the singles of our sample prove to be less constrained than plural DMUs, and couples are less constrained than families and groups of friends. In many cases, personal factors are not homogeneous in the vacation DMU. Each individual has his or her own personality, activities and interests. Further, an individual's vacation experience in the current DMU can dramatically depart from his or her experience in previous DMUs ('She almost never travelled before she knew me').

8.1. Literature Review

Group DM has benefited from a considerable interest in the socio-psychological literature. In marketing and consumer behaviour, many studies have been conducted on family DM. The husband–wife relationship first attracted considerable interest (e.g. Sharp and Mott, 1956; Davis and Rigaux, 1974; Davis, 1976; Green *et al.*, 1983), whereas the influence of children has been considered more recently (e.g. Darley and Lim, 1986; Ekstrom *et al.*, 1986; Mangleburg, 1990;

Lackman and Lasana, 1993). Tourism research has followed roughly the same path. First, many studies focused on the marital dyad (Jenkins, 1978; Filiatrault and Ritchie, 1980; Nichols and Snepenger, 1988; Fodness, 1992) from a role-taxonomical perspective (i.e. who makes the decision within the couple). A distinction between three typical situations has been suggested: husband-dominant, wife-dominant and joint decisions. This distribution of roles has been investigated for different vacation subdecisions (e.g. destination, accommodation or budget) and typical DM stages (i.e. initiation of plans, information search, evaluation of alternatives and booking).

Originally ignored and later dismissed, the influence of children has been reassessed more recently. Some authors have limited the role of children to a passive indirect influence on vacation activities and on parents' satisfaction (Filiatrault and Ritchie, 1980; Ryan, 1992). Other researchers have identified children as having a more active role as actual negotiators in the DMP (Howard and Madrigal, 1990; Cullingford, 1994; Seaton and Tagg, 1995; Thornton *et al.*, 1997). Again, these studies focused on which type of (pre-purchase) decision was most affected by children in a role-taxonomical view. For example, Thornton *et al.* (1997) included the influence of children on the activities of tourist parties while on holiday, based on a space–time budget survey. More recently, Bohlmann and Qualls (2001) examined how individual preferences could be revised through family interaction, whereas Mottiar and Quinn (2004) investigated power relationships within the couple. The latter authors concluded that 'the overall consumption of a holiday is largely a joint decision, but when the purchase is broken down into different stages, females have a dominant role in the early stages of the process, possibly making them the gatekeepers' (2004, p. 149). While the couple and family have drawn considerable interest from marketing and tourism researchers (e.g. van Raaij, 1986; Nichols and Snepenger, 1988; Fodness, 1992), joint decisions by groups of friends have been ignored. To fill this gap, Gitelson and Kerstetter (1994, p. 65) proposed 'to include friends and/or relatives as potentially equal partners in the DMP'. They considered the decision process of travel parties visiting friends and relatives and the particular influence of the latter on the decisions made during the trip. However, their study did not focus on the party of friends as a DMU in itself. The authors themselves suggested that further research should examine when (prior, during or after the trip?) friends become influential.

8.2. Group Cohesiveness

The level of group cohesiveness has a major influence on vacation decisions and DM. In many families, children leave it to their parents to decide, simply because they trust them or submit to parental authority:

Jean (M, 47, family): We were forced sometimes to take some decisions without their [i.e. children's] consent, between brackets. But also we can say that each time we went on vacation, they enjoyed what we did. Thus, a certain trust has been established. [Q8.1]

Solidarity, abnegation and altruism also often occur, as suggested by these two contrasting examples. On the one hand, parents sacrifice the family holiday for their children's own vacation plans. On the other hand, parents refuse to spend too much on a trip with friends in order not to cut down on the family vacation budget. In highly cohesive groups, the generic decision to leave is even questioned when some members cannot join the travel party ('We all go or we do not go').

Sharing vacation experiences and interests may be an important motive for travelling. It often happens that someone in the DMU wants the other members to benefit from a previous experience he or she had with another DMU. This primarily affects destination choice, as illustrated by the three following examples: a French native woman would like to show her husband many places in France; after a school trip to Greece, a young man tells his parents 'You must definitely go there'; a member of a party of friends communicates his experience of Tenerife while praising the merits of the island. Most often parents try to inculcate experiences in their children, as part of their education. There is a kind of intergenerational learning and transfer of travel knowledge: 'Thus we try, because they are our children anyway, we try to teach them our vacation style but that's not easy.'

8.3. Distribution of Roles

Emerging findings regarding the distribution of roles within the DMU are summarized in Table 8.1. It only deals with family and couple DMUs, as the distribution of roles within groups of friends is very different and difficult to grasp. From Table 8.1, it can be seen that overall DM tends to be syncretic. In other words, vacation decisions prove to be joint, as they involve all family members. However, in a few DMUs, the man (husband) is dominant. Although they have an influence, women (wives) and children play more passive roles in DM. If we go into more detail, we see that the nature of these influences varies.

Children influence what people do on vacation. Accompaniment (taking a friend with the family), accommodation ('There must be a swimming pool!'), attractions ('I want to visit the Pont de Normandie'), activities (swimming, walking, sports, dancing) and destination (not the destination itself but attributes the destination must possess) decisions are particularly affected. Moreover, children's side projects (camps, training courses) often influence the holiday timing. While influential, children are not the driving force of the family decisions. However, their involvement increases during the vacation experience. It appears from the data that most decisions taken 'on trip' (tour, activities, attractions, purchases)

Table 8.1. Family roles in vacation decision making.

DMU id.	Overall decision making	Destination choice	On trip choices	Instigation	Information search	Practical preparation	Reservation
1	M	A	M	A	F	A	F
2	S	A	F	F	S	A	A
3	S	A	C	F	M	F	–
5	S	S	A	A	A	F	–
7	F+C	C	C	F	F+C	F	–
11	S	A	–	F	F	A	F
13	S(C)	C	A	A	M	A(F)	A
14	P	C	A	C	M	A	–
15	A(P)	F	C	A(C)	M	A	F
16	M	F	A	M	M	M	M
17	S	S	M	A	F	M(S)	–
18	S	A(P)	A	P	A	A	F
19	A	A(P)	A	M	F	F	F
22	S(M)	M	C	F(C)	M	A	A
23	M	M	C	F	M	A	–
26	S	F	M	F	F(S)	F	F

Note: A = autonomic decision (decisions are taken separately and no one is dominant); C = children-dominant decision; F = female(wife)-dominant decision; M = male(husband)-dominant decision; P = parents-dominant decision; S = syncretic decision (decisions are taken together).

are dominated by children. There are more indications that the communication within the DMU increases during vacation time and that parents are more inclined to ask for children's requests and desires, and to take them into account. Parents are used to sacrificing their own desires and interests for those of their children: 'children will be king' during the trip. Each day, children give a direction and a pace to the vacation; they initiate planning and the search for information:

> *Claude* (F, 38, family): Because we have children that are always inclined to ask: 'What are we going to do today?' Already at home, but then on vacation, oh! In that case, we say first that we do not know, then five minutes after: 'What are we going to do?' We are actually obliged to do some things. [Q8.2]

Overall, final decisions (and in particular the generic decision to go or not to go) are dominated by men, while women instigate the vacation drive and propose the first (destination) ideas. In our sample, men are filtering, reorienting and giving concrete expression to those ideas:

> *Claude* (M, 40, family): I would say that my wife brings up the idea, and I direct it or restrict it …
> *Interviewer*: You filter?
> *Claude*: I filter and I try to soften in a realistic way the duties. [Q8.3]

It is typical that once a final vacation decision is made, women get back on top as they take care of most practical vacation preparations (last information search, booking the trip, packing cases and bags, preparing material support, doing the washing, urging children to prepare their things). Men also care for a substantial part of the preparations but these are of a very different nature, i.e. preparing the route and tour (including reading maps), checking (and driving) the car, going for cash and foreign currency, caring for administrative matters (insurance, visas, passports, etc.), preparing heavy material (camping, loading the car). There is thus a strong gender specialization and differentiation with respect to vacation preparation. Women are involved in preparation during the last days of work while for men it rather means the first days of vacation:

> *Michèle* (F, 41, family): However, it's a lot of additional work. And after all those preparations, it was very very very hard. And I was sick and tired, I did not want to leave anymore. In fact, it's good that the reservations were made; if not I would have said to the others: 'I am not going anywhere!' [Q8.4]

Findings further show that men care more for information search than their female partners. Women seem to be less willing to know much about the destination before leaving. They do not need substantial information, either because they prefer to discover unexpected things or because they rely on their male partners. The nature of information also varies: men collect more general, intellectual, geographic and sociocultural information about the destination in travel guides, books or maps, whereas women look for more pragmatic aspects in brochures or magazines. Again, the latter sometimes complain that the dirty work is for them:

> *Jacqueline* (F, 54, couple): Ah, the dirty work, it's always me.
> *Interviewer:* The dirty work, what do you mean?
> *Jacqueline:* To go for the catalogues, to look for prices, compare a continental breakfast with a buffet breakfast, after all, only little, insignificant things. [Q8.5]

It should be noted that the distribution of roles seems to be influenced by personal factors. For example, language knowledge has an influence on who will take care of preparation and information search. In the same way, the unequal distribution of personal resources (time, health) across the different members of the household results in particular role performance: 'I am not myself ... I don't like to organize, that's one thing. I trust my wife a lot because she does it much better than I do; maybe she has more time for it.'

8.4. Interpersonal Congruence: Conflict and Consensus

Members of the same DMU may have different vacation and travel backgrounds, which result in different vacation motives, expectations and involvement. This introduces the problem of interpersonal congruence. The lack of congruence results in conflicts, which may be solved in different ways but leave (sometimes indelible) marks on some vacation decisions and on future DM. Three conflict situations emerge from the coding process: structural, organizational and distributional. First, structural conflicts are triggered by factors external to the travel party. Members may show fundamental differences in their values and goals due to divergent personality traits, vacation and travel definitions, motives and involvement levels. Participating in several DMUs at the same time also leads to conflictual situations or 'orientation problems' (Bales and Strodtbeck, 1951). For example, the informal structure of a group of friends may be confronted with a more formal structure like that of the family or a scouting staff. This institutional type of group involves rigid rules (i.e. planning and organizing activities for the children, looking for camping places, keeping the group's accounts, etc.) that depart from the group of friends' informal norms (having fun, sharing emotions, learning new things, etc.). Structural conflicts also arise because status and role may differ in the two types of groups.

Second, organizational conflicts occur when members are not happy about the way group activities take place. They share the same travel motives and involvement but show different product preferences. They have different assessments of the attributes and alternatives that are involved in a choice solution. In yet other cases, the costs and benefits are perceived to be distributed unequally across the members of the DMU. Some members complain that they do not, or are likely not to, benefit from vacation choices as much as other members do. These distributional conflicts may be related to equity theory in social psychology (Oliver and Swan, 1989). This postulates that equitable (inequitable) relationships exist between individuals when all participants perceive the ratios of their inputs and outcomes to be equal (unequal) to the respective ratios of all participants (van Raaij and Francken, 1984). If unresolved, a distribution conflict most of the time results in a vacationer's dissatisfaction (Chapter 7, this volume).

The previous typology may be connected with Kirchler's distinction (1995) between value, preference and distribution conflicts. Value conflicts arise when the DMU members show fundamental differences in their goals resulting from different personality traits, product involvement, values, definitions and motives. Preference conflicts mean that members share the same motives and involvement in the decision domain, but have different assessments about the attributes and alternatives involved in the choice solution. Finally, distribution conflicts result from situations where the costs and benefits are perceived to be distributed unequally across the members of the DMU.

In the data, agreement and conflict situations are distributed almost evenly. Probability conflicts (133 quotations) are more frequently mentioned than value (100) and distribution (95) conflicts. Most often these conflicts are resolved through consensus (altruism), negotiation (give and take), dictatorship (one member imposes his or her ideas on the other members) or delegation (letting another person decide for oneself). More precise influence tactics can be seen at work in the data. These range from insisting to resigning (leaving the scene). Others use rewards or punishments, form a coalition, decide or yield according to habitual roles or family norms, bargain, or use logical arguments. These tactics are much in line with the listing of influence tactics of Howard *et al.* (1986), Nelson (1988) and Kirchler (1993) that spouses use to resolve conflict or divergence of wishes and opinions in joint decisions. Consequences of these conflict-resolving modes are bitterness, frustration, etc. In some cases, the conflict cannot be solved and this leads to rupture, with separate ways being taken. For example, in family DMUs, intergenerational differences may result in value conflicts. As children enter adolescence, they build their definitions of vacation with their own motives and expectations, which may obviously differ from those of their parents. In a few families, conflicting values are retained because of strong parent authoritarianism. In other families, teenagers dare to express their own values, which results in two possible situations:

1. Parents take children's requests into consideration and adapt their vacation destinations, modes and, most of all, activities.
2. Children refuse to accompany their parents any more. This may lead to a lasting modification of the DMU.

Based on this difference, we could speak of constructive conflicts that increase the understanding of issues vs. destructive conflicts that decrease group cohesiveness and may lead to the destruction of the group (Ellis and Fisher, 1994).

Overall, value conflicts are less negotiable and are more likely to end up in destruction than preference and distribution conflicts.

8.5. Delegation and Group-think

We close the findings section by describing two phenomena that are typical of the parties of friends of this sample. Personal and situational factors may strongly vary within the DMU, making it very troublesome to find a compromising solution. There are problems of conflicting time schedules, budgets, involvement, interests, etc. As a consequence, DM takes place very late and leadership is often needed in order to carry out the project. A leader emerges from the group who triggers major decisions (destination, period, transportation, accommodation). This is not to say that the other members are not consulted before the final decision is taken but, in the end, the leader takes the decision alone. He or she acts on behalf of the group. In contrast with family DMUs, unilateral DM does not result in frustration and angry moods because friends are simply willing to sacrifice all their wishes to let someone else organize things (and do all the work) for them. In that sense, we can speak of delegation. Furthermore, individual preferences are upset as participation in the group is the major criterion. The content of the vacation is much less relevant:

> *Patrick* (M, 45, family): Well every year, it's a group boss who decides: 'I would like to take you there, does that interest you?' In general, we say yes even if it is a place where we never thought of going. I would even say, it's because we would not go individually that we accept to go then as a group because the work is done, so that's it. For example, I would not go to Scotland on my own despite all the good things they say about it at the level. ... Well at the weather level, etc. At the scenery level.
>
> *Michèle* (F, 43): It's precisely because of the weather! [laughs]
>
> *Patrick*: But since the group is going to Scotland, it's the opportunity to go to Scotland, well then you go. [Q8.6]

This quote indicates that participating in the group is more important than the particular alternative that will be chosen. This may be related to group loyalty and 'group-think' (Janis, 1983), which means that:

> when a group is cohesive and in strong agreement about a decision, the opinions and preferences of the individuals in the group change to conform more to the preferences of the group as a whole. The members are so committed to the group that they use it as a basis for their own opinions, suspending their own critical thinking in favor of the group's opinions. ... And because individuals value their membership in the group and feel a strong sense of commitment, they conform quite easily. (Ellis and Fisher, 1994, p. 28)

So group-think may lead to more extreme or poorer decisions because members suspend their critical faculties in favour of consensus. The group is more concerned with agreement and consensus than with the quality of the decision to be made. It is therefore not wise to predict choice on the basis of individual preferences as far as groups of friends are concerned.

A New Typology of Vacationers[1] 9

9.0. Introduction

During a whole year, we followed the vacation DMP of 25 Belgian households. These were interviewed in-depth up to four times: three times before their summer vacation and once after it. Following the qualitative methodology of grounded theory, a number of interesting findings emerged from data collection and interpretation. In Chapter 4, we discussed the context in which vacation decisions are made. In Chapters 5 and 6, the focus was on the DMP itself, both at the generic and vacation levels (Chapter 5, this volume) and at the destination level (Chapter 6, this volume). Post-experience processes were investigated in Chapter 7, whereas group processes were the particular focus of Chapter 8.

This last chapter represents the integrative and conclusive part of the book. It starts with an overview of extant typologies of tourists or travellers. The strengths and shortcomings of these typologies are then assessed. Next, a new typology of vacationers is proposed. This typology is empirically grounded in the data we collected and integrates traditional socio-demographic, psychographic and behavioural criteria with DM variables and processes to give an inclusive view of different vacationers. The last two sections are devoted to the theoretical and managerial implications of this research and its limitations. A few suggestions for further research are given as well.

---

[1] Section 9.1 and 9.2 of this chapter are adapted from Decrop and Snelders (2005), with permission of *Tourism Management*.

©A. Decrop 2006. *Vacation Decision Making* (A. Decrop)

9.1. Review of Extant Typologies

9.1.1. Segmentation typologies

The tourism literature has proposed a large number of typologies of vacationers, tourists and travellers. Many of these typologies are based on segmentation criteria (see Table 9.1), which have been proposed to subdivide vacationers into homogeneous groups, in order to help targeting and positioning strategies. These criteria can be used separately or in combination (Lang and O'Leary, 1997). Widely used are demographic criteria, such as age (Anderson and Langmeyer, 1982), family life cycle (Fodness, 1992) and vacationers' predispositions such as benefits sought (Shoemaker, 1994; Woodside and Jacobs, 1985). Substantial attention has also been given to behavioural variables, such as vacation activities (Hsieh *et al.*, 1992; Moscardo *et al.*, 1996), amount of expenditure (Spotts and Mahoney, 1991), chosen destination (Lang *et al.*, 1997), distance travelled (Etzel and Woodside, 1982) and frequency of travel (Woodside *et al.*, 1987). More traditional geographical and economical criteria have been suggested as well (Swarbrooke and Horner, 1999).

Typologies based on segmentation criteria can be used for day-to-day marketing operations such as targeting, destination selection, pricing and media planning. However, segmentation criteria are less useful for describing more fundamental and structural aspects of the vacationer's life that are important for theoretical purposes and strategic marketing planning (e.g. product development and (re)positioning may be based on an analysis of social and cultural trends in the market). Although segmentation criteria can highlight various aspects of the vacationer's life, without an integrated theory of how to combine them they are like separate pieces of a puzzle. Therefore, more theoretical typologies have been proposed, and these have focused either on socio-psychological variables of the vacationer or on his or her DM style.

9.1.2. Socio-psychological typologies

In general, socio-psychological typologies offer a more integrated view on the vacationer because they connect descriptive aspects of the vacationer with sociological or psychological variables (see Table 9.2). Socio-psychological typologies can be based on values and lifestyles (Madrigal and Kahle, 1994; Thrane, 1997), attitudes, interests and opinions (Davis *et al.*, 1988), motives (Cha *et al.*, 1995) or personality types (Plog, 1974). In a 'meta-typology', Plog (1994) identified eight psychographic or personality dimensions of the tourist: venturesomeness, pleasure-seeking, impulsivity, self-confidence, planfulness, masculinity, intellectualism and people orientation. Of particular importance to tourism literature is Cohen's work (1972, 1979). Based on tourist roles, motives and sought experiences, he developed a fourfold classification of tourist behaviours: drifter,

Table 9.1. Tourist typologies based on segmentation criteria.

Author(s)	Major variable(s)	Tourist types
Anderson and Langmeyer (1982)	Age	Under 50 and over 50
Etzel and Woodside (1982)	Distance travelled	Distant and near home
Fodness (1992)	Family life cycle	Young couple, young parents, mature parents, mature couple, senior couple
Hsieh *et al.* (1992)	Activities	Visiting friends and relatives, outdoor sports, sightseeing, full-house activity, entertainment
Lang *et al.* (1997)	Destination	Within Asia and out of Asia (Taiwanese outbound tourists)
Moscardo *et al.* (1996)	Travel benefits and activities	Escape or excitement, self-esteem or self-development, family relationships, physical activity, safety or security, self-esteem or social status, escape, relaxation
Shoemaker (1994)	Benefits sought	Get away or family, adventurous or educational, gamblers or fun-oriented
Spotts and Mahoney (1991)	Expenditure	Light, medium and heavy spenders
Woodside and Jacobs (1985)	Benefits sought	Rest and relaxation, cultural experiences, family togetherness
Woodside *et al.* (1987)	Frequency of travel	Light and heavy

explorer, individual mass and organized mass. There have been a few attempts to develop and refine this popular typology (Pearce, 1982; Redfoot, 1984; Wickens, 2002). Mayo and Jarvis (1981) describe five types of travellers: 'peace-and-quiet', overseas, historian, recreational vehicle and 'travel now/pay later'. Finally, general socio-style typologies of US and European consumers have been adapted to tourism (Mazanec, 1994). Other typologies are reviewed by Lowyck *et al.* (1992) and Swarbrooke and Horner (1999).

While interesting for conceptualization purposes and a more thorough understanding of tourist behaviour, socio-psychological typologies lack practical relevance for DM in tourism, 'as the implied types are often difficult to identify' (Bargeman *et al.*, 2002, p. 321). One reason for this may be that many typologies have been built more than 10 years ago, at a time when the tourism market was not as developed as it is today, and when vacationing was not such an integral part of people's lives. Another reason is that most socio-psychological typologies are presented as universal, to be applied to people in

Table 9.2. Tourist typologies based on socio-psychological variables.

Author(s)	Major variable(s)	Tourist types
Cha *et al.* (1995)	Push factors (motives)	Sport seekers, novelty seekers, family or relaxation seekers
Cohen (1972)	Roles, motives and level of risk aversion or novelty seeking	Drifter, explorer, individual mass, organized mass
Cohen (1979)	Roles, motives and sought experiences	Recreational, diversionary, experiential, experimental and existential
Davis *et al.* (1988)	Attitudes, interests and opinions	Five clusters of differing degrees of attitudes towards the state's tourism efforts
Madrigal and Kahle (1994)	Values and lifestyles	External locus of control (sense of belonging and security), enjoyment or excitement, achievement, egocentrism
Mayo and Jarvis (1981)	Psychographics	'Peace-and-quiet', overseas, historian, recreational vehicle and 'travel now/pay later'
Mazanec (1994)	Socio-styles	Dandy, rocky, business, squadra, protest, scout, pioneer, olvidados vigilante, romantic, defensive, prudent, moralist, citizen, gentry, strict
Plog (1974, 1994)	Personality traits	Psychocentrics and allocentrics (plus intermediate categories: near-psychocentrics, mid-centrics, near-allocentrics)
Smith (1989)	Motives and lifestyles	Explorer, elite, offbeat, unusual, incipient mass, mass, charter
Thrane (1997)	Personal values	Modern materialist, modern idealist, traditional materialist, traditional idealist

all types of DMUs and all countries. Interpersonal influences in group DM and the cultural environment are not taken into account when looking at tourist behaviour. In addition, almost all typologies suggest mutually exclusive categories of tourists that do not allow consumers to move between categories in response to personal or situational changes, or to an evolution in their 'vacation career' (Pearce, 1988). Finally, most socio-psychological typologies lack practical relevance because they have not been empirically tested (Mo *et al.*, 1993).

9.1.3. Decision-making typologies

Bronner and de Hoog (1985) propose another view on building a more theoretical typology of vacationers. They argue that the way people decide is an important element for segmentation studies. Socio-demographic and socio-psychological variables should be complemented by DM variables like information-seeking (Oppedijk van Veen, 1983), and combined they can form a typology of decision styles. Bronner and de Hoog further identify three segments (nature seekers, sun and beach seekers, and culture seekers) based on different socio-demographics, vacation ideas and choice characteristics. They stress that 'differences between people concerning choice characteristics are real. This means that in planning a marketing strategy these differences must be taken into account' (1985, p. 114). Sproles and Kendall (1986, p. 267) define a consumer DM style as 'a mental orientation characterizing a consumer's approach to making choices' and consider it as a basic aspect of the consumer's personality. They also provide empirical support that DM styles are largely independent of culture, although this finding was later contradicted by Lysonski *et al.* (1996). These authors identified seven factors of DM profiles of shoppers in four countries, and found that 'some of the factors are not applicable in describing DM styles in other countries' (1996, p. 14).

Bronner and de Hoog's proposition (1985) to base market segmentation on DM styles has been supported by Woodside and Carr (1988, p. 2), who conclude that 'vacation travelers can be segmented meaningfully by consumer DM variables'. The latter authors propose the following variables: alternatives considered, benefits sought, decision rules used and sensitivities to changes in attributes. Much in accordance with this, Hsieh *et al.* (1997) have identified different types of travel decision patterns in the Japanese travel market using a multistage segmentation base. Three major criteria are enhanced: travel philosophies (how people think about and prefer to travel overall), benefits sought and product preferences. They conclude that 'travel decision pattern segmentation is a theoretically and statistically feasible approach to understand and segment travelers' (1997, p. 299). Fodness and Murray (1998) presented a classification of tourist information search strategies, while Bargeman *et al.* (2002) recently developed a typology incorporating information on vacation behaviour over time using sequence-alignment methods and Dutch vacation history data. These major typologies based on DM variables are summarized in Table 9.3.

While useful for both theoretical and practical purposes, typologies based on DM styles tend to consider DM variables in isolation, and decision style as a personality trait. An exception to this is the typology of Reid and Crompton (1993), who developed a taxonomy of five DM styles based on the level of involvement and the ability to differentiate between attributes. But apart from this study, there has been no attempt at an integrative empirical typology of vacationers. This chapter extends on the previous work by providing a typology based on DM variables and processes. It describes decision styles within the larger framework of socio-demographic and socio-psychological criteria. It is

Table 9.3. Tourist typologies based on decision-making variables.

Author(s)	Major variable(s)	Tourist types
Bargeman et al. (2002)	Sequence of decisions (frequency duration, timing, destination, temporal and spatial sequence, spatial repetition)	Groups I–VIII
Bronner and de Hoog (1985)	Decision styles (socio-demographics, vacation ideas and choice characteristics)	Nature seekers, sun and beach seekers, culture seekers
Fodness and Murray (1998)	Information search strategies	Pre-purchase mix, tourist bureau, personal experience, ongoing, on-site, automobile club, travel agency
Hsieh et al. (1997)	Travel philosophies (how people think about and prefer to travel overall), benefits sought and product preferences	Active, heritage or outdoor sports; reluctant, social escape or outdoor sports; budget, escape or cultural scenic; active package, being and seeing or destination attributes; low-yield and high-yield
Reid and Crompton (1993)	Level of involvement and the ability to differentiate between attributes	Hierarchy-of-effects, dissonance-attribution hierarchy, alternative attribution hierarchy, low involvement hierarchy, single or integrated hierarchy

hoped that this will avoid the respective lack of theoretical socio-psychological typologies, which have limited relevance for managers, and of typologies based on segmentation criteria that lack a conceptual orientation (Bargeman *et al.*, 2002). Finally, the typology will be related to the major DM variables and models described at the outset of this book (Chapter 1, this volume).

9.2. A New Typology of Vacationers

Given the variation in DM styles, one cannot speak of one universal vacation DMP. Depending on the project, six types of vacationers can be described: habitual, rational, hedonic, opportunistic, constrained and adaptable. These are discussed in the following sections. For each type of vacationers, the number of DMUs is listed within parentheses, describing how often the type was dominant in the DMU.

9.2.1. The habitual vacationer

Habitual vacationers ($n = 3$) are slightly involved and repeat the same vacation behaviour almost every year (e.g. going to the same place). They are ruled by habit due to their personality or structural influences (e.g. owning a cottage). In many instances, this type of vacationers is risk-averse: they cannot afford to 'miss' their vacation and like to feel at home at the destination. Optimizing the vacation time is another possible goal: by always going to the same spot, they avoid wasting time on familiarizing themselves with a new environment. It should further be noted that habitual DM often pertains to particular vacation subdecisions. For example, for an older couple, the choice of transportation has never been discussed since they always go on vacation by car. This is not to say that other vacation decision aspects are automatic.

Habitual vacationers follow decision rules in an unconscious and routine way. They hardly prepare their trip and limit their information to new possible activities in the familiar region. Habitual vacationers may be the 'victims' of their passive and inertial personality: while they may first have an intention to break with routine and fantasize about alternative destinations, they seem incapable of making it happen. Long-term planning is a difficult task for them. In contrast, they are pragmatic and prefer certainty, even if this means the renunciation of potentially better solutions:

> *André* (M, 40, family): At a certain moment, we found ourselves in front of different options: either we let go the possibility of going to Sweden because other interested people began to appear, or ... and thus one of the options, let's say the one most worked out disappeared, and we ended up in front of very vague projects and finally we told ourselves 'Well, let's take the option we know and we will search better next year'. [Q9.1]

In the literature, habitual DM is characterized by little or no information-seeking and little or no evaluation of alternatives. Repeated purchases and brand loyalty are the major consequences of a habitual DMP (Jacoby and Kyner, 1973). A lot of product decisions have been presented to involve habit as a simplifying strategy when consumers are less involved in the category or when they want to reduce risk. However, to the best of our knowledge, vacation DM has never been presented as a habitual process. In contrast, tourism has been depicted as a high involvement (shopping) product with high consumer commitment and a complex DMP (Chapter 2, this volume).

9.2.2. The (bounded) rational vacationer

Risk aversion has a strong influence on the vacation decisions and DMP of rational vacationers ($n = 7$). First, it affects generic trade-off choices: thrifty, they are not ready to go on vacation at any cost. Second, risk aversion often results in brand loyalty for particular aspects of the trip: e.g. a single vacationer always books his or her trips in the same travel agency. Third, rational vacationers are not daydreamers or fantasizers, but careful and realistic decision makers.

Rational vacationers start thinking about their vacation early enough (before January). They are characterized by careful planning, and take facilitating and inhibiting constraints into account as they appear. This is not to say that final vacation decisions are taken early, but a booking is made as soon as the context makes it possible. Choices are well thought out and predictable: the final destination is always one of the first evoked destinations; well-defined decision criteria and strategies are used (see Q 5.11).

Bounded rationality (March and Simon, 1958; Cyert and March, 1963) is the prevailing paradigm here. Rational vacationers do not go to all ends to choose the best possible vacation alternative, but rather choose an alternative that is 'good enough'. An emerging reason for not being purely rational is incrementalism: choosing the best alternative is not truly necessary since poor decisions may be changed the next (vacation) time. Further, informants do not search for that much information as they have limited information-processing abilities. However, information collection is more important and purposeful than for other types of vacationers. Preparation is extensive enough and occurs before booking and not on the spot. Everything has to be planned before leaving in order not to miss important aspects of the trip (e.g. historical sites) or to avoid bad surprises (e.g. no vacancies). During the trip, rational vacationers take care that everything happens according to plans or, at least, the situation is kept under volitional control ('If we have participated in all those additional activities, it is just because we wanted it').

This type of vacation DM can be paralleled with the problem-solving paradigm in consumer behaviour (Howard and Sheth, 1969; Engel *et al.*, 1973). DM starts with a problem within the DMU (i.e. a need or desire to go on vacation) and the vacationer tries to solve the problem by planning a course of action to satisfy this need or desire. Information search, evaluation of vacation alternatives, consumption (rather than purchase) and post-experience evaluation are the major DM steps. However, even rational vacationers do not go through each of these steps sequentially. For example, they may make a destination decision before looking for information about it. Therefore, speaking of thoughtful or reasoned action (Fishbein, 1980) is more appropriate.

9.2.3. The hedonic vacationer

Hedonic vacationers ($n = 4$) take delight in thinking, dreaming and talking about their vacation because this enhances their pleasure and emotional arousal. As vacation involvement is very strong, they grasp any occasion to collect tourist information. They do not hesitate to prompt their fellows to go on vacation and recommend particular destinations. They are so optimistic that they often neglect the importance of situational constraints: emotional drives are stronger than reasonable considerations. As a consequence, hedonic vacationers rehearse both planning and experiencing their dream trip, although it is never made or substituted by a proxy destination experience. That is why one could speak of 'surrogate' vacationers. For those vacationers, the shift from dream to reality is very pronounced: dreamt destinations are considered first, but the evoked set becomes more realistic over time. However, the final destination may not be part of the first evoked destinations. This focus on daydreaming and vacation experience, in addition to that on DMP, is supported by Hirschman and Holbrook (1982) and Holbrook and Hirschman (1982).

For the hedonic vacationer, information search seems to be a better indicator of ideals and preferences than of actual choices. For example, a 40-year-old mother of three children gathered loads of information on Brittany but finally chose another destination (Jura), which she knew hardly anything about. When realizing that the dream vacation would not be possible, this vacationer went back to a more feasible option in order to avoid frustration. This appeared to be very hard (see Q4.3).

Hedonic vacationers are also characterized by hedonic consumption, as illustrated by the following examples. A single woman never brings souvenirs because she considers her trips as pleasurable experiences that do not need to leave material marks. Another informant wants to go back to Rome because of the pleasure of dawdling and dreaming (imagining discourses in the Forum) when visiting its historical sites.

9.2.4. The opportunistic vacationer

Opportunistic vacationers ($n = 5$) do not think or talk a lot about vacation. As they minimize vacation planning and preparation, they could be considered unplanned vacationers, either as a strategy, due to contextual pressures or because of a lack of vacation involvement. First, they are willingly waiting for a social or financial opportunity or they anticipate potential situational constraints (e.g. children's summer activities, school results, time of vacation pay or a threatening illness). Heavy professional activities and the resulting lack of leisure time are a second reason for being unplanned and opportunistic. Third, personal factors such as the lack of involvement or the passive ('wait-and-see') nature of the vacationer come into play. Information is limited, not actively searched and often not used. For example, the opportunistic vacationer may find himself or herself in Vienna for two days, with the only prior knowledge that Vienna is in Austria. However, he or she is always listening to ideas and propositions from social and commercial networks.

Opportunistic vacationers do not use any well-defined strategy in making their vacation decisions. Decisions result from opportunities or special occasions. This may be an advertised commercial offer, or propositions or invitations by family and friends. Vacation choices are made haphazardly during discussions, meetings, walks or phone calls. Waiting for opportunities results in very late but sudden decisions and bears the risk of not going on vacation at all. Since flexibility is important for them, vacation plans and evoked sets are not very stable; turnarounds make destination choices particularly unpredictable:

> *Thierry* (M, 28, couple): But if an opportunity comes out from now to the end of the year, it is very possible … (from now to vacation time, sorry) that we will take this opportunity. I do not know … if we have an opportunity to go to Italy because for one reason or another, we have a house, or rather there is a friend who rents one house and who proposes us to go with him, well we'll go to Italy. [Q9.3]

Decisions here stem from the co-occurrence of a need and a choice solution, which is in line with the 'garbage can' decision model (Cohen *et al.*, 1972; Wilson and Wilson, 1988) described in Section 1.1.1. Finally, data suggest that opportunistic vacationers combine different options from plans and situations in their trips. For example, a family plans to combine a visit to one of their children vacationing in Spain with a visit to long-time friends in Montpellier (France), and showing the Pont de Normandie (France) to their children while coming back home.

9.2.5. The constrained vacationer

Constrained vacationers ($n = 4$) undergo vacation DM rather than controlling it. Some vacationers are weighted down by contextual inhibitors (Chapter 4, this volume) such as limited financial resources or the intervention of situational variables (e.g. moving house, health problems). Some of these constraints only pertain to particular individuals within the DMU. For example, members of a group of friends find it hard to make final vacation decisions due to conflicting individual preferences. Conflicts may arise within the DMU, and this may make vacationers unwilling as they are forced to make the trip and visit certain destinations because other members of the DMU demand it. This is especially true for women and children. For example, an old widow was forced to go on vacation against her will, because her son wanted her to recover from depression. Children are often constrained vacationers because the destination chosen by their parents does not match their preferences. Some women also become unwilling vacationers when they realize that the choice of accommodation (i.e. renting an apartment) will force them to do the same housework as at home. The political model of DM (Pettigrew, 1973; Pfeffer, 1981) can readily be applied to constrained vacationers. This model contends that most human decisions are not individual but rather involve groups, which may lead to conflicts in preferences and identities and a struggle for power.

As a consequence, constrained vacationers are not really involved in a DMP; information search is very limited and passive, if existing at all. In contrast with hedonic vacationers, the destination evoked set is quite stable and realistic right from the outset of plans:

> *Jacques* (M, 43, family): We dream about vacations and we know that there are vacations ... that we have dreams that we will ...
> *Chantal* (F, 35): ... never do it.
> *Jacques*: ... never carry out. For example, the United States is a country that I dream of going, that it would be the most beautiful. But, I know that I will never go. [Q9.4]

Finally, the particular case of a group of friends is worth mentioning. Each group member proposes up to three destinations and the final destination is drawn from a hat. These vacationers are constrained because they are bound to the result of the draw, even though they do not like the destination. There is a moral commitment to that random decision based on group adhesion, such as explained by the 26-year-old speaker of the group: 'We have already discussed about that: thus if there is someone who does not want, well he does not come. Generally, everybody comes because we are a very united group from the army.'

9.2.6. The adaptable vacationer

This type of vacationer is inspired by the 'adaptive decision maker' of Payne *et al.* (1993). Adaptable vacationers ($n = 3$) like vacationing and travelling. Thinking about vacation is a continuous flow, as they always have more vacation projects in mind. Those projects are often carried through because these vacationers adapt their plans according to the situation, which means that they often revise their decisions and modify their behaviour. Final decisions are taken late because they wait for the best adaptation of their plans. Adaptable vacationers go on holiday sometimes with their family (including children), sometimes with friends or sometimes with their partner for a romantic trip. Each time, decisions and DM style are adapted to the particularities of the different DMUs. This is in line with March's contention (1994, p. 198) that 'any decision process involves a collection of individuals and groups who are simultaneously involved in other things'.

Adaptable vacationers do not use well-defined decision strategies. DM is characterized by much flexibility, which makes choices very unpredictable:

> *Pierre* (M, 43, family/couple): We have some friends who would like to go to Scotland. Err ... to Scotland, I say yes: if finally the decision is taken, if they want to leave at the same period as us, we will leave together. There you go, we will go there because of them. If not, I'd like to take my wife to discover the Nordic countries which I have already visited and I'd like to make her discover that. Actually nothing has been ... I'm ready to change, you know.

Interviewer: You are ready to change?

Pierre: Yes, I mean that if another project takes shape, we will change. It's not ... as we do not reserve anything, nothing has been ... [Q9.5]

Adaptable vacationers do not prepare the trip in too much depth as flexibility is also relevant during the trip itself. As a consequence, adaptable vacationers are independent travellers who hate group constraints and organized tours. While having some anchor points (must-see sights), they make room for improvisation and the adaptation of plans:

Françoise (F, 30, group of friends): It is anyway the rule that we always have together, it is that whenever we went to a place, if there was a place that we liked, we did not hesitate to stay longer, ready to give up another thing. Thus, actually we never have something totally precise, planned, for which we cannot change the rule if we see other interesting things. [Q9.6]

The previous findings confirm the contention of Payne *et al.* (1993) that people are adaptive in that they use a variety of strategies to solve decision problems, contingent upon task and context (social) factors. According to these authors (1993, p. 248), strategy selection may be seen as 'the result of a compromise between the desire to make the most accurate decision and the desire to minimize cognitive effort'.

9.2.7. Assessment of the new typology

According to Hunt (1991, pp. 187–188), typologies used in marketing should be 'intersubjectively unambiguous', 'mutually exclusive' and 'collectively exhaustive'. The typology presented here scores well on the first criterion: our naturalistic longitudinal design allowed for a rich description of each type. With respect to the second criterion, this typology is not mutually exclusive at the DMU level, since there may be individual differences within DMUs. Even within one individual, different types of DMPs may be followed depending on opportunities, emotions, etc., as illustrated by the following quotation:

Martine (F, 37, single): The destination, well that depends. There are some trips which I have in reserve and I wait to find the best trip or when the prices have lowered; then there are the ones that I fall in love with. Sometimes, I may have not even considered any destination and then suddenly ... [Q9.7]

Although DMUs and individuals may mix DM styles, informants could easily be classified into one particular style within each vacation project. This means that the typology is mutually exclusive at the vacation project level. As for the third criterion, the typology is exhaustive within the constraints of the small sample of Belgian vacationers. The six types provide a good description of all encountered cases.

9.3. Implications

9.3.1. Theoretical implications

The need for relativism is the major theoretical lesson from this research. There is not only one but a plurality of vacation DMPs. Six types of vacationers have been depicted based on personal, social and DM variables. This breaks with existing models that propose only one typical, i.e. bounded rational (March and Simon, 1958), vacation decision process. Our findings have shown that there is a need to 'soften' traditional tenets that characterize vacation DM as high involvement (Moutinho, 1987; Swarbrooke and Horner, 1999), extensive problem-solving and information search (Middleton, 1994), and a sequential evolution of plans starting from the generic decision to go on vacation (van Raaij and Francken, 1984; Mansfeld, 1992). More particularly, one should pay more attention to adaptability and opportunism in vacation DM, which have major consequences on decision timing, information search and predictability of choices.

Another aspect deserving more attention is the daydreaming of hedonic vacationers (Hirschman and Holbrook, 1982). A lot of information about tourist destinations is collected for fantasizing and stirring the imagination. At the same time, that information is hardly predictive of actual vacation choices. So one may wonder whether daydreaming is an end in itself, or whether it serves some function during the actual vacation experience. Further research should clarify this, since the informants of this study were not contacted during their vacation. Finally, the constrained vacationer type shows that people do not always feel in control when choosing and planning their vacation. In the sample, this concerned women and children the most, who often felt forced into supporting certain decisions, becoming disinterested in the vacation as a result. Again, the implications of this finding for the actual vacation experience and family relations during the vacation deserve more attention.

When compared to other products and services, vacation and tourism appear to have particular characteristics. It is a complex, experiential and seasonally recurrent product at the same time. It is very easy to think of other products that have one of the previous characteristics: financial services and cars are complex products; restaurant meals and attending to sport or music events are highly experiential; clothes or footwear are seasonally recurrent items. However, we cannot find any product that combines all three characteristics of a vacation. Research and practice should take these into account in order to generate better predictions of attitudes and behaviour. First, vacation DM is *complex*. Three decision levels have been brought to light: generic, vacation and each vacation item. The thrust of tourism research has ignored this complexity. As shown in Chapter 2, many DM models lack a clear indication of which (level of) decision is considered. More precision is needed since, based on the comparability and exclusivity of alternatives, each level has important implications on the decision criteria and strategies that are used. Second, vacation DM is strongly *experiential*. By this, we mean that a substantial part of decisions and information collection occur during the vacation itself. It is also experiential because both the DMP and the consumption of a holiday involve emotions, daydreaming and fantasies (Holbrook and Hirschman, 1982), as well as anticipation and nostalgia (Campbell, 1987). Finally, vacations *always come back again* within particular time periods. In this book, vacation DM is found to be an ongoing (circular) process. More projects are considered at the same time with different time horizons, different types of DMUs, etc. Different CSs coexist in the vacationer's mind. Therefore, isolating well-defined stages in DMPs is difficult and may even be irrelevant. This implies that distinguishing between pre- and post- (information) search stages, between generic and vacation decisions, and even between pre- and post-purchase should be questioned in conceptualization and empirical measurement. Further, investigating DM should not cease once a decision is made. Vacation proves to be a strongly timeless phenomenon for which thinking, dreaming, talking and gathering information are ongoing.

9.3.2. Managerial implications

At the managerial level, tourism professionals should always keep listening to the changing needs and preferences of vacationers. Products should be proposed that enable them to get away from their mundane everyday life. Attention should be paid to the growing maturity and experience of vacationers because this induces a shift in vacation motives, involvement and expectation level. The distinction between variety seekers and brand loyalists could be used to segment them. As to timing and planning, Belgian vacationers often start thinking about their summer vacation early enough; January seems to be a key month for drawing their attention. The focus should not only be on destination but also on accommodation, period and transportation, which are the most important decision criteria. Tour operators and travel agents should also benefit from the opportunistic nature of DM of some vacationers by keeping in touch with them, and making them offers (early booking or last-minute discounts). Active steps are particularly recommended because vacationers prove to be waiting for, and not purposefully searching for, information.

The adaptability of vacationers should also be taken into account. As vacationers are involved in more vacation projects at the same time with different needs and desires, they should not be put into one exclusive segment. Promotional timing should thus be adapted according to the DMP of the different DMUs (e.g. early booking reductions for families and last-minute offers for couples or groups of friends). Our typology of vacationers based on DMPs could therefore be used in addition to more traditional segmentation bases. Given the stress on the DMP, this typology is more likely to be applied for the purpose of product communication than for the purpose of product development. It gives indications about vacation involvement and planning, decision timing, amount and type of information search, etc. All these elements could be used in promotion campaigns. Finally, it should be noted that vacationers may like more flexibility in their planning, that they may value information as much for its utility as for its ability to stir up the imagination, and that the actual vacation package may have to deal with uninvolved and even unwilling vacationers. These issues could be taken into account when developing packages and organized tours.

Vacationers should be addressed as groups, and not only as individuals, because: (i) most of the time, vacation DM is a joint process that involves several persons (partners, parents and children, friends); and (ii) social interaction is one of the major motives for travelling. Members of a group like to benefit from the holiday to meet again and share activities. Tourism operators should listen to group (and not only individual) needs, expectations or preferences, and be aware of the particular influence of group members on vacation decisions. In the same way, group values such as togetherness, friendship, trust or confidence could be used in communication messages. However, because motives, constraints and decision modes are different in a couple, a family and a party of friends, marketing strategies and tools should be adapted accordingly. In families, marketeers should try to reach either women or men depending on the decision stage or role (see Table 8.1). Tour operators should develop packages with one all-inclusive price and adapt to the evolving structure of many families (e.g. one parent + two children). In groups of friends, the leaders should be targeted. Of course, this would be easier in formal than in informal groups. In a formal group, such as a sport club or cultural association, leaders can be identified easily based on yearbooks or directories, and reached through direct marketing or personal selling. As to informal groups, occasions should be created for them to meet and to share leisure and travel activities, and communicate through the mass media. Firms have already taken some steps in that direction. In the 'Coca-Cola: Create your night' project, groups of two to four friends were invited to describe the party of their dreams and win the chance to live it out. More than 45,000 online votes were collected and considered by the jury! SN Brussels Airlines regularly offers special passes with favourable prices for (younger) groups of friends. In all cases, practitioners need to be careful when measuring expectations and preferences because group variables may differ from, and not be the sum of, individual variables. It is especially not wise to predict choice on the basis of individual preferences as far as groups of friends are concerned.

9.4. Limitations and Suggestions for Future Research

Probably the major question about this research pertains to the external validity or transferability of emerging findings. Two dimensions of transferability need to be discussed: statistical generalization and ethnicity of informants. In this chapter, a typology of vacationers has been built inductively from the study of a phenomenon situated in a particular context. Although analytical generalization of some emerging findings is possible, statistical generalization is not possible because of the theoretical (non-random) sampling procedure and small sample size. More particularly, the small number of parties of friends involved in this study does not allow for definitive conclusions about their particularities in comparison with couples and families. If statistical generalization were desired, the emerging propositions of this book could be tested on larger representative samples. For example, it would be interesting to investigate whether a typology similar to this new typology of vacationers could be derived from quantitative survey data using factor-analytic or clustering techniques. The present study has put forward many propositions that could be converted into questions to generate those data. Finally, particular aspects of the DMP would deserve further investigations. For example, group DM could be a focus in itself, maybe with other data collection (e.g. non-participant observation or the Nominal Group Technique) and recording (e.g. video camera) techniques. All DMU members did not always participate in the interviews, so there were both within and between case comparison problems. It was especially a problem for groups of friends where it has never been possible to interview all the members involved at the same time.

The issue of the transferability in terms of the ethnicity of informants also has to be raised, since the sample of this study only consists of Belgian vacationers. This means that the reader should be aware that the emerging propositions of this book are the reflection of a particular cultural view. In Hofstede's (2001) famous work on culture's consequences, Belgium is depicted as an individualistic society (people look to themselves before considering group interests) with strong uncertainty avoidance (people tend to be risk-averse), long power distance (people accept unequal situations), and where 'tough' masculine values (as opposed to 'tender' feminine ones) prevail slightly. These traits have implications for vacation DM. For example, power distance may influence the distribution of tasks within the household; the leadership phenomenon could be less pronounced in countries with short power distance like Denmark or New Zealand; the negotiation of individual expectations and preferences to match collective ones could be a lesser problem in more collectivistic societies such as Korea, Singapore or Taiwan; in couples and families, the distribution of roles could be more equalitarian in 'feminine' regions like Scandinavia or the Netherlands. In the same way, risk aversion may lead to higher involvement levels, extended information collection, avoiding conflicts and safer choices; as a consequence, our description of the habitual, rational and constrained vacationer types may be somewhat exaggerated when looked at from a culture that is less risk-averse. Finally, vacation DM may be influenced by the amount of discretionary time, and this is likely to be higher in Belgium than in countries such as the USA, UK and Japan, where people work longer hours and have fewer holidays, and lower in places such as Germany or the Netherlands, where people work shorter hours and have more holidays.

However, Belgians resemble French, Spanish and Italian people on Hofstede's four cultural dimensions. On individualism and masculinity, Belgium does not score very differently from the other European countries and the Anglo-Saxon world (Canada, New Zealand, USA, UK and Australia). In addition, it can be argued that culture is not the principal determinant of vacation behaviour. The emergence of a 'touristic' culture, as opposed to a 'nationalistic' culture, has been put into light for western countries from which most tourists emanate (de Vulpian, 1989; McIntosh *et al.*, 1995). As a result, international tourists tend to have similar profiles:

> The international [tourism] market is largely made up of middle-income people, including the more prosperous minority of the working class, who normally live in large cities and earn their living in managerial, professional, white-collar, supervisory, and skilled occupations. (McIntosh *et al.*, 1995, p. 235)

Statistical data suggest that preferences and behaviour patterns of Belgian vacationers do not differ much from those of the other EU countries (Hollier and Subremon, 1992; Pasqualini and Jacquet, 1992). Moreover, Sproles and Kendall (1986) argue that DM styles are largely independent of the culture, but are rather descriptive of a personal orientation. Therefore, the six types of vacationers presented in this chapter could be found in different parts of the world, of course with different distributions. In general, the Belgian society is reported to be a 'miniature Europe', where 'most general economic and consumption tendencies that have a grip over Europe, also reign the Belgian society' (Gijsbrechts *et al.*, 1995, p. 389).

References

Abelson, R.P. and Levi, A. (1985) Decision making and decision theory. In: Lindzey, G. and Aronson, E. (eds) *The Handbook of Social Psychology.* Random House, New York, pp. 231–309.

Ajzen, I. and Fishbein, M. (1980) *Understanding Attitudes and Predicting Social Behavior.* Prentice-Hall, Englewood Cliffs, New Jersey.

Allen, D.E. (2002) Toward a theory of consumer choice as sociohistorically shaped practical experience: the fits-like-a-glove (FLAG) framework. *Journal of Consumer Research* 28(March), 515–532.

Allport, G.W. (1935) Attitudes. In: Murchinson, C.A. (ed.) *A Handbook of Social Psychology.* Clark University Press, Worcester, UK, pp. 798–844.

Anderson, G. and Langmeyer, L. (1982) The under-50 and over-50 travelers: a profile of similarities and differences. *Journal of Travel Research* 20 (Spring), 20–24.

Anderson, J.R. (1983) *The Architecture of Cognition.* Harvard University Press, Cambridge, Massachusetts.

Andreasen, A.R. (1965) Attitudes and customer behavior: a decision model. In: Preston, L.E. (ed.) *New Research in Marketing.* University of California, Institute of Business and Economic Research, Berkeley, California, pp. 1–16.

Andreasen, A.R. and Best, A. (1977) Consumers complain: does business respond? *Harvard Business Review*, July–August, 94–104.

Antil, J.H. (1984) Conceptualization and operationalization of involvement. *Advances in Consumer Research* 11.

Assael, H. (1984) *Consumer Behavior and Marketing Action.* Kent, Boston, Massachusetts.

Axelrod, J. (1968) Attitude measures that predict purchase. *Journal of Advertising Research* 8, 3–17.

Bales, R.F. and Strodtbeck, F.L. (1951) Phases in group problem-solving. *Journal of Abnormal and Social Psychology* 46, 485–495.

Bargeman, B., Joh, C.-H. and Timmermans, H. (2002) Vacation behavior using a sequence alignment method. *Annals of Tourism Research* 29, 320–337.

Bauer, R.A. (1960) Consumer behavior as risk taking. In: Hancock, R.S. (ed.) *Dynamic Marketing for a Changing World.* Proceedings of the 43rd Conference of the American Marketing Association, Chicago, Illinois, 389–400.

Beach, L.R. and Mitchell, T.R. (1978) A contingency model for the selection of decision strategies. *Academy of Management Review* 3, 439–449.

Beatty, J.E. and Torbert, W.R. (2003) The false duality of work and leisure. *Journal of Management Inquiry,* 12(3), 239–252.

Becker, H.S., Geer, B., Hughes, E.C. and Strauss, A.L. (1961) *Boys in White: Student Culture in Medical School.* University of Chicago Press, Chicago, Illinois.

Belk, R.W. (1975) Situational variables and consumer behavior. *Journal of Consumer Research* 2, 157–167.

Belk, R.W. (1985) Issues in the intention-behavior discrepancy. In: Sheth, J.N. (ed.) *Research in Consumer Behavior,* Vol. 1. JAI Press, Greenwich, Connecticut, pp. 1–34.

Bell, D.E. (1982) Regret in decision making under uncertainty. *Operations Research* 30, 961–981.

Belonax, J.A. and Mittelstaedt, R.A. (1978) Evoked set size as a function of number of choice criterion and information variability. *Advances in Consumer Research* 5, 48–51.

Bendor, J. (1995) A model of muddling through. *American Political Science Review* 89, 819–840.

Bettman, J.R. (1979) *An Information Processing Theory of Consumer Choice.* Addison-Wesley, Reading, Massachusetts.

Bettman, J.R. and Park, C.W. (1980) Effects of prior knowledge and experience and phase of the choice process on consumer decision processes: a protocol analysis. *Journal of Consumer Research* 7, 234–248.

Bettman, J.R. and Sujan, M. (1987) Effects of framing on evaluation of comparable and noncomparable alternatives by expert and novice consumers. *Journal of Consumer Research* 14, 141–154.

Bettman, J.R., Johnson, E.J. and Payne, J.W. (1991) Consumer decision making. In: Robertson, T.S. and Kassarjian, H.H. (eds) *Handbook of Consumer Behavior.* Prentice-Hall, Englewood Cliffs, New Jersey, pp. 50–84.

Bettman, J.R., Luce, M.F. and Payne, J.W. (1998) Constructive consumer choice processes. *Journal of Consumer Research* 25, 187–217.

Biehal, G.J. and Chakravarti, D. (1989) The effects of concurrent verbalization on choice processing. *Journal of Marketing Research* 26 (1), 84–96.

Bjorklund, R.A. and King, B. (1982) A consumer-based approach to assist in the design of hotels. *Journal of Travel Research* 20 (2), 45–52.

Blackwell, R.D., Miniard, P.W. and Engel, J.F. (2001) *Consumer Behavior,* 9th edn. Harcourt College Publishers, Fort Worth, Texas.

Bohlmann, J.D. and Qualls, W.J. (2001) Household preference revisions and decision-making: the role of disconfirmation. *International Journal of Research in Marketing* 18, 319–339.

Boorstin, D.J. (1964) *The Image: A Guide to Pseudo-Events in America.* Harper & Row, New York.

Botterill, T.D. (1987) Dissatisfaction with a construction of satisfaction. *Annals of Tourism Research* 14, 139–141.

Braybrooke, D. and Lindblom, C.E. (1963) *A Strategy of Decision.* Free Press, New York.

Breivik, E., Troye, S.V. and Olsson, U.H. (1998) Dimensions of product intangibility and their impact on product evaluation. Paper presented at the 26th conference of the Association of Consumer Research, Montreal, Canada, September.

Brisoux, J.E. and Laroche, M. (1980) A proposed consumer strategy of simplification for categorising brands. In: Summey, J.D. and Taylor, R.D. (eds) *Evolving Marketing Thought for 1980.* Proceedings of the annual meeting of the Southern Marketing Association, Carbondale, Illinois, pp. 112–114.

Bronfenbrenner, U. (1986) Recent advances in research on the ecology of human development. In: Silbereisen, R.K., Eyferth, K. and Rudinger, G. (eds) *Development as Action in Context: Problem Behavior and Normal Youth Development.* Springer, New York, pp. 287–309.

Bronfenbrenner, U. (1992) Ecological systems theory. In Vasta, R. (ed.) *Six Theories of Child Development: Revised Formulations and Current Ideas.* Jessica Kingsley, London, pp. 187–249.

Bronner, F. and de Hoog, R. (1985) A recipe for mixing decision ingredients. *European Research* 13, 109–115.

Burrell, G. and Morgan, G. (1979) *Sociological Paradigms and Organizational Analysis.* Heinemann, London.

Burton, S. (1990) The framing of purchase for services. *Journal of Services Marketing* 4, 55–67.

Cacioppo, J.T. and Petty, R.E. (1982) The need for cognition. *Journal of Personality and Social Psychology* 42, 116–131.

Cadotte, E.R., Woodruff, R.B. and Jenkins, R.L. (1987) Expectations and norms in models of consumer satisfaction. *Journal of Marketing Research* 24, 305–314.

Campbell, C. (1987) *The Romantic Ethic and the Spirit of Modern Consumerism.* Blackwell Publishers, Oxford.

Carroll, J.S. and Johnson, E.J. (1990) *Decision Research: A Field Guide.* Sage, Newbury Park, California.

Cha, S., McCleary, K.W. and Uysal, M. (1995) Travel motivations of Japanese overseas travelers: a factor-cluster segmentation approach. *Journal of Travel Research* 34 (Summer), 33–39.

Chapman, L.J. and Chapman, J.P. (1967) Genesis of popular but erroneous psychodiagnostic observations. *Journal of Abnormal Psychology* 72, 193–204.

Charmaz, K. (2000) Grounded theory: objectivist and constructivist methods. In: Denzin, N. and Lincoln, Y. (eds) *Handbook of Qualitative Research*, 2nd edn. Sage, Thousand Oaks, California, pp. 509–535.

Chisnall, P.M. (1985) *Marketing: A Behavioural Analysis*, 2nd edn. McGraw-Hill, New York.

Chon, K. (1987) An assessment of images of Korea as a tourist destination by American tourists. *Hotel and Tourism Management Review* 3, 155–170.

Chon, K.S. (1989) Understanding recreational traveler's motivation, expectation, satisfaction. *Revue de Tourisme* 44 (1), 3–7.

Chon, K.S. (1990) The role of destination image in tourism: a review and discussion. *Revue de Tourisme* 45 (2), 2–9.

Chon, K.S. (1992) The role of destination image in tourism: an extension. *Revue de Tourisme* 47 (2), 2–9.

Chon, K.S., Christianson, D.J. and Lee, C.-L. (1994) Contemporary research issues related tourist satisfaction and dissatisfaction. In: Gasser, R.V. and Weiermmair, K. (eds) *Spoilt for Choice: Decision Making Processes and Preference Changes of Tourist – Intertemporal and Intercountry Perspectives.* Kulturverlag, Thaur, Germany, pp. 149–160.

Churchill, G.A. and Surprenant, C. (1982) An investigation into the determinants of customer satisfaction. *Journal of Marketing Research* 19, 491–504.

Cohen, E. (1972) Towards a sociology of international tourism. *Social Research* 39, 164–182.

Cohen, E. (1979) A phenomenology of tourist types. *Sociology* 13, 179–201.

Cohen, E. (1988) Traditions in the qualitative sociology of tourism. *Annals of Tourism Research* 15, 29–46.

Cohen, M.D., March, J.G. and Olsen, J. (1972) A garbage can model of organizational choice. *Administrative Science Quaterly* 17, 1–24.

Connell, J. and Lowe, A. (1997) Generating grounded theory from qualitative data: the application of inductive methods in tourism and hospitality management research. *Progress in Tourism and Hospitality Research* 3, 165–173.

Coombs, C.H. (1958) On the use of inconsistency of preferences in psychological measurement. *Journal of Experimental Psychology* 55, 1–7.

Cotte, J. and Ratneshwar, S. (2001) Timestyle and leisure decisions. *Journal of Leisure Research*, 33(4), 396–409.

Cotte, J., Ratneshwar, S. and Mick, D.G. (2004) The times of their lives: phenomenological and metaphysical characteristics of consumer timestyles. *Journal of Consumer Research*, 31(3), 333–345.

Crawford, D.W., Jackson, E.L. and Godbey, G. (1991) A hierarchical model of leisure constraints. *Leisure Sciences* 13, 309–320.

Creusen, M.E.H. and Schoormans, J.P.L. (1997) The nature of differences between similarity and preference judgments: a replication with extension. *International Journal of Research in Marketing* 14, 81–87.

Crick, M. (1988) Sun, sex, sights, savings and servility. *Criticism, Heresy and Interpretation* 1, 37–76.

Crick, M. (1989) Representation of international tourism in the social sciences: sun, sex, sights, savings and servility. *Annual Review of Anthropology* 18, 307–344.

Crompton, J.L. (1979) Motivations for pleasure travel. *Annals of Tourism Research* 6, 408–424.

Cullingford, C. (1994) Children's attitudes to holiday overseas. *Tourism Management* 16, 121–127.

Curren, M., Folkes, V. and Steckel, J. (1992) Explanations for successful and unsuccessful marketing decisions: the decision maker's perspective. *Journal of Marketing* 56, 18–31.

Cyert, R.M. and March, J.G. (1963) *A Behavioral Theory of the Firm.* Prentice-Hall, Englewood Cliffs, New Jersey.

Dann, G.M. (1977) Anomie, ego-enhancement and tourism. *Annals of Tourism Research* 4, 184–194.

Dann, G.M. (1996) *The Language of Tourism: A Sociolinguistic Perspective.* CAB International, Wallingford, UK.

Darley, W. and Lim, J. (1986) Family decision making in leisure-time activities: an exploratory investigation of the impact of locus of control, child age influence factor and parental type on perceived child influence. *Advances in Consumer Research* 13, 370–374.

Davis, D.J., Allen, J. and Crosenza, R.M. (1988) Segmenting local residents by their attitudes, interests and opinions toward tourism. *Journal of Travel Research* 27, 2–8.

Davis, H.L. (1976) Decision making within the household. *Journal of Consumer Research* 2, 241–260.

Davis, H.L. and Rigaux, B.P. (1974) Perception of marital roles in decision processes. *Journal of Consumer Research* 1, 51–62.

de Vulpian, A. (1989) L'émergence de typologies transnationales. *Revue Française de Marketing* 124, 67–72.

Decrop, A. (1999a) Triangulation in qualitative tourism research. *Tourism Management* 20, 157–162.

Decrop, A. (1999b) Personal aspects of vacationers' decision making processes. *Journal of Travel and Tourism Marketing* 8(4), 59–68.

Decrop, A. (2001) The antecedents and consequences of vacationers' dis/satisfaction: tales from the field. In: Mazanec, J.A., Crouch, G.I., Woodside, A.G. and Ritchie, J.R. Brent (eds) *Consumer Psychology of Travel, Hospitality and Leisure*, Vol. 2. CAB International, Wallingford, UK, pp. 333–347.

Decrop, A. (2005) Group processes in vacation decision-making. *Journal of Travel and Tourism Marketing* 18(3), 23–36.

Decrop, A. and Snelders, D. (2004) Planning the summer vacation: an adaptable and opportunistic process. *Annals of Tourism Research* 31, 1008–1030.

Decrop, A. and Snelders, D. (2005) A grounded typology of vacation decision making. *Tourism Management* 26, 121–132.

Dellaert, B.G., Ettema, D.F. and Lindh, C. (1998) Multi-faceted tourist travel decisions: a constraint-based conceptual framework to describe tourists' sequential choices of travel components. *Tourism Management* 19, 313–320.

Denzin, N.K. (1978) *The Research Act: A Theoretical Introduction to Sociological Methods*. McGraw-Hill, New York.

Denzin, N.K. and Lincoln, Y.S. (2000) Introduction: the discipline and practice of qualitative research. In: Denzin, N.K. and Lincoln, Y.S. (eds) *Handbook of Qualitative Research*, 2nd edn. Sage, Thousand Oaks, California, pp. 1–28.

Du Toit, B.M. (1975) A decision-making model for the study of migration. In: Du Toit, B.M. and Safa, H.I. (eds) *Migration and Urbanization*. Mouton Publishers, The Hague, pp. 49–76.

Dubé-Rioux, L., Regan, D.T. and Schmitt, B.H. (1990) The cognitive representation of services varying in concreteness and specificity. *Advances in Consumer Research* 17, 861–865.

Duke, C.R. and Persia, M.A. (1996a) Consumer-defined dimensions for the escorted tour industry segment: expectations, satisfactions and importance. *Journal of Travel and Tourism Marketing* 5 (1/2), 77–99.

Duke, C.R. and Persia, M.A. (1996b) Performance-importance analysis of escorted tour evaluations. *Journal of Travel and Tourism Marketing* 5 (3), 207–223.

Durkheim, E. (1952) *Suicide: A Study in Sociology*. Free Press, Glencoe, UK.

Echtner, C.M. and Ritchie, J.R. Brent (1993) The measurement of destination image: an empirical assessment. *Journal of Travel Research* 31 (Spring), 3–13.

Edwards, W. (1954) The theory of decision making. *Psychological Bulletin* 41, 380–417.

Einhorn, H. and Hogarth, R. (1981) Behavioral decision theory: processes of judgment and choice. *Annual Review of Psychology* 32, 53–88.

Eiser, J.R. (1986) *Social Psychology: Attitudes, Cognition and Social Behaviour.* Cambridge University Press, Cambridge.

Ekstrom, K., Tansuhaj, P. and Fowman, E. (1986) Children's influence in family decisions and consumer socialization: a reciprocal view. *Advances in Consumer Research* 14, 283–288.

Ellis, D.G. and Fisher, B.A. (1994) *Small Group Decision Making: Communication and the Group Process.* McGraw-Hill, New York.

Engel, J.F. and Blackwell, R.D. (1982) *Consumer Behavior.* The Dryden Press, Hinsdale, Illinois.

Engel, J.F., Kollat, D.T. and Blackwell, R.D. (1973) *Consumer Behavior.* Holt, Rinehart and Winston, New York.

Engel, J.F., Blackwell, R.D. and Miniard, P.W. (1990) *Consumer Behavior.* The Dryden Press, Hinsdale, Illinois.

Etzel, M.J. and Woodside, A.G. (1982) Segmentation vacation markets: the case of the distant and near-home travelers. *Journal of Travel Research* 20 (4), 10–14.

Evans, M.J., Moutinho, L. and van Raaij, W.F. (1996) *Applied Consumer Behaviour.* Addison-Wesley, London.

Feifer, M. (1985) *Going Places.* MacMillan, London.

Feldman, L.P. and Hornik, J. (1981) The use of time: an integrated conceptual model. *Journal of Consumer Research*, 7(1), 407–419.

Fesenmaier, D. and Johnson, B. (1989) Involvement-based segmentation: implications for travel marketing in Texas. *Tourism Management* 10, 293–300.

Fesenmaier, D. and Vogt, C. (1992) Evaluating the utility of touristic information sources for planning Midwest vacation travel. *Journal of Travel and Tourism Marketing* 1 (2), 1–18.

Festinger, L. (1957) *A Theory of Cognitive Dissonance.* Stanford University Press, Stanford, California.

Filiatrault, P. and Ritchie, J.R. (1980) Joint purchasing decisions: a comparison of influence structure in family and couple decision-making units. *Journal of Consumer Research* 7, 131–150.

Fishbein, M. (1963) An investigation of the relationships between beliefs about an object and the attitudes towards that object. *Human Relations* 16, 233–240.

Fishbein, M. (1970) The relationship between beliefs, attitudes and behavior. In: Kollat, D.T. (ed.) *Research in Consumer Behavior.* Holt, Rinehart and Winston, New York, pp. 216–235.

Fishbein, M. (1980) A theory of reasoned action: some applications and implications. In: Howe, H. and Page, M. (eds) *Nebraska Symposium on Motivation,* Vol. 27. University of Nebraska Press, Lincoln, Nebraska, pp. 65–116.

Fishbein, M. and Ajzen, I. (1975) *Belief, Attitude, Intention and Behavior: An Introduction to Theory and Research.* Addison-Wesley, Reading, Massachusetts.

Flipo, J.P. (1988) On the intangibility of services. *The Service Industries Journal* 8, 286–298.

Floyd, M.F., Shinew, K.J., McGuire, M.A. and Noe, F.P. (1994) Race, class, and leisure activity preferences: marginality and ethnicity revisited. *Journal of Leisure Research*, 26(2), 158–173.

Fodness, D. (1992) The impact of family life cycle on the vacation decision-making process. *Journal of Travel Research* 31 (Fall), 8–13.

Fodness, D. (1994) Measuring tourist motivation. *Annals of Tourism Research* 21, 555–581.

Fodness, D. and Murray, B. (1997) Tourist information search. *Annals of Tourism Research* 24, 503–523.

Fodness, D. and Murray, B. (1998) A typology of tourist information search strategies. *Journal of Travel Research* 37 (2), 108–119.

Folkes, V.S. (1984) Consumer reactions to product failure: an attributional approach. *Journal of Consumer Research* 10, 398–409.

Foucault, M. (1976) *The Birth of the Clinic*. Tavistock, London.

Fournier, S. and Mick, D.G. (1999) Rediscovering satisfaction. *Journal of Marketing* 63, 5–23.

Foxall, G.R. and Goldsmith, R.E. (1994) *Consumer Psychology for Marketing*. Routledge, London.

Frances, R. (1992) *La Perception*. P.U.F, Paris.

Francken, D.A. and van Raaij, W.F. (1979) A longitudinal study of vacationers' information acquisition behavior. Papers on Economic Psychology, 2. Erasmus University, Rotterdam, The Netherlands.

Francken, D.A. and van Raaij, W.F. (1981) Satisfaction with leisure time activities. *Journal of Leisure Research* 13, 337–352.

Geertz, C. (1973) *The Interpretation of Cultures: Selected Essays*. Basic Books, New York.

Gijsbrechts, E., Swinnen, G. and van Waterschoot, W. (1995) The changing consumer in Belgium. *International Journal of Research in Marketing* 12, 389–403.

Gilbert, D.C. (1991) An examination of the consumer behaviour process related to tourism. In: Cooper, C. (ed.) *Progress in Tourism, Recreation and Hospitality Management*, Vol. 3. Belhaven Press, London, pp. 78–105.

Gitelson, R.L. and Crompton, J.L. (1983) The planning horizons and sources of information used by pleasure travelers. *Journal of Travel Research* 21 (Winter), 2–7.

Gitelson, R.J. and Crompton, J.L. (1984) Insights into the repeat vacation phenomenon. *Annals of Tourism Research* 11, 199–217.

Gitelson, R. and Kerstetter, D. (1990) The relationship between socio-demographic variables, benefits sought and subsequent vacation behavior: a case study. *Journal of Travel Research* 28 (Winter), 24–29.

Gitelson, R. and Kerstetter, D. (1994) The influence of friends and relatives in travel decision-making. *Journal of Travel and Tourism Marketing* 3, 59–68.

Glaser, B. and Strauss, A. (1967) *The Discovery of Grounded Theory*. Aldine, Chicago, Illinois.

Gnoth, J. (1997) Tourism motivation and expectation formation. *Annals of Tourism Research* 24, 283–304.

Goodall, B. (1988) How tourists choose their holidays: an analytical framework. In: Goodall, B. and Ashworth, G. (eds) *Marketing in the Tourist Industry: The Promotion of Destination Regions*. Routledge, London, pp. 1–17.

Goodall, B. (1991) Understanding holiday choice. In: Cooper, C.P. (ed.) *Progress in Tourism, Recreation and Hospitality Management*, Vol. 3. Belhaven Press, London, pp. 59–77.

Gordon, I.E. (1989) *Theories of Visual Perception*. John Wiley & Sons, Chichester, UK.

Gorman, W.M. (1980) A possible procedure for analyzing quality differentials in the egg market. *Review of Economic Studies* 47, 843–856.

Graburn, N.H. (1983) To pray, pay and play: the cultural structure of Japanese domestic tourism. *Cahiers du Tourisme,* B-26. Centre des Hautes Etudes Touristiques, Aix-en-Provence, France.

Graburn, N.H. (1989) Tourism: the sacred journey. In: Smith, V.L. (ed.) *Hosts and Guests: The Anthropology of Tourism*. University of Pennsylvania Press, Philadelphia, Pennsylvania, pp. 21–36.

Graburn, N.H. and Moore, R.S. (1994) Anthropological research on tourism. In: Ritchie, J.R. Brent and Goeldner, C.R. (eds) *Travel, Tourism and Hospitality Research: A Handbook for Managers and Researchers*. John Wiley & Sons, New York, pp. 233–242.

Graillot, L. (1997) Un renouvellement de l'analyse du marché touristique français offert par l'intégration du concept du comportement exploratoire. In: Filser, M. and Bourgeon-Renault, D. (eds) *Marketing des Activités Culturelles, Touristiques et de Loisirs*. Actes de la 1ère Journée de Recherche en Marketing de Bourgogne, Dijon, France, pp. 3–13.

Green, R.T., Leonardi, J.P., Chandon, J.L., Cunningham, I., Verhage, B. and Strazzieri, A. (1983) Societal development and family purchasing roles: a cross-national study. *Journal of Consumer Research* 9, 436–442.

Grubb, E.L. and Stern, B.L. (1971) Self-concept and significant others. *Journal of Marketing Research* 8, 382–385.

Guba, E.G. and Lincoln, Y.S. (1994) Competing paradigms in qualitative research. In: Denzin, N.K. and Lincoln, Y.S. (eds) *Handbook of Qualitative Research*. Sage, Thousand Oaks, California, pp. 105–117.

Haider, W. and Ewing, G.O. (1990) A model of tourist choices of hypothetical Caribbean destinations. *Leisure Sciences* 12, 33–47.

Henderson, K.A. (1991) *Dimensions of Choice: A Qualitative Approach to Recreation, Parks and Leisure Research*. Venture Publishing, State College, Pennsylvania.

Hernandez, S.A., Cohen, J. and Garcia, H.L. (1996) Residents' attitudes towards an instant enclave resort. *Annals of Tourism Research* 23, 755–779.

Herold, E., Garcia, R. and DeMoya, T. (2001) Female tourists and beach boys: romance or sex tourism? *Annals of Tourism Research* 28, 978–997.

Hirschman, E.C. and Holbrook, M.B. (1982) Hedonic consumption: emerging concepts, methods and propositions. *Journal of Marketing* 46 (Summer), 92–101.

Hoch, S.J. and Ha, Y.W. (1986) Consumer learning: advertising and the ambiguity of product experience. *Journal of Consumer Research* 13, 221–233.

Hofstede, G. (2001) *Culture's Consequences: Comparing Values, Behaviors, Institutions and Organizations Across Nations*. Sage, Thousand Oaks, California.

Holbrook, M.B. (1984) Emotion in the consumption experience: toward a new model of the human consumer. In: Peterson, R.A., Hoyer, W.D. and Wilson,

W.R. (eds) *The Role of Affect in Consumer Behavior: Emerging Theories and Applications.* Lexington Books, Lexington, Kentucky, pp. 17–52.

Holbrook, M.B. and Batra, R. (1987) Assessing the role of emotions as mediators of consumer response to advertising. *Journal of Consumer Research* 14, 404–420.

Holbrook, M.B. and Hirschman, E.C. (1982) The experiential aspects of consumption: consumer fantasies, feelings and fun. *Journal of Consumer Research* 9, 132–140.

Hollier, R. and Subremon, A. (1992) *Le Tourisme dans la Communauté Européenne.* P.U.F., Paris.

Howard, D. and Madrigal, R. (1990) Who makes the decision: the parent or the child? The perceived influence of parents and children on the purchase of recreation services. *Journal of Leisure Research* 22, 244–258.

Howard, J.A. (1963) *Marketing Management, Analysis and Planning.* Richard D. Irwin, Homewood, Alaska.

Howard, J.A. (1977) *Consumer Behavior: An Application of Theory.* McGraw-Hill, New York.

Howard, J.A. and Sheth, J.N. (1969) *The Theory of Buyer Behavior.* John Wiley & Sons, New York.

Howard, J.A., Blumstein, P. and Schwartz, P. (1986) Sex, power and influence tactics in intimate relationships. *Journal of Personality and Social Psychology* 51, 102–109.

Hsieh, S., O'Leary, J.T. and Morrison, A.M. (1992) Segmenting the international travel market by activity. *Tourism Management* 13, 209–223.

Hsieh, S., O'Leary, J.T., Morrison, A.M. and Chiang, D. (1997) Travel decision pattern segmentation of pleasure travel. *Journal of Vacation Marketing* 3, 289–302.

Huberman, A.M. and Miles, M.B. (1994) Data management and analysis methods. In: Denzin, N.K. and Lincoln, Y.S. (eds) *Handbook of Qualitative Research.* Sage, Thousand Oaks, California, pp. 428–444.

Hudson, S. and Shephard, G.W. (1998) Measuring service quality at tourist destinations: an application of importance-performance analysis to an alpine ski resort. *Journal of Travel and Tourism Marketing* 7 (3), 61–77.

Hughes, E.C. (1937) Institutional office and the person. *American Journal of Sociology* 43, 404–413.

Hunt, S.D. (1991) *Modern Marketing Theory: Critical Issues in the Philosophy of Marketing Science.* SouthWestern Publishing, Cincinnati, Ohio.

Hyde, K. (1998) A hedonic perspective on independent vacation planning, decision-making and behaviour. Paper presented at the Symposium on the Consumer Psychology of Travel, Hospitality and Leisure Research, Hilo, Hawaii, August.

Jackson, E.L. (1997) In the eye of the beholder: a comment on Samdahl and Jekubovich (1997): 'a critique of leisure constraints: comparative analyses and understandings'. *Journal of Leisure Research*, 29(4), 458–468.

Jackson, E.L., Crawford, D.W. and Godbey, G. (1993) Negotiation of leisure constraints. *Leisure Sciences* 15, 1–11.

Jacoby, J. and Kyner, D.B. (1973) Brand loyalty vs. repeat purchasing behavior. *Journal of Marketing Research* 9 (February), 1–9.

Janis, I.L. (1983) *Groupthink: Psychological Studies of Foreign Policy Decisions and Fiascoes.* Houghton Mifflin, Boston, Massachusetts.

Jansen, C. (1969) Some sociological aspects of migration. In: Jackson, J.A. (ed.) *Migration*. Cambridge University Press, Cambridge, pp. 60–73.

Jeng, J.M. and Fesenmaier, D.R. (1997) Facets of the complex trip decision-making process. In: *The Evolution of Tourism: Adapting to Change*. Proceedings of the 28th Annual Conference of the Travel and Tourism Research Association. Travel and Tourism Research Association, Lexington, Kentucky, pp. 32–41.

Jenkins, R.L. (1978) Family vacation decision-making. *Journal of Travel Research* 16 (Spring), 2–7.

Johnson, E.J. and Russo, J.E. (1978) The organization of product information in memory identified recall times. *Advances in Consumer Research* 5, 79–86.

Johnson, M.D. (1984) Consumer choice strategies for comparing noncomparable alternatives. *Journal of Consumer Research* 11, 741–753.

Johnson, M.D. (1986) Modeling choice strategies for noncomparable alternatives. *Marketing Science* 5, 37–54.

Judd, G.E. (1964) The case for redefining services. *Journal of Marketing* 28 (January), 58–59.

Kahneman, D. and Miller, D.T. (1986) Norm theory: comparing reality to its alternatives. *Psychological Review* 93, 136–153.

Kahneman, D. and Tversky, A. (1979) Prospect theory: an analysis of decisions under risk. *Econometrica* 47, 263–291.

Kelley, H.H. (1973) The process of causal attribution. *American Psychologist*, 28, 107–128.

Kent, P. (1990) People, places and priorities: opportunity sets and consumers' holiday choice. In: Ashworth, G.J. and Goodall, B. (eds) *Marketing Tourism Places*. Routledge, London, pp. 42–62.

Kirchler, E. (1993) Spouses' joint purchase decisions: determinants of influence tactics for muddling through the process. *Journal of Economic Psychology* 14, 405–438.

Kirchler, E. (1995) Studying economic decisions within private households: a critical review and design for a 'couple experiences diary'. *Journal of Economic Psychology* 16, 393–419.

Koppelman, S.F. (1980) Consumer analysis of travel choice. *Journal of Advanced Transportation* 14, 133–159.

Kotler, P. (2003) *Marketing Management*, 11th edn. Prentice Hall, Upper Saddle River, New Jersey.

Lackman, C. and Lasana, J.M. (1993) Family decision-making theory: an overview and assessment. *Psychology and Marketing* 10, 81–93.

Lancaster, J.K. (1971) *Consumer Demand: A New Approach*. Columbia University Press, New York.

Lancaster, K.J. (1966) A new approach to consumer theory. *Journal of Political Economy* 74, 132–157.

Lang, C.-T. and O'Leary, J.T. (1997) Motivation, participation and preference: a multi-segmentation approach of the Australian nature travel market. *Journal of Travel and Tourism Marketing* 6, 159–180.

Lang, C.-T., O'Leary, J.T. and Morrison, A.M. (1997) Distinguishing the destination choices of pleasure travelers from Taiwan. *Journal of Travel and Tourism Marketing* 6 (1), 21–40.

Laurent, G. and Kapferer, J.-N. (1985) Measuring consumer involvement profiles. *Journal of Marketing Research* 22, 41–53.

Lefkoff-Hagius, R. and Mason, C. (1993) Characteristic, beneficial and image attributes in consumer judgments of similarity and preference. *Journal of Consumer Research* 20, 100–110.

Lett, J. (1983) Ludic and liminoid aspects of charter yacht tourism in the Caribbean. *Annals of Tourism Research* 10, 35–56.

Lévi-Strauss, C. (1955) *Tristes Tropiques*. Plon, Paris.

Lewin, K. (1936) *Principles of Topological Psychology*. McGraw-Hill, New York.

Lewin, K. (1951) *Field Theory in Social Science*. Harper & Row, New York.

Lincoln, Y.S. and Guba, E. (1985) *Naturalistic Inquiry*. Sage, Beverly Hills, California.

Lindblom, C.E. (1959) The science of 'Muddling Through'. *Public Administration Review* 19, 79–88.

Loomes, G. and Sugden, R. (1982) Regret theory: an alternative theory of rational choice under uncertainty. *The Economic Journal* 92, 805–824.

Lounsbury, J.W. and Hoopes, L.L. (1985) An investigation of factors associated with vacation satisfaction. *Journal of Leisure Research* 17, 1–13.

Louviere, J.J. (1988) *Analyzing Decision Making: Metric Conjoint Analysis*. Sage, Beverly Hills, California.

Lowyck, E., Van Langenhove, L. and Bollaert, L. (1992) Typologies of tourist roles. In: Johnson, P. and Thomas, B. (eds) *Choice and Demand in Tourism*. Mansell, London, pp. 13–32.

Lysonski, S., Durvasula, S. and Zotos, Y. (1996) Consumer decision-making styles: a multi-country investigation. *European Journal of Marketing* 30 (12), 10–21.

MacCannell, D. (1973) Staged authenticity: arrangements of social space in tourist settings. *American Sociological Review* 79, 589–603.

MacCannell, D. (1976) *The Tourist: A New Theory of the Leisure Class*. Schocken Books, New York.

MacInnis, D.J. and Price, L.L. (1987) The role of imagery in information processing: review and extensions. *Journal of Consumer Research* 13, 473–491.

Madrigal, R. and Kahle, L.R. (1994) Predicting vacation activity preferences on the basis of value-system segmentation. *Journal of Travel Research* 33, 22–28.

Malle, B.F. (1999) How people explain behavior: a new theoretical framework. *Personality and Social Psychology Review*, 3(1), 23–48.

Mangalam, J. (1968) *Human Migration*. University of Kentucky Press, Lexington, Kentucky.

Mangleburg, T.F. (1990) Children's influence in purchase decisions: a review and critique. *Advances in Consumer Research* 17, 813–825.

Mansfeld, Y. (1992) Tourism: towards a behavioural approach. The choice of destination and its impact on spatial behaviour. *Progress in Planning* 38, 1–92.

Mansfeld, Y. (1994) The 'value stretch' model and its implementation in detecting tourists' class-differentiated destination choice. In: Gasser, R.V. and Weiermair, K. (eds) *Spoilt for Choice. Decision Making Processes and Preference Change of Tourists: Intertemporal and Intercountry Perspectives*. Kulturverlag, Thaur, Germany, pp. 60–79.

Mansfield, E. (1989) *Principles of Microeconomics*. W.W. Norton, New York.

Mantel, S.P. and Kardes, F.R. (1999) The role of direction of comparison: attribute-based processing and attitude-based processing in consumer preferences. *Journal of Consumer Research* 25, 335–352.

March, J.G. (1994) *A Primer on Decision Making: How Decisions Happen.* Free Press, New York.

March, J.G. and Simon, H.A. (1958) *Organizations.* John Wiley & Sons, New York.

Marshall, C. and Rossman, G.B. (1995) *Designing Qualitative Research.* Sage, Thousand Oaks, California.

Martilla, J.A. and James, J.C. (1977) Importance-performance analysis. *Journal of Marketing* 41 (1), 13–17.

Mäser, B. and Weiermair K. (1998) Travel decision-making: from the vantage point of perceived risk and information preferences. *Journal of Travel and Tourism Marketing* 7, 107–121.

Maslow, A. (1954) *Motivation and Personality.* Harper & Row, New York.

Mathieson, A. and Wall, G. (1982) *Tourism: Economic, Physical and Social Impacts.* Longman, Harlow, New York.

Maule, A.J. and Svenson, O. (1993) Theoretical and empirical approaches to behavioral decision making and their relation to time constraints. In: Svenson, O. and Maule, A.J. (eds) *Time Pressure and Stress in Human Judgment and Decision Making.* Plenum Press, New York, pp. 3–25.

May, K.O. (1954) Intransitivity, utility and the aggregation of preference patterns. *Econometrica* 22, 1–13.

Mayo, E.J. and Jarvis, L.P. (1981) *The Psychology of Leisure Travel.* CBI Publishing, Boston, Massachusetts.

Mazanec, J.A. (1994) Segmenting travel markets. In: Teare, R., Mazanec, J.A., Crawford-Welch, S. and Calver, S. (eds) *Marketing in Hospitality and Tourism: A Consumer Focus.* Cassell, London, pp. 99–166.

Mazursky, D. (1989) Past experience and future tourism decisions. *Annals of Tourism Research* 16, 333–344.

McCracken, G. (1988) *Culture and Consumption.* Indiana University Press, Indianapolis.

McIntosh, R.W., Goeldner, C.R. and Ritchie, J.R. Brent (1995) *Tourism: Principles, Practices, Philosophies.* John Wiley & Sons, New York.

Middleton, V.T. (1994) *Marketing in Travel and Tourism,* 2nd edn. Butterworth-Heinemann, Oxford.

Middleton, V.T. and Clarke, J. (2001) *Marketing in Travel and Tourism,* 3rd edn. Butterworth-Heinemann, Oxford.

Miller, G.A., Galanter, E. and Pribram, K.H. (1960) *Plans and the Structure of Behavior.* Holt, Rinehart & Winston, New York.

Miller, W.L. and Crabtree, B.F. (1994) Clinical research. In: Denzin, N.K. and Lincoln, Y.S. (eds) *Handbook of Qualitative Research.* Sage, Thousand Oaks, California, pp. 340–352.

Mittal, B. (1988) The role of affective choice mode in the consumer purchase of expressive products. *Journal of Economic Psychology* 9, 499–524.

Mo, C., Howard, D.R. and Havitz, M.E. (1993) Testing an international tourist role typology. *Annals of Tourism Research* 20, 319–335.

Morley, C.L. (1992) A microeconomic theory of international tourism demand. *Annals of Tourism Research* 19, 250–267.

Morley, C.L. (1994) Experimental destination choice analysis. *Annals of Tourism Research* 21, 780–791.

Moscardo, G., Morrison, A.M., Pearce, P.L., Lang, C. and O'Leary, J.T. (1996) Understanding vacation destination choice through travel motivation and activities. *Journal of Vacation Marketing* 2, 109–122.

Mottiar, Z. and Quinn, D. (2004) Couple dynamics in household tourism decision-making: women as the gatekeepers? *Journal of Vacation Marketing* 10, 149–160.

Moutinho, L. (1987) Consumer behaviour in tourism. *European Journal of Marketing* 21 (10), 2–44.

Mullen, B. and Johnson, C. (1990) *The Psychology of Consumer Behavior.* Lawrence Erlbaum, Hillsdale, New Jersey.

Murray, H.A. (1938) *Explorations in Personality.* Oxford University Press, New York.

Narayana, C.L. and Markin, R.J. (1975) Consumer behavior and product performance: an alternative conceptualization. *Journal of Marketing* 39 (Fall), 1–6.

Nash, D. (1989) Tourism as a form of imperialism. In: Smith, V.L. (ed.) *Hosts and Guests: The Anthropology of Tourism.* University of Pennsylvania Press, Philadelphia, Pennsylvania, pp. 37–54.

Nash, D. (1996) *Anthropology of Tourism.* Pergamon Press, Kidlington, UK.

Nedungadi, P. (1990) Recall and consumer consideration sets: influencing choice without altering brand evaluations. *Journal of Consumer Research* 17, 263–276.

Nelson, M.C. (1988) The resolution of conflict in joint purchase decisions of husbands and wives: a review and empirical test. *Advances in Consumer Research* 15, 436–441.

Nichols, C.M. and Snepenger, D.J. (1988) Family decision making and tourism behavior and attitudes. *Journal of Travel Research* 26 (Spring), 2–6.

Nicosia, F.M. (1966) *Consumer Decision Processes: Marketing and Advertising Implications.* Prentice-Hall, Englewood Cliffs, New Jersey.

Nolan, S.D. (1976) Tourists' use and evaluation of travel information sources: summary and conclusions. *Journal of Travel Research* 14, 6–8.

Nuñez, T. (1989) Touristic studies in anthropological perspective. In: Smith, V.L. (ed.) *Hosts and Guests: The Anthropology of Tourism.* University of Pennsylvania Press, Philadelphia, Pennsylvania, pp. 265–279.

Oliver, R.L. (1980) A cognitive model of the antecedents and consequences of satisfaction decisions. *Journal of Marketing Research* 17, 460–469.

Oliver, R.L. and Swan, J.E. (1989) Consumer perceptions of interpersonal equity and satisfaction in transactions: a field survey approach. *Journal of Marketing* 53, 21–35.

Oppedijk van Veen, W.M. (1983) Consumentenonderzoek als basis voor strategieontwikkeling in de recreatiesector. Paper NVM-marktonderzoekdag.

Ozanne, J.L. and Hudson, L.A. (1989) Exploring diversity in consumer research. In: Hirschman, E.C. (ed.) *Interpretive Consumer Research.* Association for Consumer Research, Provo, Utah, pp. 1–9.

Papandreou, A.G. (1953) An experimental test of an axiom in the theory of choice. *Econometrica* 21, 477.

Papatheodorou, A. (2001) Why people travel to different places. *Annals of Tourism Research* 28, 164–179.

Parasuraman, A., Zeithaml, V.A. and Berry, L.L. (1988) SERVQUAL: a multiple-item scale for measuring consumer perceptions of service quality. *Journal of Retailing* 64 (Spring), 12–43.

Park, C.W. and Lutz, R.J. (1982) Decision plans and consumer choice dynamics. *Journal of Marketing Research* 19, 108–115.

Parker, S. (1983) *Leisure and Work*. Allen & Unwin, Massachusetts.

Pasqualini, J.-P. and Jacquet, B. (1992) *Tourismes en Europe*. Dunod, Paris.

Patton, M.Q. (1990) *Qualitative Evaluation and Research Methods*. Sage, Newbury Park, California.

Payne, J.W. (1982) Contingent decision behavior. *Psychological Bulletin* 92, 382–402.

Payne, J.W., Bettman, J.R. and Johnson, E.J. (1993) *The Adaptive Decision Maker*. Cambridge University Press, Cambridge, UK.

Pearce, P. and Moscardo, G. (1986) The concept of authenticity in tourist experiences. *Australian and New Zealand Journal of Sociology* 22, 121–132.

Pearce, P.L. (1982) *The Social Psychology of Tourist Behavior*. Pergamon Press, Oxford, UK.

Pearce, P.L. (1988) *The Ulysses Factor: Evaluating Visitors in Tourist Settings*. Springer-Verlag, New York.

Pechmann, C. and Ratneshwar, S. (1992) Consumer covariation judgments: theory or data driven? *Journal of Consumer Research* 19, 373–386.

Peterson, R.A., Hoyer, W.D. and Wilson, W.R. (1986) *The Role of Affect in Consumer Behavior: Emerging Theories and Applications*. D.C. Heath, Lexington, Kentucky.

Pettigrew, A. (1973) *The Politics of Organizational Decision Making*. Tavistosck, London.

Pfeffer, J. (1981) *Power in Organizations*. Pittman Publishing, Boston, Massachusetts.

Phelps, A. (1986) Holiday destination image – the problem of assessment : an example developed in Menorca. *Tourism Management* 7, 168–180.

Phillips, D.M., Olson, J.C. and Baumgartner, H. (1995) Consumption visions in consumer decision-making. *Advances in Consumer Research* 22, 280–284.

Pine, J. and Gilmore, J. (1999) *The Experience Economy*. Horward Business School Press, Boston, Massachusetts.

Pizam, A., Neuman, Y. and Reichel, A. (1978) Dimensions of tourist satisfaction with a destination area. *Annals of Tourism Research* 5, 314–322.

Plog, S.C. (1972) Why destination areas rise and fall in popularity. Paper presented to the Travel Research Association (Southern California Chapter), Los Angeles, October.

Plog, S.C. (1974) Why destination areas rise and fall in popularity. *Cornell Hotel and Restaurant Administration Quarterly* 14 (4), 55–58.

Plog, S.C. (1994) Developing and using psychographics in tourism research. In: Ritchie, J.R. and Goeldner, C.R. (eds) *Travel, Tourism and Hospitality Research: A Handbook for Managers and Researchers*. John Wiley & Sons, New York, pp. 209–218.

Plutchik, R. (1980) *Emotion: A Psychoevolutionary Synthesis*. Harper & Row, New York.

Price, L.L. and Arnould, E.J. (1999) Commercial friendships: service provider–client relationships in context. *Journal of Marketing* 63, 38–56.

Puto, C.P. (1987) The framing of buying decisions. *Journal of Consumer Research* 14, 301–315.

Ratchford, B.T. (1987) New insights about the FCB grid. *Journal of Advertising Research* 27 (4), 24–38.

Rauch, A. (1993) *Les Vacances*. Presses Universitaires de France, Paris.

Raymore, L. (2002) Facilitators to leisure. *Journal of Leisure Research*, 34(1), 37–51.

Redfoot, D. (1984) Touristic authenticity, touristic angst and modern reality. *Qualitative Sociology* 7, 291–309.

Reid, I.S. and Crompton, J.L. (1993) A taxonomy of leisure purchase decision paradigms based on level of involvement. *Journal of Leisure Research* 25, 182–202.

Riley, R. (1995) Prestige worthy leisure travel behavior. *Annals of Tourism Research* 22, 630–649.

Ritchie, J.R. (1994) Research on leisure behavior and tourism: state of the art. In: Gasser, R.V. and Weiermair, K. (eds) *Spoilt for Choice. Decision Making Processes and Preference Change of Tourists: Intertemporal and Intercountry Perspectives*. Kulturverlag, Thaur, Germany, pp. 2–27.

Rodman, H. (1963) The lower class value stretch. *Social Forces* 42, 205–215.

Rosch, E.H. (1978) Principles of categorization. In: Rosch, E.H. and Lloyd, B. (eds) *Cognition and Categorization*. Lawrence Erlbaum, Hillsdale, New Jersey, pp. 27–48.

Rosch, E.H., Mervis, C.B., Gray, W.D., Johnson, D.M. and Boyes-Braem, P. (1976) Basic objects in natural categories. *Cognitive Psychology* 8, 382–439.

Rosenberg, M.J. and Hovland, C.I. (1960) *Attitude Organization and Change*. Yale University Press, New York.

Ross, G.F. (1994) *The Psychology of Tourism*. Hospitality Press, Melbourne.

Rossiter, J.R., Percy, L. and Donovan, R.J. (1991) A better advertising planning grid. *Journal of Advertising Research* 31 (October/November), 11–21.

Rothschild, M.L. (1979) Marketing communications in non-business situations or why it's so hard to sell brotherhood like soap. *Journal of Marketing* 43, 11–20.

Rubin, H.J. and Rubin I.S. (1995) *Qualitative Interviewing: The Art of Hearing Data*. Sage, Thousand Oaks, California.

Rugg, D. (1973) The choice of journey destination: a theoretical and empirical analysis. *The Review of Economics and Statistics* 55, 64–72.

Russo, J.E. (1977) The value of unit price information. *Journal of Marketing Research* 14, 193–201.

Russo, J.E. (1978) Eye fixations can save the world: critical evaluation and comparison between eye fixations and other information processing methodologies. *Advances in Consumer Research* 5, 561–570.

Ryan, C. (1992) The child as a visitor. *World Travel and Tourism Review,* 135–139.

Ryan, C. (1995) *Researching Tourist Satisfaction: Issues, Concepts, Problems*. Routledge, London.

Ryan, C. (1999) From the psychometrics of SERVQUAL to sex: measurements of tourist satisfaction. In: Pizam, A. and Mansfeld, Y. (eds) *Consumer Behavior in Travel and Tourism*. Haworth Hospitality Press, New York, pp. 267–286.

Ryan, C. and Cliff, A. (1997) Do travel agencies measure up to customer expectations? An empirical investigation of travel agencies service quality

as measured by SERVQUAL. *Journal of Travel and Tourism Marketing* 6
(2), 1–32.
Samdahl, D.M. and Jekubovich, N.J. (1997) A critique of leisure constraints: com-
parative analyses and understandings. *Journal of Leisure Research*, 29(4),
430–452.
Schmoll, G.A. (1977) *Tourism Promotion: Marketing Background, Promotion
Techniques and Promotion Planning Methods.* Tourism International Press,
London.
Schofield, P. (1999) Developing a day trip expectation/satisfaction construct: a
comparative analysis of scale construction techniques. *Journal of Travel and
Tourism Marketing* 8 (3), 101–110.
Seaton, A.V. and Tagg, S. (1995) The family vacation in Europe: paedonomic
aspects of choices and satisfactions. *Journal of Travel and Tourism Marketing*
4 (1), 1–21.
Seddighi, H.R. and Theocharous, A.L. (2002) A model of tourism destination choice:
a theoretical and empirical analysis. *Tourism Management* 23, 475–487.
Sharp, H. and Mott, P. (1956) Consumer decision-making in the metropolitan
family. *Journal of Marketing* 21, 149–156.
Shaw, M.E. (1976) *Group Dynamics: The Psychology of Small Group Behavior*,
2nd edn. McGraw-Hill, New York.
Shaw, M.E. and Wright, J.M. (1967) *Scales for the Measurement of Attitudes.*
McGraw-Hill, New York.
Shepard, R.N. (1964) On subjectively optimum selection among multiattribute
alternatives. In: Shelly II, M.W. and Bryan, G.L. (eds) *Human Judgments and
Optimality.* John Wiley & Sons, New York.
Shields, R. (1990) *Places on the Margin.* Routledge, London.
Shoemaker, S. (1994) Segmentation of the U.S. travel market according to benefits
realized. *Journal of Travel Research* 32 (3), 8–21.
Simon, H. (1957) *Models of Man: Social and Rational.* John Wiley & Sons, New York.
Simon, H.A. (1955) A behavioral model of rational choice. *Quaterly Journal of
Economics* 69, 99–118.
Slovic, P., Fischhoff, B. and Lichtenstein, S. (1977) Behavioral decision theory.
Annual Review of Psychology 28, 1–39.
Smith, V.L. (1989) *Hosts and Guests: the Anthropology of Tourism*, 2nd edn.
University of Pennsylvania Press, Philadelphia, Pennsylvania.
Smith, V.L. (ed.) (1992) Pilgrimage and tourism. *Annals of Tourism Research*
(Special Issue) 19 (1), 1–171.
Spotts, D.M. and Mahoney, E.M. (1991) Segmenting visitors to a destination region
based on the volume of their expenditures. *Journal of Travel Research*
29 (Summer), 24–31.
Sproles, G.B. and Kendall, E.L. (1986) A methodology for profiling consumer decision-making styles. *The Journal of Consumer Affairs* 20, 267–279.
Stapel, D.A., Koomen, W. and Van Der Pligt, J. (1997) Categories of category
accessability: the impact of trait versus exemplar priming on person judgements. *Journal of Personality and Social Psychology* 33, 44–76.
Stern, B.B., Thompson, C.J. and Arnould, E.J. (1998) Narrative analysis of a marketing relationship: the consumer's perspective. *Psychology and Marketing*,
15(3), 195–214.

Strauss, A. and Corbin, J. (1990) *Basics of Qualitative Research: Grounded Theory Procedures and Techniques.* Sage, Newbury Park, California.

Sujan, M. (1985) Consumer knowledge: effects on evaluation strategies mediating consumer judgments. *Journal of Consumer Research* 12, 31–46.

Sussmann, S. and Unel, A. (1999) Destination image and its modification after travel: an empirical study on Turkey. In: Pizam, A. and Mansfeld, Y. (eds) *Consumer Behavior in Travel and Tourism.* Haworth Hospitality Press, New York, pp. 207–226.

Svenson, O. (1979) Process descriptions of decision making. *Organizational Behavior and Human Performance* 23, 86–112.

Svenson, O. (1996) Decision making and the search for fundamental psychological regularities: what can be learned from a process perspective? *Organizational Behavior and Human Decision Processes* 65, 252–267.

Swarbrooke, J. and Horner, S. (1999) *Consumer Behaviour in Tourism.* Butterworth-Heinemann, London.

Taylor, J.W. (1974) The role of risk in consumer behavior. *Journal of Marketing* 38 (April), 54–60.

Taylor, R.C. (1969) Migration and motivation: a study of determinants and types. In: Jackson, J.A. (ed.) *Migration.* Cambridge University Press, Cambridge, UK, pp. 99–133.

Taylor, S.J. and Bogdan, R. (1984) *Introduction to Qualitative Research: The Search for Meanings.* John Wiley & Sons, New York.

Teare, R. (1994) Consumer decision making. In: Teare, R., Mazanec, J.A., Crawford-Welch, S. and Calver, S. (eds) *Marketing in Hospitality and Tourism: A Consumer Focus.* Cassell, London, pp. 1–96.

Teare, R. and Boer, A. (1991) *Strategic Hospitality Management: Theory and Practice for the 1990s.* Cassell, London.

Thomas, D.S. (1941) *Social and Economic Aspects of Swedish Population Movements 1750–1933.* Macmillan, New York.

Thompson, J.R. and Cooper, R.D. (1979) Additional evidence on the limited size of evoked and inept sets of travel destinations. *Journal of Travel Research* 18 (Winter), 23–25.

Thornton, P.R., Shaw, G. and Williams, A.M. (1997) Tourist group holiday decision-making and behaviour: the influence of children. *Tourism Management* 18, 287–297.

Thrane, C. (1997) Values as segmentation criteria in tourism research: the Norwegian Monitor approach. *Tourism Management* 18, 111–113.

Tolman, E.C. (1932) *Purposive Behaviour: Animals and Men.* Century, New York.

Turner, L. and Ash, J. (1975) *The Golden Hordes.* Constable, London.

Turner, V. (1973) The center out there: pilgrim's goal. *History of Religions* 12, 191–230.

Turner, V. (1974) *The Ritual Process.* Penguin, Harmondsworth, UK.

Turner, V. and Turner, E. (1978) *Image and Pilgrimage in Christian Culture.* Columbia University Press, New York.

Tversky, A. (1977) Features of Similarity. *Psychological Review* 84, 327–352.

Tversky, A. and Kahneman, D. (1981) The framing of decisions and the psychology of choice. *Science* 211, 453–458.

Um, S. (1990) The roles of perceived inhibitors and perceived facilitators in the pleasure travel destination choice process. In: *The Tourism Connection:*

Linking Research and Marketing. Proceedings of the 21st Annual Conference of the Travel and Tourism Research Association. Bureau of Economic and Business Research, Salt Lake City, Utah, pp. 7–11.

Um, S. and Crompton, J.L. (1990) Attitude determinants in tourism destination choice. *Annals of Tourism Research* 17, 432–448.

Unger, L.S. and Kernan, J.B. (1983) On the meaning of leisure: an investigation of some determinants of the subjective experience. *Journal of Consumer Research* 9, 381–392.

Urry, J. (1990) *The Tourist Gaze: Leisure and Travel in Contemporary Societies*. Sage, London.

Urry, J. (1995) *Consuming Places*. Routledge, London.

van Gennep, A. (1909) *Les Rites de Passage: Etude Systématique des Rites*. Nourry, Paris.

van Raaij, W.F. (1977) Consumer information processing for different information structures and formats. *Advances in Consumer Research* 4, 176–184.

van Raaij, W.F. (1986) Consumer research on tourism: mental and behavioral constructs. *Annals of Tourism Research* 13, 1–9.

van Raaij, W.F. and Francken, D.A. (1984) Vacations decisions, activities and satisfaction. *Annals of Tourism Research* 11, 101–112.

Vaughn, R. (1980) How advertising works: a planning model. *Journal of Advertising Research* 20 (5), 27–33.

Veblen, T. (1899) *The Theory of the Leisure Class*. Viking Press, New York.

Von Neumann, J. and Morgenstern, O. (1944) *Theory of Games and Economic Behavior*. Princeton University Press, Princeton, New Jersey.

Wahab, S., Crampon, L.J. and Rothfield, L.M. (1976) *Tourism Marketing*. Tourism International Press, London.

Walters, C.G. and Bergiel, B.J. (1989) *Consumer Behavior: A Decision-Making Approach*. SouthWestern Publishing, Cincinnati, Ohio.

Ward, J.C. and Reingen, P.H. (1990) A sociocognitive analysis of group decision-making among consumers. *Journal of Consumer Research* 17, 245–262.

Weiermair, K. and Fuchs, M. (1999) Measuring tourist judgment on service quality. *Annals of Tourism Research* 26, 1004–1021.

Weitzman, E. and Miles, M.B. (1995) *Computer Programs for Qualitative Analysis*. Sage, Thousand Oaks, California.

Westbrook, R.A. (1980) Interpersonal influences on customer satisfaction with products. *Journal of Consumer Research* 7, 49–53.

Westbrook, R.A. (1987) Product consumption based affective purchases and post-purchase processes. *Journal of Marketing Research* 24, 258–270.

Westbrook, R.A. and Newman, J.W. (1978) An analysis of shopper dissatisfaction for major household appliances. *Journal of Marketing Research* 15, 456–466.

Westbrook, R.A. and Oliver, R. (1991) The dimensionality of consumption emotion patterns and consumer satisfaction. *Journal of Consumer Research* 18, 84–91.

Wickens, E. (2002) The sacred and the profane: a tourist typology. *Annals of Tourism Research* 29, 834–851.

Wilkie, W.L. (1990) *Consumer Behavior*. John Wiley & Sons, New York.

Wilson, E.J. and Wilson, D.T. (1988) 'Degrees of freedom' in case research of behavioral theories of group buying. *Advances in Consumer Research* 15, 587–594.

Woodruff, R.B., Cadotte, E.R. and Jenkins, R.L. (1983) Modeling consumer satisfaction processes using experience-based norms. *Journal of Marketing Research* 20, 296–304.

Woodside, A.G. (2005) *Market-Driven Thinking: Achieving Contextual Intelligence.* Butterworth Heinemann, Amsterdam.

Woodside, A.G. and Bearden, W.O. (1978) Field theory applied to consumer theory. In: Sheth, J.N. (ed.) *Research in Marketing*, Vol. 1. JAI Press, Stanford, Connecticut.

Woodside, A.G. and Carr, J.A. (1988) Consumer decision making and competitive marketing strategies: applications for tourism planning. *Journal of Travel Research* 27 (Winter), 2–7.

Woodside, A.G. and Jacobs, L.W. (1985) Step two in benefit segmentation: learning the benefits realized by major travel markets. *Journal of Travel Research* 23 (Fall), 14–24.

Woodside, A.G. and Lysonski, S. (1989) A general model of traveler destination choice. *Journal of Travel Research* 27 (Spring), 8–14.

Woodside, A.G. and MacDonald, R. (1994) General system framework of customer choice processes of tourism services. In: Gasser, R.V. and Weiermair, K. (eds) *Spoilt for Choice. Decision Making Processes and Preference Change of Tourists: Intertemporal and Intercountry Perspectives.* Kulturverlag, Thaur, Germany, pp. 30–59.

Woodside, A.G. and Sherrell, D. (1977) Traveler evoked, inept and inert sets of vacation destinations. *Journal of Travel Research* 16 (Winter), 14–18.

Woodside, A.G. and Wilson, E.J. (1995) Applying the long interview in direct marketing research. *Journal of Direct Marketing*, 9(1), 37–55.

Woodside, A.G. and Wilson, E.J. (2003) Case study research methods for theory building. *Journal of Business & Industrial Marketing*, 18(6/7), 493–508.

Woodside, A.G., Cooke, V.J. and Mindak, W. (1987) Profiling the heavy traveler segment. *Journal of Travel Research* 25, 9–14.

Woodside, A.G., MacDonald, R. and Burford, M. (2004) Grounded theory of leisure travel. *Journal of Travel and Tourism Marketing*, 17(1), 7–40.

Woodside, A.G., Caldwell, M. and Spurr, R. (2005) Advancing ecological systems theory in lifestyle, leisure, and travel research. *Journal of Travel Research*, forthcoming.

WTO (1995) *Concepts, Definitions and Classifications for Tourism Statistics.* Technical Manual No. 1. World Tourism Organization, Madrid, Spain.

Yin, R.K. (1989) *Case Study Research: Design and Methods.* Sage, Beverly Hills, California.

Zajonc, R.B. (1978) Preferanda and discriminanda: processing of affect. Paper presented at the Symposium on New Directions in Experimental Aesthetics, 86th Annual Convention of the American Psychological Association, Toronto, Canada.

Zajonc, R.B. and Markus, H. (1982) Affective and cognitive factors in preferences. *Journal of Consumer Research* 9, 123–131.

Zalatan, A. (1994) Tourist satisfaction: a predetermined model. *Revue de Tourisme* 1, 9–13.

Zeithaml, V.A. (1981) How consumer evaluation processes differ between goods and services. In: Donnelly, J.H. and George, W.R. (eds) *Marketing for Services.* American Marketing Association, Chicago, Illinois.

Appendix

1

A Summary of Existing Models of Vacation Decision Making.

Model	Theoretical foundations	Stages/steps	Major variables	Methodology	Tourist product(s)
A. Microeconomic models					
Rugg (1973)	Lancaster (1966)	None	Product characteristics (e.g. scenic beauty or historical attractions) Constraints: • consumption technology • budget (money and time transport and stay costs)	Least squared regression	Destinations
Haider and Ewing (1990)	Bjorklund and King (1982); Louviere (1988)	None	Destination preferences (DV) Characteristics of the accommodation Distance of relevant tourist facilities Price	Experimental design, discrete choice model	Caribbean destinations and accommodations

Continued

A Summary of Existing Models of Vacation Decision Making. – *cont'd*

Model	Theoretical foundations	Stages/steps	Major variables	Methodology	Tourist product(s)
Morley (1992, 1994)	Lancaster (1966); Rugg (1973)	1. Decision to travel or not 2. Time and budget allocations 3. Choice of tour	Country of destination Individual characteristics: income, time available, demographics Destination characteristics: time in transit, price	Experimental design, stated preference data and discrete choice model	Tour (involving stays at one destination, i.e. Sydney)
Papatheodorou (2001)	Lancaster (1966); Gorman (1980)	None	Expenditure and time constraints Prices Consumer preferences Quality, information and advertising Tourism agglomeration Competition (emergence of a new destination)	None	Destinations
Seddighi and Theocharous (2002)	Lancaster (1966); Koppelman (1980)	1. Vacation or no vacation decision 2. Domestic or foreign destination decision 3. Abstraction process:	Revisit intention (DV) Perceptions or feelings of product characteristics Personal characteristics Destination experience	Logit analysis	Destination (Cyprus)

Continued

	systems characteristics are used as DM criteria 4. Aggregation process: perceptions and feelings are transformed into a preference ordering 5. Choice (preferences may be modified due to situational constraints)	Political instability	Survey (longitudinal) Quantitative analysis (t-tests)	Destination

B. Cognitive models

Crompton (1977); Um and Crompton (1990)	Howard and Sheth (1969); Fishbein and Ajzen (1975); Belk (1975); Assael (1984)	1. Generic decision 2. Destination decision: • evolution from an awareness set to an evoked set • selection from the evoked set	Consideration sets, beliefs, attitudes, situational constraints

A Summary of Existing Models of Vacation Decision Making. – *cont'd*

Model	Theoretical foundations	Stages/steps	Major variables	Methodology	Tourist product(s)
Mathieson and Wall (1982)	Schmoll (1977); Wahab *et al.* (1976)	1. Felt need (travel desire) 2. Information collection and evaluation 3. Travel decisions 4. Preparations and experience 5. Satisfaction evaluation	Awareness, desire, image of destination		Focus on destination but 'the decision to travel precipitates a series of subsequent decisions, including choice of destination, model of travel, length of stay and type of accommodation' (p. 31)
Moutinho (1982, 1987)	Nicosia (1966); Howard and Sheth (1969); Fishbein (1970); Engel *et al.* (1973)	1. Tourism need arousal 2. Information search 3. Decisions on different vacation items (e.g. destination) 4. Travel preparation	Preference, decision, purchase, (dis)satisfaction, repeat-buying	Survey Quantitative analysis (facet theory + bivariate analysis)	Any Destination is a compulsory subdecision among other travel subdecisions
van Raaij and Francken (1984); van Raaij (1986)	Engel and Blackwell (1982)	1. Generic decision 2. Information search 3. Joint decision making	Interaction process, lifestyle, vacation sequence (see on the left)		Any

Goodall (1988)	Mathieson and Wall (1982)	4. Vacation activities 5. (Dis)satisfaction 1. Vacation selection process: • motivations • image formation 2. Choice of resort: • search process • evaluation of alternatives	Motivation, images, expectation, perception, preference		Ambiguous: there seems to be a distinction between vacation (including destination) and resort choices but, in fact, there is much confusion.
Woodside and Lysonski (1989)	Axelrod (1968); Howard and Sheth (1969)		Destination awareness (consideration set), preferences, intentions, situational variables, choice	Survey Quantitative analysis (constant-sum approach)	Destination
Mansfeld (1992)	Mathieson and Wall (1982); random utility theory	1. Generic decision 2. Information search 3. Elimination and assessment of alternatives 4. Actual choice	Motivation, information, evaluation, group decision making		Destination

Continued

A Summary of Existing Models of Vacation Decision Making. – *cont'd*

Model	Theoretical foundations	Stages/steps	Major variables	Methodology	Tourist product(s)
Middleton (1994)	Allport (1935); Maslow (1954); Chisnall (1985)	Stimulus-response model	Needs, wants and goals Perception, attitude		Any Distinction between: 1. Convenience goods (routinized problem solving) 2. Shopping goods (extensive problem solving)
C. Interpretive frameworks					
Woodside and MacDonald (1994)	Lewin (1936, 1951); Belk (1975); Woodside and Bearden (1978)		Consideration set, motives, information search, evaluation, intention	Open-ended structured interviews Qualitative analysis (cognitive mapping)	Eight decision areas: destination, accommodation, activities, attraction, mode of transportation and route, destination area choices and route, eating, self-gifts and other durable purchases
Teare (1994)	Teare and Boer (1991)		Product experience, involvement, evaluation (assessment, rating), joint decision making, expectations	Participant observation or semi-structured interviews Qualitative analysis (grounded theory)	Accommodation (hotels)

Appendix

Description of the Sample.

DMU id.	Type of DMU and family situation	Age	Education and occupation	Personality and lifestyle
1	Married couple: Jeanine[a] and Paul have two children who no longer live with them	She is 61 and he is 63	She is a nurse and he was a military officer (airforce) but is now retired; both have a higher education level	Paul is stubborn and organized; he is pragmatic, (self-)reflective and prospective, and likes reading; both spouses are afraid of the unknown
2	Family: Claude and Marleen have two children (Simon[a] and Andreas[a]), but are not married	He is 40 and she is 33; Simon is 2 while Andreas was born 1 week ago	He is a teacher but is looking for another job; she was a nurse but does not work any more; both have a higher education level	Both spouses are quite emotional, improvisers and adventurous; Marleen is impulsive, unstable and likes risk even more than her partner; Claude is resourceful, self-reflective, hates crowds and likes geography very much; they often go to 'bio' markets
3	Family: Rosine and Luc have brought up six children but still care for the two youngest (Damien and Gilles)	Both parents are 56; Damien is 21 and Gilles 16	Rosine is a housewife, although educated as a nurse; Luc is a teacher and has a higher degree; both children are still students (university and secondary school, respectively)	Parents are rather 'stay-at-home'; they wake early, are tidy and resourceful; Luc feels frustrated about his poor (financial) situation as a teacher, is inquisitive, critical but courteous and do-it-yourself is his major hobby; Damien is an inquisitive and reasonable boy and is engaged in music, while Gilles likes playing tennis
4	Group of friends: Françoise and Cathy[a] are both single; they see and hear from each	Françoise is 30 and Cathy 29	Both friends are teachers (physical training and Greek–Latin); Françoise has graduated from a higher	Françoise likes surprises and the unforeseen, proves to be very resourceful and prefers a cautious approach as she sometimes

	other very often Mixed DMU: it will be the third time they will go on vacation together, but they also go in couples with their boy-friends and family	school and Cathy from university		apprehends future events; both women are leaders of girl scouts, are occupied with fairy tales, legends and Celtic music and read a lot; both are members of sport clubs (diving for Françoise and cycling for Cathy)
5	Family: Jean-Pierre and Danièle are married and have five children	He is 42 and she is 44; Nicolas[a] is 19, Caroline 18, Stéphanie 16, Mélanie 13 and Emilie 6	Jean-Pierre is a state servant while Danièle cares for their children; Nicolas studies at the university, while the other children are still at school	This family likes risk and the unforeseen and are nostalgic of Africa, where they lived for many years; Jean-Pierre and Stéphanie are dreamers who are rather passive; Jean-Pierre is further crowd-aversive and optimistic
6	Single: Marie is living alone since the death of her husband 3 years ago; she has two children	She is 60	Graduating from higher school, she became a gym teacher and now helps the blind with their mobility (she accompanies some of them on vacation)	Marie proves to be a very emotional person. She is impulsive, grateful, dynamic and prospective; however, due to age, she is becoming more and more cautious and reasonable; she has a strong character: stubborn, authoritarian and proud, and also proves to be very resourceful; because of personal and health problems, she takes life day by day; she has many passions: walking, naturalism, singing in a choir, the chiming of bells

Continued

Description of the Sample. – *cont'd*

DMU id.	Type of DMU and family situation	Age	Education and occupation	Personality and lifestyle
7	Family: Peter and Anne live together (they are not married) with their three children	Peter is 40 and Anne 41; Elodie[a] is 15, Tiphaine 13 and Félix[a] 4	Both parents have university degrees and are journalists; all children are at school	Both are engaged in books and travel, they like to discover and are resourceful; Peter, a native of Germany, has a passion for the culture of his country, is introverted and passive, and now longs for more stability as he has moved house 59 times in 19 years! Anne is much more extroverted, is very dynamic and cannot remain in one place; she proves to be impulsive and obsessive
8	Single: Jean-Benoît lives alone and goes on vacation alone or with friends	He is 26	He is a researcher in economics at the university	He is resourceful and well-organized, proves to be quite risk-aversive while travelling alone, is always willing to help and likes social contact
9	Single: Jacqueline is single, lives with her mother and goes on vacation with her family	She is 43	Graduating from the university, she teaches mathematics and physics	–
10	Single: Martine lives alone	She is 37	She has a university degree and is teaching in a higher nursery school	Martine travels and likes walking, has even undergone training for being a tourist guide, is very dynamic (active), spontaneous (talks a lot), stubborn (demanding), resourceful, well-organized and likes adventure without too much risk
11	Married couple: Jacqueline and Roger	Jacqueline is 58 and Roger 63	She has a university degree in history and he has a degree	They like walking and cultural activities; they show a lot of risk aversion;

	still have two children at home, but these two do not participate in the family vacation any more; Jacqueline sometimes goes on vacation with a friend		in law; she used to be a teacher but is now a housewife; he is the chairman of a Court of Appeal	they do not spend too much because they are afraid of the future; Roger is especially quiet and cautious, and has a very busy professional life; Jacqueline is more of an improviser and is adventurous, very inquisitive and critical
12	Single: Brigitte is separated from her husband; has two dependent children (18 and 15 years old); she now considers going on vacation alone or with friends	She is 35–40	She is a tourism graduate; she worked in the travel sector before becoming an employee in the private sector	Brigitte is an improviser, is impulsive, hedonistic, and sometimes makes irrational choices as emotion is stronger than reason; she has a passion for Italy, where she has lived for 7 years; her favourite hobbies are reading and listening to music; she likes social contact and also follows a course of graphology
13	Family: Michèle and André are married and have three children; most often, they go on vacation all together, but sometimes the parents go on their own also	She is 41 and he is 40; Alexandre is 15, Catherine 14 and Hélène 9	She is a teacher, while he is an engineer in the petrol sector; both hold university degrees	It is a conservative, discrete and wise family, where excess and risk are avoided: they prefer certainty rather than adventure and improvisation; Michèle is quite apprehensive (if not pessimistic) and authoritarian while André is quiet and passive; parents are particularly crowd-aversive; Alexandre is interested in basketball, while the two girls have a passion for horse riding; Alexandre and Catherine seem to be very shy

Continued

Description of the Sample. – *cont'd*

DMU id.	Type of DMU and family situation	Age	Education and occupation	Personality and lifestyle
14	Family: Jaqueline and Louis are married and have brought up nine children; three still participate in the family vacation	Jaqueline is 54 and Louis 59; their oldest child is 32, Véronique is 28, Gilles 18 and Stéphanie 13	Both parents are teachers: she has a higher degree and he has a university degree; Véronique is a nurse, Gilles is at university, while Stéphanie is still at school	Resourcefulness is highly valued in the family since they do not earn that much; Jaqueline is an improviser and likes to enhance her self-esteem, is talkative and authoritarian; Louis is more discrete and absent-minded, likes organizing tours for his students and has a passion for ancient history; both parents read a lot (she, novels and he, guide books); children are very spontaneous and enthusiastic; Stéphanie is pernickety and sings in a choir, Gilles and Stéphanie are members of the Scouts
15	Family: Patrick and Michèle are married with two children; in addition to family, they often go on vacation with friends	He is 45 and she is 43; Jérôme[a] is 16 and Violaine[a] 12	Both parents are lawyers: Patrick is attorney and Michèle is an employee in the private sector	Parents are quite open-minded, spontaneous, talkative and extrovert, and like having social contacts; they prefer certainty to the unknown; Patrick has a busy professional life, and the children are not very independent
16	Married couple: Christian and Marie France have brought up two children who do not participate any more in vacation decisions	He is 59 and she is 53	Christian holds a university degree and works as a state servant; Marie-France holds a literary masters but is retired	This couple proves to be very rational and careful; moreover, Christian is especially a homebody and introvert, is organized and avoids improvisation, has a passion for trains and the Gallo-Roman civilization; Marie-France is more

17	Married couple: Jacqueline and René have brought up three children who are all married	Jacqueline is 52 and René 54	Both spouses hold a university degree; she is a housewife, while he is a higher officer of the Belgian Army	This couple is risk-aversive (especially René), reasonable and crowd-aversive; suffering from major health problems, Jacqueline is critical, quite pessimistic and even depressive; René looks tired, seems to be quiet and organized
18	Family: Claude and Jean (married) have two children	She is 38 and he is 47; Marie is 13 and Anne-Sophie 9	Claude holds a degree and works in economics, Jean (higher education degree) is a teacher; Marie goes to the secondary school and Anne-Sophie to the primary school	This family likes the coziness of their home, avoids crowds as they highly value quietness, and enjoy winter skiing; a reflective and sensible man, Jean likes boats and orienteering; Marie is very active and does a lot of gymnastics, while Anne-Sophie is more passive (likes 'cocooning') and likes swimming
19	Family: Pierre and Maryse[a] have made a new family: Maryse has two children; they also go on vacation with friends	Pierre is 43 and Maryse 37; Géraldine[a] is 10 and Lionel[a] 7	Pierre is an independent manager of an old people's home, Maryse is an employee, and both hold higher education degrees; the children go to the primary school	The parents have a passion for photography (they participate in photo raids and organize slide shows), are keen on travel (they have a mobile home), care for international student exchanges, read a lot, are resourceful and like adventure and improvisation; in contrast, their children do not like adventure: Pierre is stubborn, prospective, hedonist, egocentric and optimistic, and Maryse is very active, dynamic and open to social contacts

Continued

Description of the Sample. – *cont'd*

DMU id.	Type of DMU and family situation	Age	Education and occupation	Personality and lifestyle
20	Single: Marie-Thérèse has been a widow for 5 years; she lives alone and has two married children	She is 56	She studied at a teachers' training college and works as a volunteer in a clinic	Marie-Thérèse feels depressed since her husband's death: more than before, she has become a homebody, is passive, manic and careful, does not like risk and the unknown; however, she likes having social contacts and easily lets herself be influenced by others; she attends gym and goes to bed early
21	Single: Georges was living and going on vacation with his mother until she died 3 years ago	He is 66	He worked as a decorator before becoming a civil servant and is now retired; he studied accounting in a professional school	Georges is still strongly affected by his mother's death: is very nostalgic, and also impulsive, hedonistic (does not do without anything) and passive (expectation); authoritarian, he likes being independent and mobile but has a poor health, his arm has been amputated and he often suffers from arthritis; before his injury, he used to do a lot of sports; he is keen on painting (he studied 5 years at the academy)
22	Family: Jacques and Chantal are married and have three children; moreover, Jacques had two	He is 43 and she is 35; Raphaël[a] is 18, Mathias[a] 14 and	Both parents have a low education level (primary and technical secondary school); she works as a domestic help and he used	Parents do not like uncertainty: they are reasonable (avoiding any financial excess) and pragmatic, value cleanliness, are resourceful, austere and well-disciplined, and so

	children from his first marriage who do not live with them	Ludovic[a] 13	to work as a cabinetmaker, but is now an industrially disabled person; all their children still go to school	expect their children to be disciplined too; children do a lot of sports (football, taekwando, etc.) and like playing Nintendo; Jacques is very authoritarian, straightforward and independent, and has a passion for fishing (has many friends) and for birds (keeps pigeons and canaries); Chantal likes reading and is much less of a homebody (is always on the move) than Jacques
23	Family: Joel and Françoise have made a new family with her two children	He is 35 and she is 24; Timmy[a] is 6 and Erinne[a] is 4	Both have a low education level (professional and lower secondary degrees) and are employees in the private sector; both children go to school	This family proves to be risk-aversive and still not very stable, adventure and the unknown are avoided; Joël is always on the move, enjoys having fun and social contacts, is stubborn and very talkative, likes history and geography (through reading and visiting) and plays chess in an association
24	Group of friends: Vincent is single and often goes on vacation with ± five friends from the Army	He is 26; the other friends[a] are about the same age	He holds a technical secondary school degree in electronics and is working as a driver-warehouseman	The friends are often in contact with each other although they live in distant places. They like the unknown, danger, and having fun (drink a lot); Vincent seems to be passive and indolent, and collects sand bottles

Continued

Description of the Sample. – *cont'd*

DMU id.	Type of DMU and family situation	Age	Education and occupation	Personality and lifestyle
25	Group of friends: last year, Annaig and Stéphanie (both singles) went on vacation with four other friends[a]; the two girls also go on vacation with family and with their boyfriends	Annaig is 20 and Stéphanie 21; Anne-Catherine[a] is 22, Frédéric[a] 20, Jean and François[a] are both 24	The two girls are students (law and nursery), Anne-Catherine is also a student, Frédéric is unemployed, while the latter two friends are working (employee and insurer)	This party of friends is quite unstable as it is made up of young unmarried couples: they see each other quite often (each Saturday night) but going on vacation together is much more difficult, and they do not like crowds; Annaig is very spontaneous, reflective and talkative, Stéphanie is much more retiring and shy, and likes animals; both girls are financially careful as they still do not earn their living
26	Unmarried couple: Thierry and Nicole are an unmarried couple; they often go on vacation together or sometimes with friends	He is 28 and she is 25	Both hold university degrees; Thierry is a sales representative and Nicole is an employee in a pharmaceutical company	Nicole and Thierry are a modern couple: they are reflective, well-organized and reasonable, and they show a Breughelian side, as they like going out for dinner or for parties with friends; Thierry plays football, likes comfort and planning, and is easily influenced; Nicole is more proactive, thoughtful and authoritarian than Thierry
27	Married couple: Jean and Nicole have brought up children who are now married	Jean is 69 and Nicole 63	Both spouses hold university degrees, were teachers and are now retired	–

[a]Indicates that the person did not participate in any interview.

Appendix

Case-by-case Evolution of Vacation Decision Making.

DMU id.	t_1	t_2	t_3
1	Concrete projects (2) Final decisions on: PER, DUR, ACC, ACT, DES (1)	=	+ Final decisions on: TRA (1), LOG (1) Δ: ACT (1), DUR (2)
2	Vague project Ideas on: ACC, ACT, ORG	+ Ideas on: DUR, LOG, ACT, DES	= 1 new (alternative) project Ideas on: PER, ACC, LOG, ACT, ORG, DES
3	Vague project Ideas on: PER, ACC, TOU, ORG, DES	= (1) New concrete project (2) Final decisions on: PER, ACC, TRA, FOR, ORG, DES	= (1) Final decision on most vacation items (2) Δ: ACC (2)
4	Concrete project Final decisions on: ACC, TRA, ORG, DES, FOR	= (2 side projects)	Final decision on most vacation items New concrete project (3 side projects)
5	No project	Booking Final decisions on: PER, ACC, TRA, LOG, ACT, ORG, DES	

Continued

Case-by-case Evolution of Vacation Decision Making. – *cont'd*

DMU id.	t_1	t_2	t_3

6	Concrete project
	Final decisions on:
	  ACC, TRA, LOG,
	  ORG, FOR
		Final decision on
		  most vacation
		  items
			=
			Δ: PER

7	Concrete project
	Ideas on: PER,
	  ACC, TRA, LOG,
	  ACT, ORG, DES
		=	=
			Δ: DES

8	Vague project
	Ideas on: FOR,
	  ACT, ORG
		+
		Ideas on: ACC, DES
			+
			Ideas on: PER, DUR,
			  DES

9	Vague project
	Ideas on: ACC,
	  LOG, DES, ORG
		The previous project
		  is abandoned	

10	Concrete project
	Final decisions on:
	  PER, ACC, ACT,
	  ORG, DES, FOR,
	  STY
		+
		Δ: TRA, DES
			Booking (TRA, LOG)
			Δ: TRA, ORG, DES

11	Concrete projects (2)
	Ideas on: PER, DES
	Final decision on:
	  ACC
		Reduction to one
		  project
		+
		Final decision on:
		  PER, TRA, LOG,
		  ORG, DES
			Δ: PER

12	Vague projects (2)
	Ideas on: ACC, DES,
	  DUR (2)
		=
		Δ: ACC, DES (2)
		New project
		Ideas on: PER,
		  ACC, LOG, ORG,
		  DES
			The previous projects
			  are abandoned

13	No project
	Idea on: FOR
	  (desire to innovate)
		Vague projects (2)
		Ideas on: PER, ACC,
		  LOG, ACT, ORG,
		  DES
			Booking of two vacations
			  (one is different
			  from t_2)
			Final decision on: PER,
			  DUR, ACC, LOG,
			  ACT, ORG, DES, FOR

14	Concrete project
	Ideas on: PER, ACC
	Final decisions on:
	  ACT, FOR, ORG
	  DES
		Δ: ORG, DES
		Final decision on:
		  PER
			Δ: PER, DES
			Final decision on:
			  most vacation items

15	Concrete project
	Final decision on:
	  PER, ACC, LOG,
	  ORG
	Ideas on: DES
		Booking (LOG)
		Δ: ACC	

Case-by-case Evolution of Vacation Decision Making. – *cont'd*

DMU id.	t_1	t_2	t_3
16	Final decision on most vacation items	Booking (LOG)	
17	Concrete project Ideas on: PER Final decision on: ACC, FOR (TRA + LOG), DES, CIR	= Δ: TRA, LOG Idea on: DUR	+ Δ: DES, CIR, DUR Final decision on: LOG, DES
18	Vague project Ideas on: PER, DES Final decision on: ACC, ORG	Booking (LOG)	
19	Concrete project	Final decision on most vacation items	=
	Final decision on: ACC, FOR (TRA + LOG), ACT, ORG Ideas on: PER, DUR, DES	+: PER, DUR, DES	Δ: ACC +: DES
20	Concrete projects (2) Ideas on: • PER, DUR, ACC, LOG, ACT, DES (1) • PER, ACC, TRA, ACT, ORG, DES (2)	Booking (project 2) +: LOG, DES Δ: PER	
21	One concrete project + one vague project Final decision on: ACT Ideas on: • PER, ACC, ORG, DES (1) • PER, DES (2)	The two previous projects are abandoned One new concrete project Final decision on: ACC, TRA, LOG, ACT, ORG, DES	The previous project is abandoned
22	Vague project Ideas on: FOR, PER, DUR, ACT, ORG, DES	Concrete project +: ACC, LOG Δ: DUR, DES	Final decision on most vacation items +: PER
23	Concrete project Ideas on: PER, DUR, ACC, LOG, ACT, ORG, DES	– Δ: DES, DUR	Final decision on most vacation items Δ: DUR, ACC, ACT
24	Final decision on most vacation aspects	= Δ: PER	= +: CIR

Continued

Case-by-case Evolution of Vacation Decision Making. – *cont'd*

DMU id.	t_1	t_2	t_3

25	Vague projects (2)
	Ideas on: PER,
	   DUR, ACC, TRA,
	   DES
		+: LOG, ACT
		Δ: PER
			– (generic decision but
			   no project anymore)

26	No project
	Ideas on: PER,
	   ACC, ACT
		=
		Ideas on: TRA,
		   LOG, ORG
		Final decision on:
		   PER
			=
			Final decision on: ACT
			Idea on: DUR

27	Final decision on
	   most vacation
	   items (routine:
	   vacation cottage)		

Note: ACC = accompaniment; ACT = activities; DES = destination; DUR = duration; FOR = formula; LOG = accommodation; PER = period; ORG = organization; TRA = transportation.

=: Status quo of projects; +: project has progressed (new aspect(s) is (are) considered); −: project has regressed; Δ: project has been modified; (x): number of projects; (i): number of the project.

Appendix

4

Case-by-case Evolution of the Number of Vacation Projects and Evoked Destinations.

DMU id.	t_1 Projects	t_1 Set	t_2 Projects	t_2 Set	t_3 Projects	t_3 Set	t_4 Projects	t_4 Set
1	2	3	2	3	2	2 (–)	No	–
	1			2 (+)		1 (–)	Yes	Yes
2	0	0	1	1	1	2 (+)	Yes	Yes
3	1	3©	2	2© (–)	2	2©	Yes	Yes
				1	1	Yes	Yes	
4	1	4	1	2 (–)	2	1 (–)	Yes	Yes
						1 (*)	Yes	Yes
							Yes	Yes
5	0	0	1	1			Yes	Yes
6	1	2	1	1 (–)	1	1	Yes	Yes
7	1	2	2	4 (+)	1	3 (2*)	Yes	Yes
8	1	3	1	2 (1*)	1	1 (–)	Yes	Yes
9	1	0	0	–			No	–
10	1	3 (2©)	1	1 (–)	1	2©	Yes	3© (+)
11	2	2	1			Yes	No (*)	
	1			2 (+)	1	3 (+)	No	–
12	2	1	2	2 (+)	0	–	Yes	No (*)
	2			2 (*)				
13	0	0	1	2	2	1 (–)	Yes	Yes
					1	Yes	Yes	
14	1	4	1	4 (2*)	1	1 (–)	Yes	Yes

Continued

Case-by-case Evolution of the Number of Vacation Projects and Evoked Destinations. – *cont'd*

DMU id.	t_1 Projects	t_1 Set	t_2 Projects	t_2 Set	t_3 Projects	t_3 Set	t_4 Projects	t_4 Set
	Evoked		Evoked		Evoked		Evoked	
15	1	2	1	1 (−)			Yes	Yes
16	1	1	1	1	Yes	Yes		
17	1	2 ©	1	2 ©	1	1 (−)	Yes	No (*)
18	1	1	1	1			Yes	2 © (+)
19	1	2	1	2 © (−)	1	1 (−)	Yes	Yes
20	2	1	1					
		2		1 (−)	Yes	Yes		
21	2	1	1		0	−	No	−
		1		1 (*)			No	−
22	1	2	1	1 (*)	1	1 (*)	No	−
23	1	2	1	3 (2*)	1	1 (−)	Yes	No
24	1	1	1	1	1	1	Yes	2 © (+)
25	2	1	2	1	2	1	No	−
		1		2 (+)		2	No	−
26	0	0	1	0	1	0	Yes	No (*)
27	1	1					Yes	Yes

Note: (+): extension of the evoked set with new alternative(s) in addition to the previous ones; (−): reduction of the evoked set; (*): new alternative; ©: combination of different alternatives in the same vacation plan; yes/no: indicates if an evoked vacation project or destination has really been achieved.

Appendix

5

Case-by-case Matrix of Major Vacation Choice Criteria.

| DMU id. | Price | Destination | Product | | Other major influences of choice | | |
			Other aspects	Other marketing variables	Variety seeking/ loyalty	Emotion	Opportunity
1		Yes	Accommodation Transportation Period	Communi- cation	VS		
2		Yes but secon- dary	Period		VS	Yes	Yes
3	Yes	No*					
4		Yes but secon- dary	Accommodation Theme Formula (transpor- tation) Route Duration			Yes	Yes
5	Yes	Yes but secon- dary	Activities Accommodation				Yes
6		Yes	Period		VS		
7		Yes*	Period Formula (transpor-	Availability			Yes

No.			Characteristic	Level		
8	Yes	Yes but secondary	tation + accommodation) / Activities			
9	Yes	Yes	Formula (transportation) / Budget	VS	Yes	
10	Yes		Duration		Yes	
11	Yes	Yes*	Activities / Theme	VS/L	Yes	Yes
12	Yes	Yes but secondary*	Period / Accompaniment		Yes	Yes
13	Yes	No*	Transportation / Accommodation	L/VS	Yes	Yes
14	Yes	No*	Accommodation	VS	Yes	
15	Yes	No (yes)	Accommodation / Communication	L/VS		Yes
16	Yes	Yes*	Accompaniment / Period / Availability	L/VS		Yes

Continued

Case-by-case Matrix of Major Vacation Choice Criteria. – *cont'd*

DMU id.	Product			Other marketing variables	Other major influences of choice		
	Price	Destination	Other aspects		Variety seeking/ loyalty	Emotion	Opportunity
17	Yes	Yes*	Period Route Tour	Communication			
18	Yes	Yes but secondary	Accommodation	Availability			
19	Yes	No*			VS		
20	Yes	No	Accompaniment	Communication	L		
21		No	Accommodation Meals		L/VS		
22	Yes	Yes*	Activities Budge Period Duration	Communication	L/VS		
23	Yes	No*					
24	Yes	Yes*		Communication			
25	Yes	Yes*	Budget Transportation Accommodation			Yes	
26	Yes	No	Period Budget	Communication Availability			

Note: Yes/No: indicates whether the criteria is important or not for the DMU; VS/L: is mentioned when variety seeking and/or loyalty is an important criteria; *: indicates a strong affection for one particular destination.

Appendix

6

Frequency Table of Destination Attributes in Perception and Evaluation Judgements.

Attribute	Perceptions					Evaluations[a]				
	t_1	t_2	t_3	t_4	Total	t_1	t_2	t_3	t_4	Total
Attribute is more frequent in evaluations										
Climate	31	16	20	19	**86**	66	28	32	76	**202**
General	39	7	5	12	**63**	110	20	13	31	**174**
Infrastructure	29	19	9	18	**75**	22	15	19	32	**88**
Attractions	26	13	12	9	**60**	24	9	13	27	**73**
Cost	18	15	11	12	**56**	13	10	8	38	**69**
Crowded/ deserted	13	3	7	9	**32**	22	13	10	24	**69**
Friendliness	15	5	5	12	**37**	24	4	10	27	**65**
Nature–holistic	11	6	5	8	**30**	25	15	5	19	**64**
Culture	19	2	2	2	**25**	24	13	6	12	**55**
Change of scenery	3	1	1	4	**9**	15	6	9	10	**40**
Surroundings	4	7	4	8	**23**	13	4	5	16	**38**
Language	5	2	3	8	**18**	6	7	11	9	**33**
Ambiance	8	2	3	2	**15**	12	4	3	12	**31**
Authenticity	9	4	0	3	**16**	8	7	2	11	**28**
Cleanliness	10	4	5	6	**25**	10	4	6	8	**28**
Space	9	5	4	3	**21**	7	5	5	8	**25**
Variety	8	4	2	2	**16**	6	3	8	8	**25**
Unique	12	5	3	1	**21**	7	4	3	10	**24**
Quietness	6	3	1	2	**12**	8	9	2	1	**20**

Continued

Frequency Table of Destination Attributes in Perception and Evaluation Judgements.
– *cont'd*

Attribute	Perceptions					Evaluations[a]				
	t_1	t_2	t_3	t_4	Total	t_1	t_2	t_3	t_4	Total
Nature–fauna	7	0	1	5	**13**	5	2	2	8	**17**
Social intervention	4	0	0	2	**6**	2	3	0	8	**13**
Population	0	0	0	0	**0**	5	5	0	0	**10**
Smells	0	0	0	0	**0**	0	0	0	2	**2**
Almost no (< 10%) difference										
Nature–geology	42	19	18	16	**95**	32	15	16	39	**102**
Mentality	23	4	3	15	**45**	14	7	6	20	**47**
Nature–flora	12	5	11	5	**33**	15	5	3	10	**33**
Customs	6	0	2	8	**16**	8	2	0	7	**17**
Food	19	5	6	5	**35**	8	1	3	26	**38**
Security	9	3	0	8	**20**	3	1	5	9	**18**
Light	10	1	1	3	**15**	9	0	2	3	**14**
Attribute is more frequent in perceptions										
Image	65	6	2	2	**75**	52	6	4	5	**67**
Visits	17	16	15	16	**64**	20	8	9	15	**52**
Localization	13	12	9	11	**45**	11	2	4	7	**24**
Cliché	22	3	7	8	**40**	7	3	4	1	**15**
Economy	10	4	4	21	**39**	1	2	2	4	**9**
History	19	7	4	8	**38**	15	3	6	6	**30**
Monuments	15	6	2	7	**30**	13	6	3	5	**27**
Housing conditions	11	4	5	8	**28**	4	2	6	3	**15**
Social	1	2	5	9	**17**	0	3	1	6	**10**
Common	2	3	3	3	**11**	5	0	1	2	**8**
Politics	4	3	1	1	**9**	0	0	0	0	**0**
Craft	2	2	2	2	**8**	0	0	2	3	**5**
TOTAL	588	228	206	303	**1325**	652	257	249	526	**1684**

[a]Evaluation judgements also include satisfaction judgements, i.e. evaluations of the destination performance.

Case-by-case Evolution of the Attribute Background of Destination Judgements.

	Perceptions			Evaluations		
DMU id.	t_1 or t_2 vs. t_2 or t_3	t_{1-3} vs. t_4	t_1 or t_2 vs. t_2 or t_3 vs. t_4	t_1 or t_2 vs. t_2 or t_3	t_{1-3} vs. t_4	t_1 or t_2 vs. t_2 or t_3 vs. t_4
1	3	2	2	1	2	0
3	0	2	0	1	1	1
4	1	1	0	1	2	0
5	2	3	1	1	1	0
6	1	2	0	1	1	0
8	3	4	1	1	1	0
10	4	4	2	2	2	1
12	NA	3	NA	NA	1	NA
13	2	0	0	2	0	0
14	NA	5	NA	NA	4	NA
15	5	6	3	2	1	0
16	6	6	4	2	1	1
17	4	NA	NA	3	NA	NA
18	2	2	1	2	2	0
19	3	3	2	3	4	3
20	1	3	1	1	1	1
22	4	NA	NA	0	NA	NA
24	2	3	0	2	1	0
25	3	NA	NA	2	NA	NA
Mean	2.70	3.06	1.21	1.58	1.56	0.50

Note: t_i = ith series of interviews; NA = the data is not available because the DMU was not interviewed at that point in time.

Index

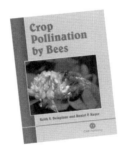
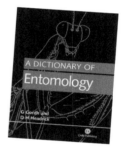
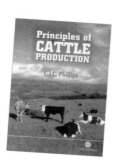